THE WEREWOLF
In Legend, Fact & Art

BASIL COPPER

ST. MARTIN'S PRESS, NEW YORK

ROBERT HALE LIMITED, LONDON

© *Basil Copper 1977*
First published in Great Britain 1977
First published in the United States of America 1977

St. Martin's Press, Inc.
175 Fifth Avenue
New York, N.Y. 10010

Library of Congress Catalog Card Number 76-62755

Library of Congress Cataloging in Publication Data
Copper, Basil.
  The werewolf.

  Bibliography: p.
  Includes index.
  1. Werewolves. I. Title.
GR830.W4C66   001.9'44   76-62755
ISBN 0-312-86222-9

Robert Hale Limited
Clerkenwell House
Clerkenwell Green
London EC1R 0HT

ISBN 0 7091 6193 X

Typeset, printed and bound
in Great Britain by
REDWOOD BURN LIMITED
Trowbridge and Esher

CONTENTS

CONTENTS

IN ART: THE CINEMA

ILLUSTRATIONS

The illustrations come from the Gerald McKee Collection

ACKNOWLEDGEMENTS

The author wishes to acknowledge, with deepest thanks, the advice, assistance, information, material and facilities afforded, without which this book could certainly not have come into existence.

I owe a special debt to Dr Lee Illis; the British Medical Association; the Royal Society of Medicine and the Honorary Editors of the Proceedings of the Royal Society of Medicine.

Derek Lewton-Brain; Gerald McKee; the Superintendent, Department of Printed Books, British Museum; Staff of the Reading Room, British Museum; Goldberg and Rimington; Hammer Films; the British Film Institute and Len Harris.

Rhona Pite; Kirby McCauley; New York Public Library; Carl Routledge; Robin James; the Gothique Film Society of London; the late David Edwards; the Hutchinson Publishing Group and Richard Davis.

I should particularly like to thank Marion Pender for the care, scholarship and patience she has displayed during the preparation of the typescript.

B.C.

Remembering *David Edwards:*
Friend, Colleague and Enthusiast for
the Macabre: and for *Andrew Gledhill,*
who carries on the Tradition

"In early days it was recognized that a werewolf might be a person who was afflicted with a horrible mania; lycanthropy is a disease, a kind of insanity or mania when the patient is afflicted with hideous appetites, the ferocity and other qualities of a wolf; men are attacked with this madness chiefly in the beginning of the year, and become most furious in February; retiring for the night to lone cemeteries and living precisely in the manner of ravening wolves."

Dr Montague Summers

Pescara: Pray-thee, what's his disease?
Doctor: A very pestilent disease, my lord.
          They call it licanthropia.

Webster
The Duchess of Malfi

FOREWORD

When introducing my companion volume *The Vampire: In Legend, Fact and Art* in 1973, I said, "[It] is not intended to be read as a work of solemn scholarship. Indeed, in a field where so much is speculative, obscure and dependent on ancient records and dubious eye-witness accounts, such a book would be a near impossibility."

The same set of circumstances apply to the present volume. *The Vampire* was such a fascinating task to write and has aroused such interest since its publication that I decided to go ahead with a planned sequence of companion volumes, of which the present is the first.

Lycanthropy, as the condition of the werewolf is called, is an equally ancient and fascinating myth and worthy of as much study as the better-known vampire. It has suffered, in comparison, possibly because its treatment in literature and the cinema has not been so striking, though there are surprises even here.

But there was a bonus in this, inasmuch as many facets and details of the werewolf and its habits remained to be uncovered. Whole areas of the literature were relatively unexplored and unanthologized and therefore less familiar.

The legends are, if anything, equally exciting and bizarre as those of the vampire; and from the factual aspect the possible cause of outbreaks of a rare and little-known disease resembling the actual state of lycanthropy in the Middle Ages has been one of the most fascinating discoveries of this study.

The history of the wolf and the werewolf are intertwined and this book also touches on the wolf in legend and fact. For much of the information in this sphere I am greatly indebted to a number of people; they are listed in the acknowledgements elsewhere but I would be less than fair if I omitted to pay suitable tribute to them here.

Foremost among them must be mentioned Dr Lee Illis of Hampshire who has made a special study of lycanthropy from the purely medical point of view. He has come up with some plausible and – to me at least – entirely convincing theories to account for some of the hysterical denunciations of so-called werewolves in medieval times.

With a generosity and breadth of spirit not always manifest among medical men, he has kindly put his findings and medical papers on the subject at my disposal. My own researches had directed me to a number of extraordinary and well-attested cases of disease where patients behaved in all respects in the same way as the werewolf of popular fiction. In medieval times the victims of the 'werewolf disease' may have been the unwitting catalysts through which bloodbaths of judicial terror and execution were triggered off.

But Dr Illis is the first authority to my knowledge who has assigned a valid reason for these extraordinary events; his researches have made him perhaps the foremost figure in this esoteric field and I am glad to be able in this study to pay tribute to his fascinating pioneer work.

In this connection I must also thank the Royal Society of Medicine and the British Medical Association who kindly gave me permission to reproduce Dr Illis's findings which were presented at a seminar held under their auspices; and the authorities of the Reading Room of the British Museum where I spent many fascinating afternoons on research. Deep thanks too, to my old friend Gerald McKee for his invaluable photographic researches on my behalf and for the outstanding skill he has brought to the photographic side of this book.

In the field of natural history the grey, somewhat maligned figure of the wolf has a part to play in the dark legend of the werewolf, and I must record here my thanks to others, too numerous to mention by name, for directing my attention to areas which I might otherwise have neglected in my search for *The Werewolf*. Their books, papers, articles and newspaper reports have diverted me down some odd and fascinating byways.

There is also the strange, relatively little explored world of the savage child, the true wolf-boy, brought up in primitive circumstances, of whom there have been many recorded instances. He too forms a vivid strand in the story of the lycanthrope down the ages.

In the field of literature, it is true, no one volume has attained the classic stature of Bram Stoker's *Dracula*. But the nearest thing to a classic in the genre, Guy Endore's brilliantly written *The Werewolf of Paris*, is a work far superior to that of Stoker and undeservedly neglected. It is analysed in detail in the chapters on the literature of the subject; and the other treatments in the field of fiction, from the early nineteenth century to the present day, have yielded up many gems.

These range from George Reynolds' *Wagner the Wehr-Wolf*, Clemence Houseman's *The Werewolf* and Erkmann-Chatrian's *The Man-Wolf* to examples by Robert Louis Stevenson and Kipling through to the modern short-story form and writers such as Algernon Blackwood, Peter Fleming, W. B. Seabrook and many others.

As always, Montague Summers has provided a rich field for the researcher both in England and France, where the legend of the *loup-garou* is one of the most potent folk-myths.

The dictionary defines lycanthropy as "the transformation of witch into wolf; form of madness in which patient imagines himself some beast and exhibits depraved appetites, change of voice etc". A classic description of the subject of this book, which also delves richly and deeply into the theme in the cinema. Though the Hungarian Bela Lugosi is best known for his immortal portrayal of Count Dracula in the 1931 film of *Dracula*, he also played the wolf-man on screen.

Perhaps the nearest thing to a film classic on the subject is the 1941 film *The Wolf Man*, an original essay in the weird, which starred Lon Chaney and Claude Rains. *The Werewolf* traces the subject in the cinema from early days to such modern examples as Hammer Films' *The Curse of the Werewolf*, a distinguished effort by the director Terence Fisher, which brought the actor Oliver Reed to wide prominence in the name part. And, of course, the best-known Wolf Man of all, Lon Chaney Jr, bearer of a famous name, receives a chapter to himself in a book which intends to cast as wide a net as possible.

In this last respect my thanks too to Robin James and the Gothique Film Society of London for enabling me to review some of the rarer films dealt with in the chapters on the theme in cinema, and in so doing to recapture an ancient thrill.

Uniquely, in all the weird and terrible picture gallery of monsters, the werewolf stands alone as the object of pity as well as terror; for he was as much victim as ravening beast and the curse of the lycanthrope could descend on him without any discernible reason, unlike the vampire which was evil of itself and had to attack its victim to spread the taint.

The legend of the werewolf has been known since Roman times and earlier; in our present age of space-travel and the atom bomb it is still a forceful and colourful figure. I have had a great deal of pleasure in tracing its genesis from earliest times down to the present day and in so doing I hope I have been able to communicate something of this to the reader.

BASIL COPPER

Semur-en-Auxois
Côte d'Or
1973–1977

In Legend

ONE

DEATH BY NIGHT

The earth is bound in the iron grip of frost. It is dusk and a chill wind sets the branches of leafless trees scratching drily in the twilight, like dead men's bones. A path stretches white along the ragged spines of the hills where firs spread a thick mantle said to conceal wolves at this time of year, forced down from the mountains beyond. The moon will soon be up but now, in that strange area between day and night, where all things may happen, everything is as blurred and insubstantial as a dream.

A heavy cart passes, creaking along the rutted dirt road in the dusk, its driver and his mate heavily muffled against the advancing cold. Their breath rises like smoke, reinforced by the steam from the horses' flanks. They and their load of logs pass the crossroads to the village beyond and all is silent once again in that remote place, apart from the idle chatter of two crows perched on the branch of a pine tree a hundred yards off.

The crows have seen something farther up the valley and presently one of them flies off from the tree to investigate. He sweeps low down beneath the belt of trees. Something is moving in the valley below the firs. The second crow, alone on the tree, hears the alarmed cries of its mate. Then the first bird reappears and alights on the branch. The two fly off as night begins to blanket the road. Lights twinkle from the village and the faint music of a distant violin insinuates itself into that wild land-scape, now beginning to be bleached by the rising moon.

A quarter of an hour passes and a twig snaps suddenly, like the slap of a pistol, so still is the night. Even the animals abroad seem to be holding their breath. Some heavy beast is evidently moving toward the road from the fir thicket beyond. Then, just as soon as the tension has begun, it seems to relax and the small, stealthy animal noises begin again. So it continues until almost an hour has passed and the moon commences to flood the landscape.

The noise of the violin and sounds of revelry from the inn in the village are at their height when another sound obtrudes. A furtive scratching on the flinty surface of the road resolves itself into footsteps. Presently a tall, unkempt man comes in sight. He is bearded and warmly wrapped against the freezing wind. His sandals too have strips of cloth round them and his canvas leggings have seen better days.

He wears a greasy, wide-brimmed black hat, pulled down low over his shaggy hair and a heavy scarf holds the hat to his head, passing across the crown and down either side of his face, where it is knotted securely beneath his chin. Seen this way, only the middle portion of his face is visible. He wears a wispy moustache and his cheeks are red and raw with the wind. He carries on his back a plain wooden framework, criss-crossed, with a heavy canvas bundle lashed with cords to the frame.

The man is a pedlar who has been walking since early morning. Now he is tired and hungry and momentarily brightens as he senses rather than sees the faint lights of the village ahead. For the moment he is unable to walk any farther and spotting a tumbled heap of boulders at the roadside near the spot the crows have quitted an hour or so before, he unloosens his pack and seats himself upon the smoothest and flattest of the stones.

The wind whistles uneasily in the pine trees and their creaking in the rising gusts masks a more furtive scratching noise from a small ravine beyond the thicket of fir. The pedlar has apparently noticed nothing untoward for he now leans forward to adjust the thongs binding his legs. This accomplished to his satisfaction, he straightens up and rubs his hands together to free them from the cold.

But the pedlar's rest is shortly to be disturbed. The crackling noises in the thicket are now too obtrusive to be ignored. The man sits up and listens intently. The sounds have momentarily ceased and all that can now be heard is the low soughing of the wind in the pines. Then comes the distant howling of wolves downwind. The pedlar is uneasy, reminded of his vulnerability in this frozen wilderness. He turns his head, looks longingly at the distant pinpoints of light which denote the village.

He eases himself to his feet, rubbing his aching calves with his hands. All the weariness of the long day's march is in his bones and he is reluctant to move for he really needs more rest. Then the brilliance of the moonlight reassures him; every leaf, every blade of grass about him is etched in minute detail in the silver glare. He re-seats himself. He is still sitting there five minutes later when a low snarling in the thicket bordering the ravine falls upon his ear. He forces himself to his feet for the second time.

The pedlar is obviously disturbed. He rummages in his pack and straightens up with a thick cudgel which has been thrust between the fastenings. The wind whistles eerily through the tops of the pines and a distinct crackling noise is heard, as of some heavy body forcing its way through the undergrowth. The pedlar picks up his pack and half-drags it behind him as he moves away from the group of stones.

The snarling noise is not repeated but the stealthy progress of some unseen creature continues, seeming to keep pace with the pedlar as he stumbles across the uneven ground. He is making for the rough track which leads to the village but to get to it, he must skirt the thicket from which the noises are coming. While it appears as if the track leads to security, in reality it must take him closer to the source of the disturbance. The pedlar hesitates, as this is borne in on him. He is tired but not so frightened as to abandon all caution.

He is reluctant to abandon his pack, which represents his livelihood; yet at the same time its weight must handicap him and speed may be of the essence if he is to reach the safety of the village. He pauses to change his grip on the bundle, stiffens as a full-blooded snarl comes from the thicket below. From the direction of the sound it is obvious that the creature, wolf or some other beast, has gained the strategic position. The pedlar must now go directly along the track and risk a direct confrontation with the creature with his club; or across the shoulder of hill in front of him which must, however, take him away from the direction of the village.

With another savage snarl from the trees the pedlar hesitates no longer. He starts off with tottering steps across the broken terrain, dragging his pack behind him. He sways from side to side as he hurries along, the pack first swinging free of the ground, then bouncing for a few yards until the man again summons enough strength to ease it clear of the rocks.

He is not yet alarmed enough to abandon his precious load

but all the while he casts anxious glances about him in the moonlight; firstly behind, where the main danger might yet lie; then from side to side in slow sweeps, in case some beast bursts forth from cover on his flanks; and lastly at the skyline ahead in case anything bars his way. For the moment he sees nothing to cause trepidation and so hurries on, his club swinging loose in his left hand, ready for use if need be.

He covers perhaps twenty or thirty yards in this fashion and then the weight of the pack begins to tell. Perspiration starts to bead his forehead, despite the cold of the night and his face presents a shiny aspect in the moonlight. Inevitably, he slows and eventually comes to rest on a ridge of higher ground which affords him some protection from whatever danger threatens. He again drops the pack and puts his hand to his chest. As he does so another, even louder snarl, sounds from the trees beyond.

The pedlar is now thoroughly frightened. He decides to leave the pack where it is and press on with all speed to the village. Transferring the cudgel to his right hand he starts to make his way across the upland to the higher ground beyond. Suddenly a low, crouching form passes across the horizon. The figure is clearly limned in the bright light of the moon. It is lean and gaunt and seems to press toward the ground in a posture like that of a wolf.

But the pedlar, with increasing terror, realizes that the figure is not really lupine. In the few seconds it was in the open and in clear view he was able to take in the details of the head which was distinctly not that of an animal. And there was something vaguely familiar about the configuration of the limbs and the pose. The pedlar realizes, with a quickening of the heart, that the figure resembled nothing so much as that of a man on all fours, running with incredible rapidity as though to cut off his retreat to the village.

Moreover, it was a figure that gave him a momentary impression of being covered with fur, like that of an animal. Despite the coldness of the night it appeared to be naked save for the natural covering and the matted and twisted growth flashed like quicksilver in the moonlight. The pedlar's throat grows dry and his eyes roll piteously as he looks about him for help. But there is none in this lonely and deserted place and the faint reflections of light from the distant village, with their connotations of comfort and safety, seem to mock him in the desperate situation in which he finds himself.

The pedlar now alters course. Conserving his breath he walks instead of running; holding the cudgel firmly he sets off downhill on the more direct route along the path which skirts the ravine and the thickets of trees. But it appears that this is exactly the course the unknown creature wishes him to take for a moment or so later, in a renewed access of terror, the wretched man sees the same figure, covering the ground at an apparently incredible speed, passing back along the skyline to cut him off from the village.

He hesitates but a moment longer, looks desperately around him; nothing moves in the pitiless moonlight save the tops of the pine trees, tossed in the rising wind. The uplands are bleak and featureless and he knows there is no help to be had in that quarter. The only safety afforded is that of the village. It is not more than half a mile at the outside but to gain it he must run the gamut of the thing which is lurking on the fringe of the dirt road. He is convinced that it intends him harm and that its movements are part of some elaborate manoeuvre to entrap him.

The biting wind is now beginning to trouble the pedlar. It stings his cheeks which are running with perspiration and tears ooze from his eyes. His teeth begin to chatter as much from fear as from the cold. He grasps the cudgel tightly, mutters a fearful prayer and sets off with a burst of scarecrow energy to face the terrors of the village pathway.

Nothing happens until he approaches the spot where he last saw the shadowy figure disappear. Then a twig snaps. But fear has set the pedlar on his path and fear keeps his legs going mechanically despite the sick chaos of his mind and the stealthy terror which keeps his heart pumping wildly and the perspiration pouring in rivulets down his cheeks. His eyes search the path on either side and every furrow and hollow, etched bright in the moonlight, which might conceal some fearful phantasm.

His breath whistles jerkily in his throat and the wind keeps up a melancholy fluttering of his rags so that the pedlar's tattered dignity would look slightly pathetic if there were any unseen watcher in that lonely place. But there is no-one. Save one. And he, securely hidden beneath a low jumble of rocky outcrops bides his time with infinite cunning, measuring the distance

which separates him from his prey and using his keen sense of
smell as well as his sharp eyesight.

The pedlar is nearly up to the junction which debouches
directly on to the village now, a point where another dirt road
loops round and passes along the spines of the hills. A shadow
sweeps across the ground and the hunted man gives a convulsive leap to one side. His relief when no attack comes is
short-lived; for the moon is passing behind thick cloud and the
tranquil landscape, so lately bathed in silver light, is plunged
into gloom.

As though encouraged by this there comes a mournful howl
from the beast-thing concealed in the thicket which makes the
pedlar's heart jump in his breast. The breathless man's plight is
now serious indeed; he is still some way from the village, at the
point of greatest danger where the rocks skirt the path; and now
the light is rapidly fading into the darkness of night.

As he reaches the rocks he faces towards them and, gripping
the cudgel as firmly as his straining nerves allow, edges his way
sideways across the rough terrain. The threatening howls have
now ceased but are replaced instead with a low growling noise
like that of a savage dog. The pedlar is almost past the greatest
point of danger and the fitful moonlight is pricking the gloom
when a figure suddenly emerges from behind the outcrop and
rushes toward the pedlar in silence.

The unfortunate man, faced with this terrifying apparition,
drops his cudgel and takes to his heels. Then begins a silent and
terrible pursuit in which the pedlar realizes his life is at stake.

His heart threatening to burst his breast, he twists and turns,
the terror of desperation propelling him at a tremendous speed
across the uneven terrain. But the beast, grimly intent on pursuit, is not to be so easily thrown off. It doubles and turns with
all the ease and facility of an animal, though it runs upright on
two legs.

From time to time the pedlar throws a hasty glance over his
shoulder but he needs all his wits and energy for the uneven
chase. What he sees in these brief glimpses gives his labouring
lungs and aching legs yet more stamina in the battle for his life.

For his pursuer, though a man to casual appearance is in
reality more like something fashioned from a nightmare. He is
covered in shaggy, silver-grey hair and though naked to the
waist wears a pair of trousers of some dark material like a man.

A large leather belt with a buckle encircles his middle. His feet are bare and scratch at the surface of the ground with minute clicking noises, like the claws and pads of a beast.

The arms are long and powerful and the creature crouches forward as though running on four legs would be more natural to it. The head, roughly shaped like a human, is beast-like in most of its aspects. Completely covered with hair, the face narrows to a muzzle-like nose which is black and squat, like that of some great dog. Saliva dribbles from its mouth and beneath the fur, powerful yellow teeth glisten. The eyes are close-set and red, burning like coals in the vileness of the face.

No wonder the pedlar leaps and swerves in his incredible facility. But the uneven race is soon done. No human heart and lungs can keep up such a pace and the man is already tired from his long day's tramp. As the moon again emerges from behind the clouds he trips and falls. His beast pursuer gives a snarl of triumph and then he has hurled himself upon the pedlar and is worrying at his throat. The unfortunate man has time for but one shriek which brings drinkers at the inn to their feet.

Then bestial teeth have met in his throat and the muscled, furry creature has torn away muscle and windpipe in the ferocity of his assault. Blood gushes from severed veins and arteries as the wolf-thing bites and tears at its prey until all life is extinct. Then it leaps to its feet and sends its ferocious howl echoing across the miles of lonely mountain and forest.

When a search-party from the inn, heavily armed with weapons ranging from fowling-pieces to cutlasses, reaches the spot where the bloodied and torn remains lie, the pedlar is long beyond earthly help. Far across the valley the bestial howls of an implacable being filled with blood-lust and the urge to destroy, echoes and re-echoes, striking a chill to the hearts of the villagers. Once again, the ancient curse of the werewolf has claimed another victim.

TWO

BEASTS AND SUPER BEASTS

The legend of the werewolf is one of the oldest and most primal of man's superstitions. It shares with the vampire, the witch, the phantom and the warlock a history which reaches thousands of years back in time and which has terrified generation after generation of people in sophisticated cities as well as in the world's most primitive places.

For the thing which killed the pedlar is common to nearly all lands, races and climates and appears in the folklore of most nations which have a written language. Even in those which do not, it has been handed down in an unbroken oral tradition so that the werewolf, equalled only by the vampire in its potency and dread, has remained one of the most frightening and invoked beings from the mist-haunted legends of the past.

Lycanthropy, to give it its proper term, means literally wolf-man, being derived from the Greek *lukanthropia*. The Oxford Dictionary, as we have seen, defines it as "transformation of witch into a wolf". In studying the history and origins of the man-beast this book will examine closely the legends and habits of the creature.

We shall be following medical cases in which patients in the Middle Ages imagined that they were savage beasts and, as we shall see, behaved like wild creatures; in actual fact they were probably suffering from a rare disease, which will be analysed in its proper place. The field of medical science has also known many instances of feral children; that is, children which were brought up among wild beasts in a natural and savage state and to all intents and purposes were wolf-like animals themselves. There were no less than fifty-three well-authenticated and recorded cases of such wolf-boys between the fourteenth century and the present day and we shall be dealing with some of the most famous in the course of the narrative.

The history of the wolf itself, one of the most fascinating and savage creatures of the wild, will be explored and the terrifying circumstances of such classic examples as the Beast of the Gevaudan touched upon. The wolf-man theme has been a rich mine for both the oral narrators of legend and those of the written sort and this study examines the habits, characteristics and geographical locations of this fabulous beast, known as the *loup-garou* in France, the werewolf or wereman in other parts of Europe and the *volkodlak* in haunted Transylvania.

In literature, as I have hinted, the gifted writer found a rich field and most of the more notable fictional works in the genre of lycanthropy will be dealt with, ranging from classics by such writers as Frederick Marryat, Kipling and Guy Endore who fathered the Werewolf of Paris, to such modern masters in the field as James Blish and Peter Fleming.

To youngsters of the modern generation the werewolf is perhaps personified only by the rather cheaply made but nevertheless potent movies of the macabre actor, the late Lon Chaney Jr, who almost literally became the "wolf man" Lawrence Talbot, in the late Thirties and early Forties in a whole series of Werewolf films, and whose productions have often been reissued and screened on television today.

To the older generation of cinema-goers, Bela Lugosi, the creator of the film *Dracula*, was perhaps the most notable actor who played the wolf man, while Henry Hull appeared in one of the best-known productions in the genre, *The Werewolf of London* in 1935. Hammer Films created the nearest thing to a modern classic in *The Curse of the Werewolf* in the 1960s, in which Oliver Reed gave an anguished performance that was the prelude to a distinguished career.

The werewolf is perhaps less well known than its brother-fiend, the vampire, and some fascinating material has been unearthed in the course of research. From Romulus and Remus onwards the tale of the wolf, the man-beast and the werewolf itself, has engrossed minds of the calibre and the diverse talents of such people as Rousseau, Linnaeus and Swift.

We shall be dealing with the habits, characteristics and traits of the werewolf in following chapters but it is as well to remember from the outset that the subject of lycanthropy is a little more complex than that of the vampire. The legendary aspects can fairly easily be disposed of in the light of modern science but in earlier centuries actual diseases which swept whole populations turned people into ravening beasts and the patients bore all the classic symptoms of the lycanthrope.

Small wonder then that there were veritable bloodbaths in Europe in the sixteenth century and earlier when those wretched victims suspected of the taint were harried and hounded to their deaths by the thousand. So we have in effect four main strands of the subject.

Firstly, the wolf itself: that most savage and cunning of creatures who has learned to outwit man in the wild places of the earth since time began. Then the werewolf, the creature of legend; the man-wizard who could turn himself into a wolf at will and seek out his victim by day or night and who could only be destroyed in certain ways, notably by being shot with a silver bullet.

Thirdly, there is the phenomenon of natural history: the feral-child, the wolf-boy; an ordinary human being brought up among animals and who had passed his life in eating raw meat and killing his own food, so that he had lost almost all recognizable human traits, including the gift of speech.

And lastly, there is the medical victim; the patient struck down by a strange disease; a form of insanity, in which the wretched victim leapt and howled, behaved like a wolf and exhibited all the savagery and physical characteristics of the species.

These, then, will be some of the main themes in a study of a fascinating and extraordinary creature, half-man half-animal, which has absorbed the attention of mankind for many thousands of years. It is time now to turn to definitions and some of the more notable traits of these monsters of fact and legend – the beasts and super-beasts.

The werewolf and its foul activities were known when Rome was young. It was a being feared in Ancient Greece and the shadow of the running man-beast has cast terror on primitive and sophisticated alike almost since time began. But, like the vampire, its most potent spell has been in Eastern Europe, where the *volkodlak* was a name that blanched the cheek and caused the peasant to glance round uneasily as the wind of sunset stirred the leafless branches.

France too suffered greatly from the *loup-garou* and folk legend tells many tales of the man-beasts which were hunted in far-off times in the mountainous regions. Naturally enough, the legend was strongest in rural and mountainous areas such as the Auvergne and the Jura, where wolves caused much depredation among shepherds' flocks and over the centuries the line between legend and superstition and the facts of natural history began to blur.

Certainly, some of the most horrific tales of werewolves of fantastic power originated in the blue distances of these historic French mountain ranges and we shall be hearing much of such districts in the course of this book. Germany was also a favourite haunting ground for this curse and though England did not seem to be greatly plagued, records show the werewolf as active as far north as Ireland.

Unlike the vampire, which returned from the grave to ingest the blood of the living, the werewolf was not an undead creature. Rather the condition was a manifestation of a disease which might strike anyone, noble or commoner alike and therefore all the more to be feared. True enough, anyone bitten by a werewolf would himself bear the taint but the appalling symptoms might come upon a man when he was safe in his own chamber and had done nothing himself to bring on such a fate. It was this aspect which resulted in holocausts in the Middle Ages when suspected werewolves were burnt and put to the sword to free the earth from a curse almost as much feared as the vampire.

So marked was the frenzy with which the symptoms were greeted and the lengths to which the authorities resorted – on mere suspicion it must be added – that the rudimentary proceedings and the mass executions bore something of the same hysteria as such manifestations as the Salem witch trials. A man need only be slightly touched by lunacy; or be of lupine aspect, or perhaps have sharp teeth or a lean cast of countenance and that would be sufficient to condemn him at a period of such outbreaks.

The time of the full moon was particularly feared, as it was known that this was the period when the disease was most likely to strike. Those so 'moon-struck' would find their bodies physically changing in vile and repugnant ways so that they looked like and behaved like wolves. While so transformed they would roam the night attacking and killing anyone who ventured across their path. Small wonder that the curse of the werewolf was so dreaded.

A vampire had to attack a person before the latter could become a vampire in turn. But the disease of lycanthropy could strike an innocent person at any time and there was no known cure. We shall be dealing with the characteristics and symptoms of the lycanthrope in the following chapter. But before we do that, we must pause awhile to relate a typical instance of lycanthropic terror, which vividly illustrates the awfulness with which the subject was surrounded in an earlier age.

Late in the sixteenth century, in the Auvergne district of France, lived a well-to-do gentleman called Sanroche who was happily married and had most of the material comforts which enabled people to live opulently and keep servants in those days of cheap labour and materials. The Auvergne was then, as now, a richly wooded area, mountainous and fed by streams which debouched from the steep hillsides.

Sanroche's substantial estate was set on the slope of a hill and commanded fine views to the south. From his mullioned windows the landowner and his family could look across the rolling slopes down to a stream and then, rising steeply in stand after stand of fine timber, the nearer ridges swept across to the blue haze of the distant hills. One afternoon in the early autumn of 1580 Sanroche was sitting by the window when a servant appeared to inform him that a friend of his, Monsieur Fayrolle, had called.

Fayrolle was noted as an enthusiastic hunter and the Auvergne abounded in game; there were plentiful fish in the clear-running streams and the forest teemed with game birds, deer and wild boar. Fayrolle had come to ask his friend to join him in an excursion after deer. Reluctantly, his host had to decline the invitation; he had his lawyer coming to see him on business within the hour and so could not join in the chase.

So, after accepting some refreshment Fayrolle took his musket and game-bag and set off through the rolling gardens below the house. Sanroche watched his friend's lithe figure as it strode down the hillside and was presently lost within the trees. The lawyer called as arranged and the pair were busy about estate affairs for upwards of an hour so that Sanroche put his friend's visit out of mind. It was not until he had bade the lawyer good evening and had returned from the supper-table that he recalled his friend's invitation.

His wife was away for the day so the gentleman, having nothing more urgent to do, resolved to follow in his friend's path and meet him on his homeward journey. The shadows were lengthening upon the ground as he set off through the garden and Sanroche paused a moment to watch the glory of the sun declining behind the western hills.

Then he pressed on down a woodland path which led to the valley below. He had been walking for something like twenty minutes when he heard a voice hailing him from the hillside ahead. On the opposite slope he could see the figure of his friend, stained scarlet by the last of the sunset which splashed the distant landscape. As the two friends drew closer to one another Sanroche could see that something was agitating Fayrolle.

When they at length met in a narrow ravine between the two opposing slopes of hill the landowner could see that Fayrolle's clothes were torn, dusty and stained with what looked like blood. Fayrolle was perturbed and out of breath so his friend at first contented himself with taking his musket and game-bag. The two friends walked some way back toward the estate in silence.

By degrees, with long intervals for breath, Fayrolle told Sanroche of a startling adventure which had befallen him in the depths of the forest. He had seen several deer in the distance but had been unable to approach near enough to secure a shot. Eventually he had penetrated a long way into the woods and felt it was about time to return.

It was in the darkest portion of the forest that Fayrolle had heard a horrendous snarling. It proceeded from a dank gully overgrown with ferns; retreating slowly, step by step, and facing in the direction of the danger, the hunter had gone about two hundred yards back toward safety when an enormous wolf bounded out of the gully and dashed toward him.

Perhaps because of the suddenness of the beast's appearance or because of the dimness of the light for shooting, Fayrolle was taken aback. He halted in mid-stride and raised the gun to his shoulder but at almost the same instant he stumbled, his boot caught on a tree-root, and the shot went wide. The wolf merely swerved in its onward rush and then, with a murderous snarling, it launched itself at the hunter's throat.

Fortunately, Fayrolle had the good sense to swing at the

beast with the butt of his reversed gun and the blow sent the animal sprawling. It was up again almost immediately, its rear paws scrabbling furiously at the fallen leaves on the forest floor, but by this time Fayrolle had managed to reach his hunting knife. With considerable courage he went forward to meet the savage animal which was menacing him. The two closed in deadly combat but Fayrolle was an old hand at woodcraft.

He had already bundled his cloak round his left forearm and he thrust this in the beast's jaws; while the animal tried vainly to sink its sharp fangs in the muscles of his arm Fayrolle was slashing at its throat with his heavy hunting knife. These forest knives were massive things with razor-sharp edges, their broad blades and enormous hilts almost as heavy as a small hand-axe.

Man and beast fell to the ground and rolled over and over in the fury of the struggle. As the battle continued, Fayrolle and the wolf, its reddened eyes glaring into his own, fetched up against a fallen log. The wolf's right forepaw rested over the curve of the trunk and in a moment Fayrolle had brought the heavy blade of his knife down in a chopping movement, severing flesh, bone and sinew. The wolf gave a long, mournful howl and tore itself from the hunter's grasp.

It went limping off up the glade as Fayrolle fell exhausted to the ground, splashed with the beast's blood. His cloak was torn to ribbons but he was relieved to find that his arm had suffered only superficial scratches, owing to his foresight in improvising such protection. He reloaded his musket and intended going in search of the wounded animal to despatch it, but it was now growing late and it would be dark before he regained his friend's estate if he delayed much longer.

One may imagine with what excitement Sanroche had followed his friend's recital; with many pauses for breath and exclamations of surprise or horror, the two friends had wandered on, stopping every now and then to emphasize a point or rest; they now found themselves in the host's garden. Fayrolle pointed impatiently to the sack and his friend passed it to him.

"I have brought the forepaw with me," he said. "So that you can attest to the truth of my story."

He put down the sack on an ornamental balustrade in the knot-garden and fumbled with the laces which held its mouth shut. Sanroche watched with unfeigned interest, his blood stirred by the exciting and perilous adventure of his friend.

Fayrolle was bent over the sack, his back to his host so that Sanroche could not at first see what he brought from the bag. He heard his friend's muffled cry and something slipped from the hunter's fingers on to the grass. Fayrolle turned a face of blanched horror to him.

"I do not understand," he said in agitated tones. "It was the forepaw of a wolf."

Sanroche followed the trembling forefinger down to the grass. His own horror equalled that of Fayrolle as he saw lying on the innocent carpet of green a recently severed human hand. Even more frightful was his emotion as he noticed that the delicate fingers of the hand bore several rings. One of them, an elaborate spiral pattern set with a blue topaz, he recognized. The hand was that of his wife.

Sanroche stumblingly excused himself and, wrapping the hand in a cloth, hurried to his house. He found his wife had returned home. She was resting, said his steward, and could not be disturbed. When the master of the house had the chamber door forced he found his wife, deathly pale, lying in bed. There was blood upon the sheets and she was only half-conscious. A doctor was called and was able to save Madame Sanroche's life. Her right hand had been severed at the wrist.

Sanroche passed several agonizing weeks before he confronted his wife with Fayrolle's story. Eventually the wretched woman broke down and confessed that she was a werewolf. It may be felt that Sanroche was a little lacking in husbandly affection for he went to the authorities a short while later and denounced her. She was in due course brought to trial and after torture made a full confession of her evil deeds. She was later burned at the stake for her crimes and the district was troubled no more with the curse of the werewolf.

The story is a well-known one, and appears, with various embellishments in a number of records of the period. Certainly it is one of the most colourful and exciting manifestations of a dreaded scourge. It is time now to examine the symptoms and traits of the lycanthrope and to trace something of his earlier history.

THREE

CRY WOLF

The dread the name of the werewolf evoked in earlier times is difficult to understand in the age of electronics and scientific sophistication in which we now live. The transformation of man into beast, of course, has been familiar in folk-tales and fairy stories from the earliest times.

Such ideas, as in *Beauty and the Beast* and tales like that of the Frog-Prince were charmingly evoked, but it was inevitable that they should become used for purposes of horror; and the Brothers Grimm were to put such themes to chilling effect in their Fairy Tales, surely a misnomer for nightmare stories more reminiscent of Edgar Allan Poe than those of trifles meant to amuse children of nursery age.

The true lycanthrope is not only physically changed so that he comes to resemble the beast of his dementia but his mind becomes changed so that he thinks and acts like a beast. Unlike the vampire he is not restricted to the night and the disease, or mania, can strike at any hour of the clock. Then again, moonlight was said to be a particular time of peril and at the height of the full moon when dogs and other wild beasts bayed at the pale burning light, the human afflicted with the taint was particularly at risk.

Those so affected would find physical changes beginning as well as mental. The features would first begin to coarsen and blur; thick hairs would appear in the palms of the hands; and the hands themselves would curve like the talons of a beast and the nails would appear to lengthen and assume the aspect of claws.

The face was gradually covered with a thick stubble of hair; the eyes would redden and glow like an animal; speech would become replaced with guttural snarls and beast-like snorts; the nose would run; the jaws salivate; and the teeth themselves appear as those of an animal. Beneath the clothes too, the victim's skin would be thickly furred like a wolf and when the werewolf moved, he would more naturally drop into a posture on all fours.

All this could happen with but the briefest of warnings, so that people suffering from this curse were forced to take special precautions to prevent their discovery. Those whose houses were large enough would lock themselves in a private room until they were themselves again. Others, if the fit came upon them by night, would take to the woods and spend their time snarling and rolling in the undergrowth, biting and slashing at stems and branches in an agony which was as much of mind as of body.

For the true lycanthrope had to bear not only the taint but the burden of guilt; one of the most terrifying things about the condition was that a man returned to his normal state after an attack had passed. If he had injured or perhaps killed another unfortunate human being during his nocturnal prowlings, then the guilt of the murderer would be added to his mental agony.

Truly, the situation of the werewolf was a most terrible one and a curse which posed a whole set of human, moral and religious problems in an age in which the church had much voice in everyday human affairs.

Even such a dread plague as the vampire admitted some slight hope; a vampire's victim might – if the vampire himself were destroyed in time – recover and return to normal life. There was little chance of this for the lycanthrope. He was doomed to wander the night until some creature stronger than himself destroyed him or a silver bullet put an end to his misery.

If his condition were discovered by the authorities an even more dreadful fate befell him; he would be haled before the magistrates, who gave short shrift to such monsters. The most he could then expect would be a quick and merciful death; but that was seldom vouchsafed. More likely he would be exposed to public trial, interspersed with torture and finally executed or burned. Very often the latter punishment was carried out with the victim still alive.

So it can be seen that the victim of lycanthropia had little to hope for, either in this world or the next. And in these straits it was no surprise that the victims sought desperate remedies, ranging from the help of wizards and witches to drastic and occasionally self-inflicted surgery.

The onset of the disease often manifested itself in what appeared to be a slight cold which later changed to fever. The patient had headaches and suffered from violent thirst. The hands would swell and appear to elongate and, like the victim of leprosy, the extremities and the skin of the face would coarsen and begin to blur. Early writers sometimes speak of a bleb or a rash which appeared as a pink sore on the chest.

Perspiration and difficulty in breathing were other aspects of the malady which, as we have indicated, then assumed a more positive form. The feet would become too cramped in their boots and the victim would be forced to remove them; the toes would appear distorted and prehensile. The victim's mind too, would be affected; he would long for the space of outdoors and feel confined inside a house. When this stage was reached the werewolf would be forced to shed his clothes and in that state of nature would naturally seek the privacy of his chamber.

With the physical nausea and cramps would come mental confusion; the chest burned, the tongue seemed to give itself reluctantly to human voice and a guttural murmur would escape from the patient's mouth.

Following the removal of clothing there would be a tendency to drop to all fours and a burning, insane desire to rend or kill some living creature would invade the brain. The heart beat faster, something ancient and primal moved heavily in the blood and the body darkened slowly with a thin matting of hair.

This extreme condition also seemed to bring with it an insensitivity to pain; a hardening of the soles of the feet and a toughening of the skin; so that the naked man-beast could run across patches of sharp stones or through sharp-spiked undergrowth in a manner which would be impossible with the sensitive skin of the normal human being.

The head was now almost completely covered with coarse hair so that it resembled the mask of an animal; the beard joined with the eyebrows and the mane ran onward up over the forehead to mingle with the hairline. Then, especially at the time of the full moon, it was impossible to avert or turn aside the blood-lust which completely seized the lycanthrope to the exclusion of everything else. He must run through the night, baying at the moon and slaughtering anything – animal or man which crossed his path.

He usually killed by biting directly through the jugular vein, as most carnivorous animals, and then later, his blood-lust sated, would fall to the ground in the forest and sleep deeply. In the morning, his features and physical aspects returned to normal, he would remember little or nothing of the night's adventures. Only if a human being had died during the night or perhaps the blood of an animal be still discernible on his bedding, would the true enormity of his condition come home to him.

Murder by night; remorseful weeping by day. Such was the awful lot, the death-in-life of the brute-victim, the werewolf. Only one thing had he to look forward to; merciful death. For, unlike the vampire, he would not return again to plague the earth.

What then were the ways in which the werewolf-victim could conceal his condition from the world at large? And perhaps, more important still, from the point of view of the community, the methods by which society could protect itself from such a monster? We shall now take a look at some of the principal procedures taken in those far-off times to rid the world of such a scourge. And the defences developed, with great cunning and resource, by the werewolf to avert suspicion and to carry on a normal life within society, while reverting to a beast-like state – often with but little prior warning.

The victim of lycanthropy – for he was more to be pitied than such a monster as the vampire – had little hope of evading discovery, unless he had an accomplice who would shield and protect him. Though this happened in the case of parents with a lycanthropic child, it was often impossible for the victim to rely on any other human being for his salvation. He developed boldness and invention in his fight to avoid detection.

At a time of full moon, when the lycanthrope would be particularly vulnerable, he would lock himself in his room and fling the key from him in the dark so that his madness would have passed by the time he found the means of egress from his prison. Others would make ingenious straps by which physically to pinion themselves to their beds. A favourite measure was for the werewolf deliberately to build himself a refuge in a remote spot in his house, probably under the eaves, where noise would be muffled.

Bars would cover the window and a grille the door. But it would still take a tremendous amount of willpower in such instances for the afflicted person not to use the key. So ingenuity would have to be used to prevent the prisoner from gaining the open air.

Specially elaborate bolts and locks, which would defeat the beast-mind, but not that of the restored human being, were evolved. But all these measures, elaborate as they seemed, were but temporary palliatives; a slender barrier between the victim and ultimate discovery. For there was no medical cure and that was the most horrifying thing about the condition.

As earlier noted, the authorities had a short way with such a monster. Apart from hanging and beheading, a convicted werewolf was frequently burned alive, often on the most slender evidence. In the age of superstition it took little for neighbour to suspect neighbour of unholy practices or pacts with the devil and once denounced, there was but little hope of the hapless person so accused being able to clear himself.

It was also believed, of course, that the true werewolf could physically change himself into an actual wolf, and many were the instances where, after a series of attacks by a wolf in individual neighbourhoods – the legends of France, Spain and Italy are thick with such examples – a local person would be accused of the 'crimes' committed by an animal and not a supernatural being.

We shall be dealing with some of these stories in later chapters. Traps were often set to catch the wolves and the authorities must have been remarkably puzzled when the animals obstinately refused to change back into human form. Female werewolves, as in the case of Madame Sanroche, were quite common too and the affliction seemed to attack both sexes impartially. The skin of the wolf also assumed magical properties in ancient times, and it was believed that humans who donned wolfskins would attain some of the beast's vitality, ferocity and other properties.

And what of the werewolf who was not a victim but merely a wicked man who actually enjoyed such a life of bestial ferocity? Herbs were believed by some to be efficacious in transforming man into beast and there were some amazing concoctions brewed in the periods between the thirteenth and nineteenth centuries in attempts by those who wished to change their shape and assume the form of wolves. We shall be meeting them also in the course of this study.

As the plague spread, so did the ferocity of the authorities' repressive measures grow to meet the menace. We have mentioned fire, the rope and the axe. Unspeakable tortures were used by the civil and ecclesiastical arm to make those accused of lycanthropy talk. And it is not difficult to understand why so many of those accused of such a heinous offence should have confessed so readily, bearing in mind the methods employed to loosen their tongues.

Werewolves, unlike vampires, could be killed by ordinary bullets but to be really effective, such a remedy should employ a specially minted silver bullet which would be sure to drop the brute dead. In some parts of Europe right up to the eighteenth century this was widely believed, as was the old story that the werewolf could never disguise his thick, bushy wolf tail. People were of the opinion that this physical trait always endured in cases of lycanthropy and this was one of the infallible tests doctors carried out.

Folklore is almost ineradicable and with such a wealth of detail it is not surprising that legends and fairy tales like Red Riding Hood, *Beauty and the Beast*, where a wolf was often used as the beast-image; and, in Russia, *Peter and the Wolf*, should have come down almost undiluted in force from earlier ages.

The wolf-fangs, like the wolf-howl, have great potency, not only in the primeval places of the world; and the dark history of the werewolf is inextricably tangled with the physical presence of the great grey beast itself in the European forests and the heartlands of Russia.

FOUR

MARK OF THE BRUTE

Philosophers and learned men through the ages have argued over the legend of the werewolf and whether such a beast could have existed. While admitting the medical form of the condition in which men believed themselves to be transformed into ravening beasts, many authorities were of the opinion that the true lycanthrope was a natural impossibility.

Speaking of the true werewolf which was able to transform itself into a wolf by means of black magic or other power, James Sprenger and Heinrich Kramer, two Dominican monks, the authors of the learned *Malleus Maleficarum*, first published in 1486, assert categorically, "It is not possible". They add that by various drugs or spells a wizard or sorcerer might cause those who gazed upon him to believe that he had transformed himself into a wolf, or another animal, but that it was impossible for him physically to change in such a way.

Other authorities had much the same opinion regarding the physical changing of man into wolf and some of them held that the devil could not form any soul or body into brutal members. But lycanthropy, in the sense that the disease could cause a person to believe he or she had been so transformed and behave in a like manner has long been recognized, even in the very earliest times.

As far back as the reign of the Roman emperor Hadrian, *c*. A.D. 125, a poet called Marcellus Sidetes wrote on lycanthropy, saying that a kind of mania afflicted the patient who was cursed with hideous appetites and the ferocity of a wolf. According to Sidetes men were mainly affected in that way at the beginning of the year, particularly in February, the month in which the disease was most rife and was to be seen in its most furious form.

The victims would then retire to the seclusion of lonely

cemeteries and live exactly as did ferocious and half-starved wolves. In classical times the werewolf was thought to be the transformed body of a wicked person who had been punished by the vengeance of the gods. In the medieval period, particularly in Central and Eastern Europe, it was believed that the werewolf had been changed through the evil designs of a witch or a wizard and many elaborate procedures for warding off this fate were evolved by the superstitious of those days.

The term itself, as we have noted, had the precise meaning of wolf-man and most countries and languages used an appellation which was remarkably similar. We have observed 'werewolf' in English and *loup-garou* in France. In Scotland the beast was called 'warwolf' and in Germany *werwolf*.

Most Slavonic tongues use similar terms, such as *vulkodlak*, *vukodlak* or *volkodlak*, the first half meaning wolf. The second appears to be a corruption for the term 'hair' so the meaning approximates very closely to the English and other European terms as applied to the man-wolf. In Romania the term *vircolac* was used for the werewolf and indeed all the countries which make up today's Eastern European bloc use remarkably similar terminology.

References abound through history to the behaviour of the person affected by lycanthropia or wolf-madness. A famous case at Padua in 1541 was that of a man who was utterly convinced that he was a wolf and ran about raving mad and behaving in all respects as a wild beast. Bohemia and Hungary were common ground for the scourge and, as we shall find, the legend of the true werewolf and that of the wolf-disease were inextricably intertwined.

An interesting example of what appears to be a victim of the werewolf disease appears in Radu Florescu and Raymond T. McNally's *Dracula*, a biography of Vlad Tepes, the Wallachian sadist and patriot, who is usually taken as the original of Bram Stoker's Dracula.

In describing a gallery of portraits of perverts and monsters in a picture gallery in Castle Ambras in the Tyrol they mention the "Wolfman" Gogonza, a native of the Canary Islands who caught a mysterious disease "which covered him with hair from top to toe".

Apparently his two children were hairy and described as "wolf-children", though his wife was quite normal. This is no doubt a medical freak but is an interesting sidelight on the mythology of the time.

In Eastern Europe in the Middle Ages certain men were said to remain hidden most of the day and to go abroad at night, barking and howling at graves and deserted cemeteries. The victims – true werewolf or those afflicted by disease, it was not clear – were described as being very dry and pale. They had heavily scabbed thighs and legs and extremely hollow eyes. They were also said to have had an "unquenchable thirst". Modern medical theory has the answer to this, as we shall see.

The werewolf theme plays a big part in the grim sagas of Norse legend. In these tales it was said that Ingiald, the son of King Aunund was an extremely timid youth. According to the scholar Muller in his *Historia Danica*, published in Copenhagen in 1839, Ingiald gained strength and courage and became the boldest of heroes after eating the heart of a wolf. Such superstitions are common to many countries of Central and Eastern Europe, as well as Scandinavia.

The fear of the wolf is deeply ingrained and manifests itself in a wide variety of ways, some of them extremely subtle. For example, it was believed in Ancient Greece that a garment made from sheep fleece could have a bad effect upon the wearer and set up an infection of the skin, in the form of a rash and itching. If this were so, said the country people, then the sheep from which the garment was made had either been killed or attacked by a savage wolf.

One of the methods by which a werewolf could be brought to book was the simple one which led to the unmasking of Madame Sanroche, as related earlier. That is, by tracing a wounded wolf by the blood-trail which in turn would lead to the human being masquerading as a beast. Or by a later identification of a known person who was wounded or injured in the same place as that in which a wolf had been shot or wounded a short time before.

This sort of evidence, purely circumstantial of course, was widely taken as overwhelming, particularly in the eighteenth century and earlier periods. But it could lead to many instances of injustice, notably in circumstances where a real wolf had been wounded and gone to ground and subsequently an innocent person, miles away at the time of the attack, had suffered an accident resulting in injury and subsequent "identification".

One hesitates to estimate the numbers of people who must have been hanged or burned after being accused under these circumstances, but the numbers involved, as ancient records testify, were considerable. It therefore follows that a great many of them must have been innocent, judged by modern standards of jurisprudence.

There are many references in Greek legend to wolves and the transformation of men into beasts. In Arcady, it was said that men could change themselves into wolves in a form of initiation ceremony. Those selected for this honour were taken to a lonely area of marshland. There they removed their clothing and left it on the shore. Once they had plunged into the marshes and swam or waded their way to the opposite bank, they would be accepted by the wolves of the region and live as one of themselves.

But, unlike the true werewolf, they were able to resume their normal lives by simply returning across the swamp and taking up the threads of their old existence as human beings. Greek myth also speaks of the ancient ritual in honour of Zeus on a mountain in Arcadia when men transformed themselves into wolves by eating a nauseous mixture of wolf entrails and those of humans, a diet akin to that of the wolf itself, an animal not above cannibalism in regard to its own species, on occasion.

In the time of Ancient Greece lycanthropy was referred to as *Lupinam Insaniam*, literally wolf-madness, but even in those days many learned men doubted that the werewolf existed. Some scholars referred to it rather as a form of melancholy; but most were agreed on it more correctly being described as a dementia or madness.

From earliest times men had used the skin of the wolf, the fiercest of beasts, as clothing and decoration and it would have been strange if something of the wolf's courage and aggressiveness had not become, in the course of time, associated with its wearer. Just as, many centuries later, the hideous cult of the Leopard Men of Africa was to evolve, where sects wore the skins, teeth and claws of leopards to strike terror into their victims when murdering them.

The wolf was not, of course, always painted as the blackest of creatures. Under certain circumstances the wolf-mother has suckled human infants. From Romulus and Remus onwards there exist many recorded instances and we shall be dealing with the more celebrated cases when we come to consider the wolf itself and feral children.

The theme of the transformation of a human into a wolf is common to most European countries and indeed, to most of the world. Invariably the treatment of the werewolf has been fairly standard; despatch by fire, sword or axe. In later centuries the bullet was the favourite method chosen. Usually a silver bullet specially minted by a gunsmith in a home-mould. Not infrequently the bullet was blessed by a priest and in some cases the ball itself even had a cross engraved upon it.

Particularly in the Middle Ages in Europe men believed the devil could enter into animals and the werewolf legend was extended to include other beasts; sometimes men were thought to be able to transform themselves into bears, swine, lions and leopards and even sheep, though it is difficult to imagine that the latter would instill much fear into their 'victims'!

The beast varied with the century and the climate but the belief remained basically the same and some amazing stories have come down from the fragmentary records of the past, which have caused much speculation among scholars and historians.

Among modern authorities who view the werewolf with a good deal of scepticism is Pennethorne Hughes, whose fascinating work *Witchcraft* was first published in 1952. In a passing reference to lycanthropy Mr Hughes observes that it had an historical origin but in Europe no real activity. He makes the exception that in sixteenth-century Europe there was an outbreak of murder and cannibalism associated with the belief in the werewolf.

An interesting reference to the werewolf belief is made by the famous writer Restif de la Bretonne in his eighteenth-century memoirs, which mention a number of peasant superstitions in the district round Auxerre in Burgundy, a district of France with which I am very familiar. France, as we have seen, and such regions as Burgundy, the Dordogne and the Auvergne in particular, has a rich history of folk legend associated with lycanthropy.

Restif mentions a number of stories of local bandits and brigands who had made pacts with the devil by which means they were able to change themselves into animals such as wolves.

Naturally, their purpose in this was to further their evil designs in the fields of robbery and murder and were not exclusively concerned with the wolf-cult. Nevertheless they are of extreme interest and France, together with such regions as the Black Forest of Germany, seems to be richest in lycanthropic detail of this kind.

The beliefs still persist even today in such districts of France as Normandy and Brittany, the latter region with which I have a family link by marriage. In Brittany the folk-tales follow the classic pattern of men either wearing wolf-skins to enable them to assume some of the savage habits of the beast; or that they literally change into wolves, generally at night-time. In other districts of France it was held that excommunication by the church brought with it the taint of lycanthropy. In Normandy in particular a man who was cast out by the church was believed to become a werewolf.

Similar tales are still held to be true in many other parts of Europe today. In my own district of Côte d'Or, the legends were embellished with quaint detail, notably that a certain term of years was assigned to the victim's state. The period usually favoured was ten or seven years. Though why this should be so is not always clear. Perhaps as a form of probation? We are never likely to know. In Brittany again it was said that if the lycanthrope be scratched above the nose so that three drops of blood were extracted, then the charm was broken.

Though most of the best-attested stories of lycanthropy appear to be French or German in origin, there is a well-authenticated body of tales involving actual werewolves and the medical state of lycorexia – where the victims experience wolfish delusions and appetites, together with other dreadful symptoms – in such countries as Austria and Russia. In the Slav countries the stories were further embellished with geographical detail. In Germany the werewolf had to be stabbed with a knife or pitchfork through the brows before it could be disenchanted.

In my earlier volume *The Vampire*, I pointed out that the practice of vampirism in many instances was held to be connected with such wild and lonely places as cross-roads in the remote places of the earth. Similarly, the werewolf has earned his own dark hunting ground and the stories, though they may vary in detail from country to country, bear an astonishing resemblance as far as the geographical locations go.

The werewolf also favoured lonely places but those where human commerce bisected them. Apart from cemeteries, his lair was often a dark and heavily wooded ravine, or perhaps a cave on the edge of an escarpment; here, preferably where a road or a cattle track wound its way through a gorge, he would lie in wait for the unwary traveller. Other favourite haunts were the paths to wells, where a wretched peasant drawing a bucket of water would be attacked or devoured. These attacks took place, of course, either by day or by night, so the werewolf was actually a more fearsome adversary than the vampire.

In France a man called Gilles Garnier actually confessed in the sixteenth century to lycanthropic practices; he admitted attacking and devouring young children, using his teeth and his claw-like hands in the manner of a ravening beast. If the story is to be believed he actually ate his victims or at least parts of them.

Dozens of witnesses gave evidence at his trial in 1573. Garnier, who admitted to murdering over a dozen children, would seem to be a victim of lycorexia, rather than a true werewolf, but certainly his practices were those of a werewolf in all respects.

As was the savage custom of those times he was condemned by his judges to be bound to the stake and burned alive. Afterwards, a common practice, his ashes were scattered to the winds and the countryside was rid of another scourge.

Dr Montague Summers, the learned English scholar and writer on occult subjects, said in one of his massive tomes on myth and legend, published more than fifty years ago, that in Slav superstition it was often very difficult to distinguish the legends of the werewolf from those of the vampire. But there are important distinctions, as we have already noted, and even in those peasant tales which approach apocryphal proportions, there is a fairly well-drawn dividing line.

In the next chapter we will examine some of the most striking cases of lycanthropy which have been recorded in past centuries.

FIVE

THE WEREWOLF STRIKES

The sixteenth century seems to have been the high-water mark of lycanthropy in France. There are literally dozens of ancient records in which attested instances are given with the names, dates, districts and details of executions of the wolf-victims. I say wolf-victims advisedly because to the modern sensibility the lycanthrope seems more to be pitied than the true monster like the vampire, the warlock and the super-sadist like Gilles de Rais.

In 1598 in the Conde district of France local people were terrified by several macabre incidents, during which the story became widely current that a monster or wolf-man was active in the area. Matters came to a head when a small girl was killed and later no less than three wolves were seen near the body.

Then a forester actually saw the wolves feeding from the human remains and the alarm was raised. A party of peasants, with considerable courage went out into the wild country where the body lay, to recover the child's corpse. Only one wolf was seen by the party and that bounded down a bank and disappeared into some fields. Later, a ragged-looking man with unkempt beard, long hair and wild eyes was discovered hiding behind a bush.

He was seized and taken before a magistrate. During cross-examination the man admitted being a *loup-garou*. Further, he averred that the other wolves seen at the scene of the child's death were his brother and sister and that they were all able to transform themselves into wolves by the use of a magical ointment. Where the man, who appeared to be simple-minded, had obtained such an ointment was never made quite clear.

The accused, who was probably demented in the terms of modern medical knowledge, was named Jacques Rollet and he was treated extremely leniently, judged by the rough standards

of the time. At his trial he was sentenced to death but the judiciary in Paris later held that he was unhinged and unfit to plead.
The sentence was commuted and he was put in care of an
asylum for the term of his natural life.

That the conclusions drawn from the evidence put forward at
the trial of Rollet were reasonably accurate cannot be doubted;
certainly the brother and sister he spoke of were never found and
the truth of the matter was that probably the child had been
attacked and killed by real wolves. Though Rollet had confessed to actually helping to kill the child and eating parts of the
body, his mental state was such as to make such testimony
extremely unreliable. This is one of the long list of similar cases
in the sixteenth century where the real facts of the matter will
never be known.

The Jura district of France too, had a great reputation for
lycanthropy and there are many stories of the atrocities committed by werewolves in that mountainous, heavily wooded
area. Late in the sixteenth century the local parliament issued
an edict laying down dire punishment for those inhuman devils
who practised the horrible crime and the authorities were extremely alarmed at the great increase in the terror in the district.

Of course, as we know, except in rare instances, the punishment for such crimes was invariably death but by threatening
torture and the long-drawn-out agony of such a fate the local
magistrates and the judiciary hoped to eradicate the menace.
There is no evidence that they succeeded, judging by the plentiful court and assize records of the hangings and burnings which
followed.

At Poligny in 1521 three werewolves caught at their grisly
tasks were publicly executed and their dreadful deeds widely
publicized, to act as a warning to others. As though the werewolf had a choice in the matter! The victim of lycanthropy
could no more prevent himself from going berserk and hunting
down his prey in the moonlight than could the beasts of the
forest.

The holocausts of hangings, burnings and summary executions were no answer to the curse of the werewolf and they
gradually died out in later centuries, though not before thousands – innocent and presumed guilty alike – had perished.

Typical of the records of the sixteenth century was that of the
extraordinary case of a Frenchman who admitted having inter-

course with wolves and of having assumed the shape of the beast through a pact he had made with the Devil. Jean Peyral, who was executed in 1518, confessed to his judges that he had killed a number of people while bodily transformed into a wolf.

Unlike most instances of lycanthropy of this period, his case exhibited other unusual features. He claimed that he could not, for instance, transform himself during daylight; all his terrifying expeditions were made during the dark hours of the night. He confessed that after his compact with the Devil he had taken part in sabbats.

His transformation also was apparently made with the aid of a magic ointment, which had been created in a particularly nauseating manner. In fact, it was said that at the trial, the ingredients were so sickening that several people in the court-room fainted. Peyral's presumed intercourse with she-wolves gave his case a cachet which many others lacked and his story became famous in the Jura Mountains. The wretched man, after suffering many tortures, was sentenced by the court and later burned. His ashes were then scattered to the winds.

Bavaria was another country where the legend of the were-wolf was particularly strong; indeed, the tales are still believed today in the more remote country districts. It is not difficult to understand this when one visits some of these brooding hills and dark forests and it is easy to imagine the most horrifying and bizarre happenings being commonplace in such surroundings.

It was in Bavaria that the legends became intermingled with those of the vampire; for instance, it was held that both had extremely long fingernails and teeth. But the main distinction of the tales of those districts, as well as those of Germany itself, was the detail that the werewolf had maddened, staring eyes with extremely narrow pupils. Certain people, though handsome in other respects, were often shunned because of these physical characteristics, against all reason or common sense, particularly in medieval times.

In Russia too, such tales were common, and it is not difficult to imagine the scene where a perfectly ordinary wolf, drawn to the outskirts of a village by hunger and a particularly harsh winter, could cause terror and havoc among the population. We shall be meeting some famous cases of man-eating wolves which were taken for supernatural monsters, in due course.

The late eighteenth century also saw one of the most famous

cases of lycanthropy of the period, that of the Werewolf of
Bordeaux. This took place in the Landes district, today a favourite resort of holidaymakers, but in those far-off times a lonely
and remote area much given to primitive superstition.

For some time the countryside round about the village of St
Sever had been the scene of horrifying and mysterious happenings
involving a wolf. A number of people had been attacked and in
time there were several deaths. Things got to such a state that
people barred their doors at night and were afraid to go out. But
it made little difference as the terror continued to strike with
impunity, by day as well as by night.

The wolf-man was eventually caught after a chase in which a
number of people joined. Uniquely, he was of tender years,
being only about fifteen. His name was Jean Grenier, and he
worked as a cow-herd for a wealthy farmer who lived near St
Sever. The farmer's own stock had suffered badly from the
depredations of the werewolf, and the reason was now plain.

Questioned by the judicial authorities, the boy confessed that
one day he had come upon a demon in the woods. He referred to
him as the Lord of the Forest and he had taken an oath to
serve him, in return for which he was given the power to change
himself into a wolf.

Grenier's youth did not save him. Like nearly all those tainted
with lycanthropy he was convicted and publicly executed.
Afterwards, the depredations among both humans and cattle in
the area ceased, and the district was troubled no more.

One of the infallible tests to determine the authenticity of a
werewolf has not yet been touched upon. It followed that because the wolf-man's flesh was covered with thick fur, his blood-
lust was combined with the practical urge to strip off all his
clothing; both in order to be free from restraint and to run about
and pursue his victims the more swiftly.

From this the natural result was that his skin was torn and
cut by his passage through undergrowth and on thorns and
branches. When the pursuing and often vengeful villagers,
usually including victims' relatives, burst into the home of a
suspected person, the suspect was often made to strip when his
tell-tale flight would be only too evidently visible on the now
human skin.

Some people also believed that if they removed or burned a
suspected werewolf's clothing he would be unable to resume his

human form. This latter superstition was widely held in Europe, Eastern Europe and Russia.

Like the vampire, the tale of the werewolf, both in its legendary form and as a medical case, seems rare in the British Isles. Perhaps the climate was too damp for it; certainly, the lycanthrope had to run about naked a great deal of the time and the drier air of the Continent would no doubt be more congenial.

The last wolf in Britain was, as is well known, shot in Scotland in the eighteenth century. It must have been a lonely beast who probably welcomed its end.

In Britain the true lycanthrope as well as the medical case would undoubtedly have suffered from rheumatism! No matter what the reason, the records of its appearance in Britain and Ireland are so sparse as to be almost non-existent. There are a few legends from Ireland, notably that of a werewolf of Meath who called a priest to attend his wolf-wife who was seriously ill. In places like Ireland, Poland and Armenia it was generally believed that the taint of the werewolf could infect whole families.

Though a natural belief, there is no general reason to believe this, nor do the records bear it out. As we have already seen, the average person's horror and revulsion was so strong as to lead him or her to denounce the marriage partner to the appropriate authorities. Certain herbs were believed to possess supernatural powers of transformation and many vile brews were concocted, often with fatal results to the would-be werewolf who drank them.

Like the case of the vampire, holy water was held to be efficacious in some countries as an antidote to the curse. When poured on to the suspected lycanthrope it physically burned the fur and purged the victim. But so far as is known, it was in no sense a cure or even a temporary relief, causing as it did more mental anguish than beneficial effect. And in some regions of the earth it was denied that holy water had the slightest efficacy at all. As we shall see, the curse of the werewolf was an even more fearful and formidable problem than that of almost any other fiend from the darker realms of the demoniacal.

The vampire's depredations seem to be more generously recorded in the eighteenth and nineteenth centuries, and there are many well-attested tales from Victorian times. Conversely, the best-documented examples of lycanthropy range from the Middle Ages forward to the late eighteenth century and thereafter become exceedingly sparse.

One unusual and particularly vivid case of lycanthropy occurred in a remote district of France in the mid-nineteenth century and because such incidents were comparatively rare in the last century the details are worth recording. Two magistrates had been out hunting in the forests of the Gironde and after a long and tiring day were caught miles from shelter. They had sent away their servants and after losing their way in deep woodland realized they were in the open for the night.

After two hours of aimless wandering they chanced upon a rough woodstore in a clearing and in this large timber shed prepared to settle down for the night. They were just about to collect the materials to light a fire in the glade beyond when they heard stealthy footsteps on the dried leaves of the forest floor. Something about the furtive approach cautioned them to remain concealed. After a minute or two they saw from their hiding-place an old countryman advancing through the woods toward them.

He was known to both magistrates as a person of ill repute and the two men wondered what he could be doing in that lonely spot. In fact, one of the officials had sentenced this very man some two years before to a term of imprisonment for a minor wrong-doing; the court had been unable to prove his guilt on the major charge and the accused's triumph had considerably enhanced his reputation for chicanery and cunning. Certainly, his actions this night were weird and bizarre in the extreme, even in a district where strange things had been known to happen.

But this was 1858, in an age of railways, progress and civilization, and in a modern country that prided itself on good government and law and order. The man was making strange signs in the air now and the magistrates shrank back behind the bushes as the bizarre, solitary display continued. The old poacher resembled nothing so much as one of the practitioners of the black arts which the two friends had often seen in books of old woodcuts.

After the preliminary motions were over the pair were startled and disconcerted when the old man threw back his head and gave a long, mournful and blood-curdling howl. The noise was like that of an animal and it aroused curious echoes in the minds of both watchers.

The man repeated his mournful cry for several minutes on end and presently it appeared as if there was an answering howl from the far distance of the forest. To the sharpened sensibilities of the two men behind the bush a sense of horror was added to the scene when they became aware of the sharp rustling of leaves in the wooded aisles, as if alien feet were running stealthily toward them. Indeed, one of the magistrates was already half-turning away in panic, when his companion's arm on his own brought him to himself, and he again sank down beside his colleague.

There was a deep and awful silence, broken only by the faint keening of the wind in the tree-tops. Then the elder magistrate felt the fierce grip of his companion's hand on his wrist. He followed the direction indicated by the trembling finger and saw faint points of light in the dark shadows at the edge of the clearing. With a shudder of horror the elder man saw the lights move and then a snarling howl again answered the weird cries of the old poacher.

The grey, shaggy form of an enormous wolf materialized in the shadow at the clearing's rim and advanced forward, every hair of its rough coat stippled and sharp-edged in the silvery moonlight. Other shadows advanced at the huge wolf's heels until the whole glade seemed full of the menacing, predatory shapes, jaws slavering, red eyes gleaming, teeth flashing as they gave back answering howls.

To the two hidden men's astonishment, the old man stood calmly in the centre of the clearing, looking expectantly as the shapes of the bounding wolves advanced towards him. The biggest detached itself from the group and flung itself against the old poacher's legs. The gesture resembled that of a great dog and the watchers' astonishment increased when they saw the ancient reach down to fondle roughly behind the wolf's ears.

The remainder of the pack, about nine or ten strong, had now joined man and wolf, and pirouetted in circles about them, howling loudly until it seemed as though the entire night was filled with their shrieking chorus. So menacing was the sound that the two magistrates behind their screening bushes fell to the ground at one point, their hands over their ears. When they again looked the old man in the glade was nowhere to be seen; there was nothing but the surging mass of the wolfpack, baying and howling excitedly.

But a new, whitish-grey brute of a wolf, almost as big as the pack-leader had joined them, and presently the whole band of ravening animals passed away to the north, their howls getting fainter and fainter until they died out among the great trunks of the forest trees. When they were certain they were safe the two men emerged from their hiding-place, built an enormous fire and huddled sleepless by it until morning, when they returned to tell the story to their incredulous families.

The old poacher – both men believed he had been the ancient grey wolf they had seen – was more cunning than the magistrates had believed. They could prove nothing and later he answered all the questions of local people with bland indifference.

If he were indeed one of the dreaded lycanthropes – and who can blame the magistrates for remaining unshaken in their belief? – he was more discreet in future and practised his black art farther afield, for the district saw that particular pack no more.

In Fact

SIX

THE HOUR OF THE WOLF

The activities of the wolf and the werewolf of legend have been inextricably intertwined in the primitive mind since the dawn of time. It must be remembered also that the wolf was found all over Europe and native to the British Isles until comparatively recently in historical terms.

The wealth of stories and legends which accreted round the beast as the centuries passed was hardly exaggerated, so fierce was the wolf's character and so horrifying some of the circumstances surrounding the deaths of its human victims.

Yet the wolf as an animal has much to commend it: courage in the face of adversity; loyalty to the pack and to its young; and a highly developed maternal instinct in the female which has led to many famous and attested cases of she-wolves suckling human young. Like the ape/human legend which inspired Edgar Rice Burroughs' *Tarzan of the Apes* series, the tales of wolves protecting and bringing to maturity abandoned human young have grown to assume epic proportion across the centuries.

The most famous of these stories is, of course, that of Romulus and Remus, the founders of the city of Rome, which now includes the wolf-boys in its official coat of arms. The two babes, twin sons of the vestal virgin Rhea Silvia as a result of her liaison with the god Mars, were illegitimate and therefore condemned.

It being the custom to abandon such children or ensure their death by exposure, the two infants were hurled into the River Tiber. But they came to shore at a spot where a she-wolf was drinking from the bank. The wolf was first prompted to approach them by the infants' screaming but the mother-instinct prevailed over the savage reflex that would normally have prompted her to kill human children.

Instead she suckled and protected them, the children drinking from her teats as new-born wolves would have done. She then carried them as a wolf would carry its cubs, to a dry cave on the Palatine Hill. Here, the children were again fed and kept warm by the protective fur of the she-wolf's body. Later, a shepherd came across the two children and brought them up as his own.

Legend does not record what stage of their development the children had reached and later speculation has rather decried credence of the story. Yet it is perfectly true that she-wolves have successfully reared human young, though of course, as in the cases of the wild boys we shall be examining later, a child brought up under such conditions and who has reached more mature years is no longer able to take his place as a member of the human race.

An infant reared in such a manner loses all capacity for speech and communication; has all the manners and traits of a beast; eats his food raw and exhibits all the wild animal's ferocity and suspicion of man. He is then incapable of training and education; and in fact the most patient and loving care on the part of human teachers in all the cases recorded since the fourteenth century has mostly failed to establish rapport with beings brought up so.

The mind appears to be incapable of learning in such situations once childhood has passed and in none of the classic examples, such as Victor, the wild boy of Aveyron, was even simple speech capable of restoration. And this, in the latter case, despite herculean efforts by a young doctor of genius, Jean Itard, who spent years on the task. We shall be meeting *homo ferus* again in the course of this study.

The wolf, *canis lupus*, was formerly widely distributed over the earth but because of over-shooting and the spread of cities and urban populations survives mainly today in Canada, Russia, Eastern Europe and parts of Asia. The Canadian timber wolf is one of the largest species outside Russia and one of the most savage and powerful of mammals; hunting in packs as it does, it is a formidable foe, especially when hungry and packs have been known to hunt down and eat even armed parties of well-equipped hunters.

The weather favours its operations in winter in such countries as Russia and the far north of Canada though regrettably, in the second half of the twentieth century, timber wolves in the latter country are being decimated by the barbaric practice of hunting from sleds.

These petrol-driven vehicles on skis propel the hunters at tremendous speed over the snow; eventually, the tiring and hard-pressed quarry is despatched by high-powered rifle or even, in some cases, by the use of automatic weapons. Needless to say the numbers of wolves slaughtered by these unsporting and brutal tactics is such that the species is bound to decline wherever the practice prevails.

The wolf as a species has much to commend it; courage in adversity; loyalty to its mate and cubs and to the pack; tactical cunning in stalking and despatching its prey, such as deer and other small animals; and a certain nobility of character. Kipling recognized this when he made the wolf the friend of Mowgli in his famous *The Jungle Book*.

Yet there is no denying a darker side to the wolf. He represents the stealthy death which comes silently by night and the legends of the wolf – as of the werewolf – hardly need embellishing, the facts in many cases of wolf attacks on humans being so horrific in detail.

The terrain of the wolf also necessarily adds to the horror; we are dealing with the wild and desolate places of the earth, where the strong reign and he who is long of tooth and claw and ferocious by nature must prevail over the weak. Small wonder that Jack London made wolves the protagonists and chief characters in many of his sombre and powerful short stories.

It needs little imagination to picture the thoughts of the lonely traveller in the icy wastes of Russia or of the Canadian Arctic as he sits by his meagre log fire in the wilderness, and hears the fierce baying of the wolf-pack somewhere beyond the fringe of firelight, where the distant stars glitter in the cold, indifferent sky.

Dr Montague Summers, the authority already mentioned, in one of his volumes on lycanthropy, which appeared in the '20s of this century, recognized the mystic bond between the figure of the wolf and the man-beast, the werewolf.

He says, "The distinctive features of the wolf are unbridled cruelty, bestial ferocity, and ravening hunger. His strength, his cunning, his speed, were regarded as abnormal, almost eerie qualities; he had something of the demon, of hell.

"He is the symbol of Night and Winter, of Stress and Storm,

the dark and mysterious harbinger of Death. In Holy Writ the wolf is ever the emblem of treachery, savagery and bloodthirstiness."

The quotation seems to sum up all the qualities I have been at some pains to point out and re-emphasize, if emphasis were needed, just how strongly the figures of the wolf and the werewolf were linked in public imagination. When we add to them the strange and bizarre figure of the wolf-boy the chain is complete.

Dr Summers makes the interesting point that the reason why the Devil is more ready to change the sorcerer into a wolf than to any other animal is owing to the natural ferocity of the wolf, who ravages and devours and does more harm to man than any other animal marauder.

And he adds, significantly, "Moreover, the wolf typifies the eternal enemy of the lamb, and by the Lamb is symbolized Our Lord and the Saviour Jesus Christ."

The wolf, unfairly as we have seen, was often blamed for the dark and terrible deeds of the werewolf, the true lycanthrope; it needed only one lone wolf to appear on the outskirts of a village in Eastern Europe or Russia in the Middle Ages for the rumours to fly. Even if the beast were relatively harmless and only foraging for scraps of food from the table during the hard season, all the crimes of the district were sure to be fastened at its door.

Such beasts were hunted mercilessly, even though relatively innocent, and an older wolf, grown cunning in the ways of men and easily able to elude the hunters with its superior woodcraft, often gained the reputation of being a true werewolf. It was only after a wolf had been shot that villagers would be able to assess the situation. If depredations in the neighbourhood ceased then the shot beast had been a *loup-garou*.

This rough and ready judgement added to the legends and the wolf, already a dreaded animal in the days when the average household had only sticks or agricultural implements with which to defend itself, became an almost supernatural figure with its glaring eyes, sharp teeth and shaggy coat.

In those primitive times the average peasant had much to fear; his feudal overlords were little less savage than the beasts of the forest and in an age noted for brutish behaviour and stern precepts for both man and beast, the wise built stout walls against weather and predator and clung to the pale solace of

Christianity or pagan superstition. The cross, as we have seen, might keep off the vampire but it was of no use against the wolf – or the werewolf.

When the weather hardened, the temperature going down many degrees below zero, then indeed the peasant might fear the wolf; for, growing bolder as the pangs of hunger grew keener, he not only came into the centre of villages but might well break into the more flimsily constructed of the houses and carry off the householder or a member of his family.

Records of the time emphasize the cruel and terrible fate of such victims, particularly those who were still alive and weakened by their savaging. For them there was nothing left but a barbaric and lingering death as they were dragged toward the waiting pack at the outskirts of the settlement.

The pack itself, the basic unit of the wolf's family structure, might range from seven or eight to more than twenty animals, according to local circumstance. A wolf pack made hungry by severe weather is a formidable entity and legend was often outdone when such a pack struck. Their victim might be a lone forester caught unaware and cut off from his village; or perhaps a sledge party.

In Eastern Europe particularly, packs have been known to run down such parties after chases lasting many miles. The horse or lead-dog would first be marked and when the quarry was brought down it was only a matter of time before death would come to all the victims, human and animal alike.

With the advent of gunpowder and the rifle such packs found it more difficult to claim human victims and often the shots would bring a rescue party from the nearest settlement. But the wolf's human prey was very often children, a defenceless woman out gathering firewood, or perhaps one or two trappers sitting round their lonely fire. The wolf feared fire, it is true, but hunger soon overcomes fear and primitive man's reliance on fire as a weapon against the wolf-pack was sometimes brutally disillusioned.

Small wonder then that the wolf's fearsome reputation – only slightly exaggerated – should have fused with the legend of the werewolf so that the line between reality and fiction became blurred, people in the Middle Ages being unable to distinguish between the two. The depredations of the wolf may have contributed to the hysteria which gripped Europe in medieval times so that thousands of suspected lycanthropes perished by the axe, by the rope and by the flame.

It has been estimated that in France alone between the early sixteenth century and the beginning of the seventeenth, well over thirty thousand people perished in a holocaust of revenge, when neighbour denounced neighbour to the authorities as a lycanthrope.

An even more horrible aspect of this black time was the widely held belief in Germany, France and Eastern Europe, that the werewolf could change his skin by literally turning it inside out. So that when he appeared as a man he wore his human skin outwards. But when he transformed himself into a wolf he reversed his covering and wore the furry side uppermost. Incredible as it may seem, many people were literally cut to pieces by their accusers, who attempted to reverse their skins to reveal the fur beneath.

It is not recorded whether any werewolves were ever discovered by this barbarous method or why, for that matter, the authorities did not desist when it became obvious that such a procedure was pointless. But then one might just as well ask why the cruel traditions of the ducking stool, the rack and the thumbscrew were not abandoned, instead of persisting for hundreds of years.

Human nature is perverse; it believes what it wants to believe; and the empiricists among the inquisitors pressed on, hoping for more tangible evidence in their righteous battle against the forces of darkness. Given the age and circumstances it is perhaps understandable, though inexcusable.

Through it all the wolf, that mysterious and elusive beast, went his dark way, indifferent to the habits and practices of mankind. We turn now to some specific examples of the terrifying and terrible acts by which individual animals gained reputations that almost rivalled those of the werewolf itself.

SEVEN

THE GREAT BEAST

There are many recorded examples of individual wolves between the eighteenth and late nineteenth century which established veritable reigns of terror and were responsible for many
human deaths, leaving aside the indiscriminate slaughter of
domestic stock. But none of these histories were more terrible
or horrifying than that of a gigantic wolf which terrified a
corner of France in the eighteenth century and which, during a
career spanning more than two years, was responsible for the
deaths of over sixty human beings.

The story began in the summer of 1764 when a huge wolf
bounded into a clearing in the mountain district of Lozere and
attacked a woman who was watching over a herd of cattle.
Fortunately for the woman, she survived though badly injured
because, as often happens, her oxen, which work together in
face of common danger, charged and attacked the wolf, hurling
it to the ground and causing it to slink away.

But the beast had apparently gained a taste for human blood
and though the attack was little noted at the time, it was to
mark a dark period in this remote corner of France which
has only been paralleled in modern times by the attacks of
man-eating tigers in the Kumaon district of the United
Provinces of India, about which the great hunter Jim Corbett
writes so vividly in a number of books; and by the depredations of the lions known as the Man-Eaters of Tsavo during
the building of a railway in East Africa in the early part of
this century.

The wolf which bounded away snarling on that warm June
day, carrying off with it fragments of the fortunate woman's
clothing instead of her body, was to gain its own immortal niche
in the sombre pages of folk-mythology. The animal, which
seemed to bear a charmed life and to have the devil's own luck

in surviving all the efforts made to track and kill it, has gone
down in the records as the Beast of the Gevaudan.

But wolves were common in the district and some are still
believed to survive there to this day and the incident, horrifying
though it had been, was shrugged off and after a few weeks was
almost forgotten by the inhabitants of that sparsely populated
area. The affair assumed a more sombre turn when in July a
young girl of about fifteen was attacked and killed near a small
village called Habats. The girl's body had been partly devoured
by the animal.

Then, with shocking suddenness, there came three more
attacks and three more deaths; the first that of another young
girl and then of two boys in September of 1764. The wolf responsible was believed to be the same animal and its favourite
method of attack was to launch itself straight at its victim and
rely on knocking him or her down with the violence of its rush.
A wolf is a big animal and its weight at speed, particularly when
the forepaws are used on the chest, is quite enough to send the
heaviest man to the ground.

The beast would usually despatch its victim with a single bite
to the face, which it would tear away with its razor-sharp teeth.
If the wound did not kill the victim immediately shock and loss
of blood would shortly do so. By the time the autumn set in, the
animal had perfected its tactics and had added a grown woman
to its victims. It was emboldened too, by the ease with which it
had accomplished its purposes. When ten persons had already
perished by the beginning of November, it was little wonder
that terror stalked the forests of the Gevaudan, and the fear-
stricken inhabitants of the small villages were in a state of
siege.

Eventually the public unease became so great that the
government ordered a unit of dragoons stationed at Clermont-
Ferrand to hunt down the animal and the troops left the barracks under the command of Captain Jean Duhamel confident
that the man-eater would soon be despatched. In passing, it is
strange to reflect that this area of France has seen some of the
most sinister and bizarre manifestations of lycanthrope-like
behaviour.

For it was only some thirty years later than the incidents con-
cerning the Beast of the Gevaudan, that Victor, the wolf-boy
was discovered not so very far away in the district of Aveyron.

Were it not too fanciful for conjecture, one might surmise that such haunted regions of mountain, ravine and forest seem to conjure up their own savage and unearthly manifestations to become the stuff of legend.

Unfortunately for the people of the Mende district the soldiers who jingled their way through the sunshine and the dust so smilingly and confidently that day in 1764 were doomed to failure, though they were destined to kill almost a hundred wolves in the series of hunts they organized with the help of villagers in the forests of the area during the next few months. By December, when the Captain had finished his work of extirpation, it was believed by both lay and military authorities alike that the menace had been destroyed.

The dragoons had no sooner left the district than the great wolf struck again. For, by an added irony, it was Christmas Eve when death came to a young boy of seven, who was badly mangled. Within days a shepherd was added to the roll and before the year was out two more young girls were killed and partly eaten by the wolf. The panic into which this threw the population may well be imagined and the stories which flew about the district added colour to the tale that the authorities were attempting to deal not with a wolf but a werewolf, a supernatural being which could strike with impunity and return to kill again. Added strength was given the legend by the fact that the troops had killed so many wolves on their drives in the district, but that the killer wolf itself had escaped.

Several more victims were claimed in the early January of 1765 and the church too declared war on the beast. The Bishop of Mende himself directed public prayer for the safety of the populace but despite these ecclesiastical and secular measures, the wolf continued its reign of terror. Several women and girls were eaten within the space of a few days and the horror of the attacks spread when the beast enlarged its area of activities to take in widely flung villages.

It is essential to know something of the circumstances of such rustic populations in those far-off times to get something of the flavour of the fear and loathing which such attacks inspired. The supernatural overtones only added fresh terrors to an already horrific situation, which was doubly emphasized by the primitive living conditions, the remoteness of the dwellings from such aid as that afforded by a town, and above all by the brooding silences of the great forests backgrounded by harsh and frowning mountains.

It got dark early in winter and it was dark too when the predominantly rustic peasant population rose to begin their simple chores. The people earned their living as farmers, cattle herdsmen, charcoal burners, verderers, stockmen, carpenters and in other such pursuits and the few educated people such as priest, squire and schoolmaster were too thin on the ground to stiffen the population in face of such a peril.

Also, the forest and mountain paths were lonely and exposed and made it easy for such a ruthless and cunning beast as a wolf to take every advantage of terrain. The population, though it possessed a few flintlocks and other primitive weapons, was too ill equipped to meet such a menace and the wolf indeed displayed almost superhuman acumen in selecting only women and children and the weak as its victims. To all intents and purposes the Beast of the Gevaudan was a supernatural creature.

It was all the more laudable therefore that almost incredible feats of heroism were witnessed in those black days, particularly on the part of simple schoolchildren, who displayed enormous courage and resource in the face of a menace which often cowed their elders. One such example occurred in mid January of 1765 when the great wolf burst into a small group of children which were playing by themselves near the village of Villaret.

The wolf seized the smallest child but reckoned without the heroism of his playmates; three of the bigger children seized sticks and stones and attacked the wolf in their turn, driving it off its victim and forcing it into flight. Though in fact the beast did bite most of these courageous children, the life of the smallest child was saved and none died of their wounds.

This was a victory for the population and an example to follow but the wolf eschewed groups for a while after this and within a few days had killed and partly eaten a young girl of twenty and a boy of about fourteen. As already observed, the creature had until then confined its horrifying activities to women and children in the main. The pattern was about to change.

It was in late January that the wolf appeared to alter its tactics. The incident, fearful enough in itself, was notable in

Hairy glory—Lon Chaney Jr in the remarkable make-up evolved by Universal's Jack P. Pierce for his role as the lycanthrope Lawrence Talbot in *The Wolf Man* (1941), the first film role of a series in which Chaney starred. (Compare with the real Chaney, facing page 65)

Lon Chaney in his striking werewolf make-up, in a posed shot from one of Universal's *Werewolf* series of the Forties, in which he appears as the unfortunate Lawrence Talbot

other ways, for the several men involved were able to give clear and coherent accounts and a complete description of the animal. The attack took place in daylight against a group of three farm-workers. These were, luckily, carrying stout metal pitchforks and they were thus able to give a very good account of themselves when the gigantic wolf burst snarling among them.

The struggle continued for what seemed like minutes but probably lasted for something like thirty seconds. The men struck and prodded at the beast, with frightened shouts and curses, as it tried to leap at their throats. They did not know whether they had inflicted any damage on it as it leapt off snarling after a short while.

The fortunate trio hurried to the nearest village to tell their story and were able to inform the authorities that the wolf was a big, full-grown animal with rough, reddish fur. It attacked alternately from a horizontal position and then reared up like a horse to strike with its forepaws. How lucky the three men were and how vengeful their attacker, can be gauged from the stark fact that the beast killed two women and a child within a few days following its abortive encounter with the farm labourers.

There was some scepticism from those fortunates outside the area of the wolf's depredations, who averred that it could not be a wolf at all. The majority, of course, put its activities down to those of a werewolf of the supernatural variety; others felt it could be some other ferocious animal. But after each kill, when the pathetic remains were recovered, the head of the victim was always found detached from the body. This was invariably the earmark of a wolf attack and is that beast's infallible practice.

One of the major difficulties confronting the authorities was that in such a wooded, mountainous area as the Gevaudan, the wolf's movements were almost impossible to follow. It had only to bound off for a few yards to be in thick cover immediately. The almost insuperable problem, however, was its unpredict-able pattern of attack; it operated over hundreds of square miles of forest and mountainous slopes and as its natural cunning became sharpened through the constant assaults on humans, so did it vary its pattern of behaviour just as though it could out-think its opponents.

It did, in fact, resemble a superhuman monster in the clever-ness of its operations and the murderous ferocity and pitiless-ness of its activities. So feared had the wolf become in a few short, bloody months of attacks against a fear-stricken populace that a number of drives took place. On one of these several thousand men took part. Disappointingly, though a number of large wolves were flushed from the forest and killed, there was no beast resembling the man-eater among them. That the efforts had been in vain was made clear by early February when a young man was attacked in the district.

He was severely injured but owed his life to the courage of his dog which in turn attacked the wolf and with almost incredible bravery forced the animal to release its hold. Nearer the scene of its former activities the monster tore a young girl to pieces toward the middle of the month, and it had become obvious that the problem was no longer merely a local one. The fame of the man-eater had reached the seat of government in Paris by this time and the King, Louis XV ordered immediate measures to be taken against the Beast of the Gevaudan.

The choice of a man to despatch the terrible beast that was ravishing the district fell to a famous hunter of the period, who had notable success with the killing of ferocious wolves. He was a man called Philippe Donneval, who had despatched upwards of a thousand wolves in Normandy. On receipt of the summons from his king, Donneval immediately set out for the Gevaudan. With him travelled his son, his assistants and his strongest and most reliable hounds.

While aid was making its best progress southwards, the man-eater had not been idle. He had attacked and killed a woman and two children and injured a number of others. More and more rumours were flying about the villages; the beast was now said to be as big as a donkey, with a monstrous tail and a brown streak across its back. Though one must allow for the exaggeration of the peasants there was no doubt that the brute was bigger than average and there was no mistaking its ferocity and cunning.

The killings went on through the spring of 1765 and in the meantime the king had put a price on its head. Several more children were killed, one father courageously rescuing his young son, though the boy subsequently died. Between the end of February and the end of May the beast attacked and killed no less than fourteen people, mostly children and young women, and injured a number of others.

A shepherd had a lucky escape when he was guarding a herd,

but fortunately his cattle rallied to his rescue, charging the wolf and forcing it to abandon its attack. The cunning of the wolf was incredible, as it seemed to sense when it was dealing only with unarmed children or simple herdsmen equipped with sticks or agricultural implements.

There do not appear to be any records of it stalking and attacking a full-grown man carrying firearms. By this time Donneval and his son had commenced their operations and though they scoured the area, killing about twenty wolves, the man-eater was not among them. Their activities, at first greeted with enthusiasm by the villagers, were latterly viewed with increasing cynicism by the wretched inhabitants of the Gevaudan.

One strange feature of the Beast of the Gevaudan, which gives some colour to the old stories that it was a supernatural creature, was its choice of prey. There were innumerable instances when the wolf could have satisfied its appetite by eating sheep or cattle. It did not do this. Instead, it preferred to stalk and attack human prey, a far harder and more exacting task and one not devoid of danger for the wolf. There is something odd here that cannot entirely be explained away in the light of modern-day knowledge.

Man-eating tigers, for example, become man-eaters through hunger, mainly because their teeth are blunted or perhaps through injury, so that they are unable to catch their natural prey. Instead, they turn to human beings, who are not so fleet of foot as antelope or gazelle. But no such reasons impelled this great wolf of the eighteenth century and its motives must remain shrouded in obscurity.

Certainly, its actions and the whole scope of its operations seemed demoniacally motivated to the people of the region at that time and it is not difficult to understand their attitude. Towards the end of May another hair-raising escape from death at the jaws of the beast pin-pointed the problem facing Donneval and his men.

The wolf, with ever-increasing boldness, this time chose to attack a horseman who was riding along a road toward one of the local villages, a place called Amorgne. The beast sprang from a thicket at the rider as man and horse came abreast its hiding-place but though the rider was unseated by the ferocity of the assault, he managed to beat off the wolf and, remounting his horse, escaped with his life.

A whole year had now gone by since the first attack by the wolf on a human being and it will be remembered that the would-be victim, a woman, escaped with her life. Now, as if to celebrate the anniversary with some more positive action, the man-eater killed a young girl at nearby Amorgne, at the beginning of June.

Another little girl with her effected her escape by climbing on top of a formation of rocks at the side of the road. But her ordeal was just beginning, for she was not discovered in her hiding-place until three whole days had elapsed. By that time the child's reason had entirely gone and she was quite demented.

The attacks on young children mounted during the next few weeks to what can only be described as a fury of senseless slaughter. The wolf was never seen on these occasions, except by its victims, and that was almost always too late. One fortunate instance concerned a young girl whose herd of pigs kept the wolf at a distance until she was rescued by her mother.

In another case a child was bitten but a party of villagers came to the rescue. Tragically, help was too late on this occasion, as the girl died of her injuries a short while after. Another little girl was more fortunate for, as often happened, her herd of oxen formed up into a phalanx and charged the wolf, which was driven off without harming the girl.

But several other girls and women were slaughtered in dark and tragic circumstances and the villagers must often have been in despair as they gathered in parties to collect the pathetic decapitated fragments of loved ones which the wolf scattered in its wake. It was now obvious that Donneval had failed. More effective measures were needed. King Louis thought he had them to hand.

Lieutenant Antoine de Bauterre was the next choice of the king. A young and vigorous officer, he had the confidence of Louis and was, in fact, his personal Lieutenant des Chasses. So he was probably not at all surprised when he was instructed to report to His Majesty at the Palace of Versailles in early July. There he was given his brief and told to select the best possible pack of wolfhounds.

Bauterre was a shrewd and efficient officer, good at his job and one of the king's favourite officials, so he had no difficulty in meeting Louis' brief. He requested the best hounds from a number of royal princes of the court and his needs were readily met by courtiers who were the lieutenant's constant companions in the field. As soon as he had gathered together the strongest possible pack, the lieutenant left for the Gevaudan with the hounds and a large detachment of men.

He arrived on the wolf's hunting ground about a fortnight later and in early August Donneval and his son gave up their attempts to make contact with the wolf and returned to their native countryside. Their experiences in pursuit of the Beast of the Gevaudan had left them sadly chastened and they doubted whether the king's lieutenant would have any better luck.

As though to show its contempt for the new foe which had arrived on the scene the great wolf struck almost immediately. It first tore to pieces an old woman at her spinning-wheel. Her body, badly savaged – most of the injuries being inflicted before death – was discovered by a small child, a girl whose screams apparently sent the wolf off. In the next few weeks five children and a young woman were cruelly slaughtered by the voracious animal which seemed to be challenging Bauterre to do his worst.

The local people were greatly cheered therefore, when at the end of August the hounds set up a gigantic wolf which was sleeping in the woods which were the property of the nuns of the Abbaye Royal. Lieutenant Bauterre himself shot at the beast and wounded it. Tremendously encouraged – because the great size of the beast surely proclaimed it the dreaded man-eater – the hunters spurred on their horses and gave chase. But before they came up to the fallen wolf it got to its feet and bounded off.

Another member of the hunting party fired at it a little while later and this time it eventually collapsed. It was quite dead when the main party came up. Amid great excitement the beast was carefully examined. It was in fact the biggest wolf the lieutenant had ever set eyes on and on being weighed, scaled at just under ten stone. Hopes rose higher still when a number of people gave it as their opinion that it was the same man-eating wolf which had attacked them in the past year.

The corpse of the great wolf was transported to Clermont-Ferrand where the carcase was dissected by the authorities. One extraordinary factor was that the animal's eyes glared so ferociously that no-one was able to stare into its hypnotic gaze without flinching. Other details of the post-mortem examination seemed to clinch the wolf's identity. It had an enormously long tail, which tallied with eye-witness descriptions of the Beast of the Gevaudan; and a number of strips of clothing, red in colour, were found in the wolf's belly, which indicated that it was an eater of human flesh.

When the attacks on humans ceased, Lieutenant Bauterre and his party were congratulated by His Majesty, who rewarded the wolf-killer with suitable gifts. But an even more sinister and tragic postscript to the lieutenant's exploits was about to be written. Bauterre and his followers, together with the pack of hounds left for the comforts of Versailles. Biding its time the cunning killer – after a discreet interval – struck again.

In the event it was early December before the unfortunate people of the Gevaudan were made to realize that they were still at the mercy of an implacable and ruthless enemy. The first intimation came with a wolf attack on a young man who, however, escaped with his life. The warning was followed by two more deaths, that of infant girls who were eaten by the animal. After more escapes and several deaths the local people organized their own hunts for the beast but, as hitherto, without success.

The year wore away and in the following spring of 1766, it became clear that the man-eating wolf was more active than ever; it had cunningly waited until Lieutenant Bauterre and his party had completed their operations and had probably gone right out of the district, possibly catching its natural prey, before returning to its old, familiar hunting grounds.

One is irresistibly reminded of the tactics of man-eating tigers, though such sagacity and such incredible luck and cunning as that of the Beast of the Gevaudan is fortunately rare in the wolf. In March 1766, the deaths of small children started again; the grief of rustic parents, simple peasants, often robbed of their only child, is hard to imagine at this distance in time, but the depredations of the great wolf only hardened people in their resolve to rid the earth of it.

The wolf was now penetrating extremely close to homesteads in its eagerness to seek its defenceless victims. Towards the end of March a boy of eight was snatched from play near his house and when the distracted father made search for his offspring he found the pathetic, mangled remains of the child nearly a mile away. An old man was the next victim but though he was badly mauled he was lucky enough to be saved by the intervention of a passing villager. He recovered from his wounds without any medical complications.

There was a lull for a while and it was not until the summer was well advanced that the attacks began again with savage suddenness. Two children looking after their family's sheep were killed in two incidents some miles apart and the melancholy catalogue of murderous attacks, miraculous escapes and shocking deaths dragged on into the autumn of the year. The slaughter of the innocents had commenced in earnest in the spring of 1766 and many desperate measures were tried to destroy the inhuman fiend that seemed to be haunting the misty forests of the Gevaudan.

Poisoned bait was one of the methods and though this might have succeeded with an ordinary animal, the great wolf was far too cunning to be taken in by such unsophisticated schemes. Traps too were staked out but these were left severely alone so even the few sceptics who supposed it to be an ordinary wolf involved, felt their conviction waning and the thought that it might be a supernatural being taking its place.

As so often happens, when the population was in despair, relief was just around the corner. But several more children and three more women were to die before the menace was lifted for ever from the district. It was left to the local people to liberate themselves from a monstrous tyranny which made every lonely hamlet, every forest path, every sunlit glade a place of terror and dread. The Beast of the Gevaudan had reigned over the forests of the area for more than two years, showing a contemptuous indifference to all efforts made to shoot or trap it.

Perhaps it was this very indifference which was to lead to its downfall. A local nobleman, the Marquis d'Apches was appealed to by the inhabitants and he organized a series of hunts for the man-killer, which were enthusiastically supported by the local population. None of these was successful, though a number of wolves were killed as they were flushed by the lines of hunters. No less than three hundred odd people were gathered for a great beat on 19th June 1766, which took place in the Forest of la Tenaziere.

Once again prayers were being said in the local churches and it must have seemed to many of those gathered in the meadow on that far-off day that this new hunt was doomed to be as abortive as all the others. But circumstances were changing and the devilish luck that had favoured the great wolf was about to turn in favour of the hunters. The beat began and the forest resounded with shouts and bugle-calls and the occasional discharge of fowling pieces.

One of the hunters was a middle-aged man called Jean Chastel who was standing in the forest near a place called la Sogne-d'Auvert. It was early afternoon and the beaters were coming closer. Chastel was bored and like most of his companions thought little would come of the hunt and that it would end abortively like all the others.

To his great surprise there was a crackling in the undergrowth and a huge reddish wolf bounded into the clearing. Rapidly taking aim Chastel fired and the animal collapsed, kicking convulsively. Excitedly, the forester ran forward and saw, to his intense delight that this was no ordinary wolf. His shot had killed it almost immediately and Chastel, together with the other men who rapidly came up at his shouts, were convinced that they had at last laid low the man-eater.

To begin with the wolf was of enormous size, though its weight was not so great as that of other large wolves killed in the earlier hunts. Then, as noted, it had a distinctive reddish tinge to its fur and that had been a characteristic of the wolf which had killed so many people in two years of tragedy and terror. And finally, when the animal was dissected in a nearby town, it was found that the stomach contained the shoulder-bone of a girl who had been killed only the previous day.

The affair had an ironic anti-climax and the heroic Chastel was robbed of his just reward because the beast's hide had not been cured properly. The man-eater was stuffed and sent to Louis at Versailles in order that the old man could claim his reward. But unfortunately the specimen became putrid with the great heat of that summer and the king made fun of Chastel and his claims and ordered the forester to bury the carcase.

But one cannot help feeling satisfaction at the knowledge that Chastel was suitably rewarded by his friends and neighbours because a public subscription was taken up for him in the Mende diocese and a considerable sum subscribed in gratitude to the man who had delivered the Gevaudan from a curse which had hung over it for more than two years.

During that time over sixty people had perished horribly and a great many others had either been permanently lamed or badly injured. That the beast Chastel had shot was the man-eater could not be denied, for the attacks ceased immediately with the wolf's death.

Some puzzles still remain. Was one animal involved or several? Why did the beast, if one beast were responsible, exhibit such cunning and evade trap after trap and the extensive hunts which were organized by famous and skilful wolf-hunters year after year? The Beast of the Gevaudan, to the good people of the area, was literally a werewolf in the supernatural sense, in the horror and terror it evoked.

Fortunately, like the werewolf itself, it remained vulnerable to a well-aimed bullet. Few men so richly deserved their reward as Jean Chastel, the instrument of justice, slayer of the Great Wolf, the Beast of the Gevaudan.

EIGHT

THE WEREWOLF DISEASE

The holocausts of judicial slaughter which spread across Europe in the Middle Ages and in which zealous and bigoted judges, officials and law officers dispensed rough justice to suspected werewolves have already been touched upon. Thousands of hapless and innocent individuals went to their deaths by fire, sword, summary execution by bullet and the rope for no other reason than that their habits appeared peculiar to their neighbours or that they had a furtive look or a strange way of walking.

We have already spoken too, of the terrible practice of subjecting the suspected lycanthrope to rough surgery in an effort to discover whether his fur was on the underside of his normal skin. Yet while it is easy to condemn these barbaric practices in the light of modern science and medical knowledge, these were primitive times; there was little education, even less mercy and in the brutish circumstances in which men found themselves in those dark days who shall blame them if they fought the devil with the only weapons to hand.

The comforts of religion and the rough edge of the sword were the two elements which stood between men in those times and the all too palpable demons of darkness. This was vividly recognized as late as the final third of the nineteenth century, and when it is recalled that the spectacle of public hanging in England ceased only in the last century, it is less easy to condemn.

The novelist Sir Walter Scott recognized the difficulties and touched on the terrors of lycanthropy in one of his less familiar works, *Demonology and Witchcraft*, which was published by John Murray in 1830 as part of an eighty-volume collection called *Murray's Family Library*.

The volume – to give it its full title – *Letters on Demonology and Witchcraft*, was written after Scott had first suffered a stroke in the February of 1830, the initial warning of the condition which was to lead to his death in 1832 in his early sixties.

In it, he wrote shrewdly of the werewolf but for the most part contented himself with repeating other people's opinions. Of this curse which laid waste Europe he said, "Lycanthropy, a superstition which was chiefly current in France, but was known in other countries and is the subject of great debate between Wier, Naude, Scot, on the one hand, and their demonological adversaries on the other.

"The idea, said the one party, was that a human being had the power, by sorcery, of transforming himself into the shape of a wolf, and in that capacity, being seized with a species of fury, he rushed out and made havoc among the flocks, slaying and wasting, like the animal whom he represented, far more than he could devour.

"The more incredulous reasoners would not allow of a real transformation, whether with or without the enchanted hide of a wolf, which in some cases was supposed to aid the metamorphosis, and contended that lycanthropy only subsisted as a woeful species of disease, a melancholy state of mind, broken with occasional fits of insanity, in which the patient imagined that he committed the ravages of which he was accused."

Scott was in error though, when he supposed that lycanthropy was heard of no more after the time of Louis XIV. But he showed remarkable prescience in some of his observations. Though he was referring to ghost stories, his remarks apply equally to the werewolf when he observes (of the public), "They want evidence. It is true that the general wish to believe, rather than the power of believing, has given certain stories some such currency in society."

Scott is equally apposite in his remarks on Matthew Hopkins, the notorious Witch-Finder General of 1644 who was responsible for the deaths of over a hundred 'witches' – innocent people whom he had tortured in order to confess their associations with the devil. Hopkins, a craven and gullible sadist whom Scott refers to as "an impudent and cruel wretch", first became the scourge of his native Essex and then descended like a plague on Suffolk. In the manner of Robespierre devoured by the Revolution he was eventually destroyed by his own methods, flung into a pool where he floated and therefore found himself condemned as a witch by his own self-made rules.

The hunting of witches bears a close relationship to that of those self-righteous commissions which sought to stamp out the crime of lycanthropy hundreds of years earlier and Scott strongly condemns the atrocities of Hopkins and his ilk. In perceptive passages which might be referring to those condemned of lycanthropy, he observes, "It was Hopkins' custom to keep the poor wretches waking, in order to prevent them from having encouragement from the devil, and, doubtless to put infirm, terrified, overwatched persons in the next state to absolute madness; and for the same purpose they were dragged about by their keepers till extreme weariness and the pain of blistered feet might form additional inducements to confession."

Precedent enough here, one would have thought, for all the self-justified torturers of modern Communist and Fascist states who extract 'confessions' from their victims under similar circumstances.

This was exactly the practice of many of those judges and judicial officers set to examine the plague of lycanthropy in the Middle Ages and, of course, accounts for the thousands of confessions extracted from the unfortunate wretches under interrogation.

We have already spoken of the symptoms, practice and traits of lycanthropy; it will be remembered that the werewolf/victim wandered about at night, disclosed bestial habits, had excessive hair on his face and hands; and in addition the skin bore score-marks and sores akin to those on the humans who associated with wolves and were brought up among savage beasts. The scars were, in fact, the classical signs of bites and claw-marks such as those wolves might make when associating with humans to whom they were acting as foster-parents.

But an English doctor in modern times has put forward a remarkably convincing explanation for the 'werewolf disease' which afflicted Europe in the Middle Ages and in other periods. We shall now proceed to examine his thesis.

Dr Lee Illis of Hampshire presented a paper on the subject to the Royal Society of Medicine in October, 1963. I am indebted to him for his generosity in putting his findings at my disposal and to the Royal Society itself for their permission to make use of their Proceedings.

Dr Illis' paper, "On Porphyria and the Aetiology of Werwolves", is a well-documented and, to my mind, unassailable argument to the effect that the outbreaks of lycanthropy which afflicted Europe and other parts of the world at various times had a solid medical basis.

Dr Illis, who prefers the term 'werwolf', says, "I believe that the so-called werwolves of the past may, at least in the majority of instances, have been suffering from congenital porphyria. The evidence for this lies in the remarkable relation between the symptoms of this rare disease and the many accounts of werwolves that have come down to us."

After dealing with instances of classical history and legend, which we have already examined, he adds, "The transformation into a wolf is not exclusive to men. Armenian and Abyssinian legends clearly implicate women and Boguet, a sixteenth-century judge who was responsible for the burning of about six hundred witches and werwolves, recounts the story of a farmer's wife who changed into a wolf and attacked a neighbour."

Illis makes the interesting point too that at a time when (men who were) werewolves were considered heretics on the Continent, they were in England regarded as victims of delusion brought on by an excessive melancholy.

He continues, "This was not due to any reasoned thinking or indulgence (since witches were being obsessionally and cruelly persecuted at that time), but to the fact that wolves [in England] were extinct.

"Throughout the world, the most common or feared animal is the one into which men were transformed. Where wild animals were extinct, the myth tended to die out."

Later the doctor observes in developing his thesis, "A Borussian werwolf was brought before the Duke of Prussia, and John Frederic Wolfeshusius of Leipzig University (1591) describes him: "He was an evil-favoured man, not much unlike a beast, and he had many scars on his face . . . although he was long and vigilantly watched, this werwolf never cast what little he possessed of human shape".

And Dr Illis adds, "Amongst the Toradja natives of Celebes (Dutch East Indies), werwolves are described as having unsteady eyes with dark green shadows under them. They do not sleep soundly. They have a long tongue with red lips and teeth which remain red in spite of chewing betel nuts. Their hair stands on end.

"Boguet describes werwolves as having a pale skin with numerous excoriations from frequenting with wolves or perhaps as a consequence of their attacks on human beings. One, he writes, was so disfigured as to be scarcely recognizable as a human being, and people could not regard him without shuddering."

The physical descriptions of these people are extremely important to the Illis theory and it should be noted that they correspond exactly to the physical symptoms of the extreme forms of porphyria as known to medical science.

Dr Illis adds, perhaps not surprisingly in view of his profession, "Physicians, on the whole, were rather more humane in their attitude to werwolves than were lawyers or priests," but it is an assertion with which few people would, I imagine, disagree.

He continues, "Oribas, physician to the Emperor Julian, says the disease [of lycanthropy] was manifested by a going out of doors at night; the patient was pale with dry, dull and hollow eyes, and his legs covered with sores from frequent stumbling. He recommended treatment by venesection and evacuation, followed by a generous diet and sleep. . . .

"It is difficult to build up a picture of a werwolf, but the most consistent one would be of a man, or occasionally a woman or child, who wanders about at night. The skin is pale, with a yellowish or greenish tint, with numerous excoriations, and with a red mouth. The eyes are unsteady.

"Occasionally werwolves are described as being hairy. They show (to say the least) disordered behaviour. Their distribution is virtually world-wide but with particular pockets of strong belief in their existence, such as South Germany. They date back at least to Greek times.

"A belief so widespread both in time and place as that of the werwolf must have some basis in fact. Either werwolves exist or some phenomenon must exist or have existed on which, by the play of fear, superstition and chance, a legend was built and grew.

"Tracing the origins of the werwolf myth is a difficult exercise. One is continually met with conflicting evidence. There would seem to be two suggestions for the origin of this myth. One is that it is a result of fear, and an invocation of evil spirits, or near witchcraft, to account for some strange happenings

which could not be explained by the contemporary philoso-
phies.

"This is attractive but, by itself, carries us no further. It
cannot explain the widespread belief and it makes no contribution to the exact aetiology of the fear. My suggestion is that the
myth arose in several isolated areas in various parts of the
world, as a result of some rare, but widespread happenings, and
spread into the common consciousness."

Dr Illis speaks of the enlightened treatment of the insane in
pre-Christian days and the contrast to that meted out in later
periods with the advent of Christianity and "the dreadful
doctrines of heresy". Similarly the savage cruelty of the Middle
Ages was practised at a time when there was a wide general
belief in lycanthropy.

"It must have been heightened by the climate of fear and by
the convenience of disposing of one's enemies by denouncing
them as witches or werwolves. This was helped by the incredible
readiness of the accused to confess; a feature which marks all
stories of witch-hunting.

"Although essentially a pre-Christian belief based on the
need to externalize fear, once a story of a werwolf of sufficient
credibility was established, it would persist for several generations and become the focus of explaining other dreadful and
otherwise inexplicable happenings. Indirect help would come
from the religious teachings of the time which played strongly
upon the ignorance and credulity of the uneducated."

Congenital porphyria is a rare disease, as already stated, but
it may be that when a person in the Middle Ages became affected by it, his subsequent actions were seen by the authorities as
bearing the taint of lycanthropy. It needed only one case for a
whole district to become infected with a collective hysteria, in
which neighbour denounced neighbour.

What then are the symptoms and the outward manifestations of this rather strange disease? Dr Illis explains that porphyria is caused by a recessive gene which leads to "severe
photosensitivity in which a vesicular erythema is produced by
the action of light".

Or in layman's terms a sensitivity of the skin which is so
affected by light, particularly sunlight, that the patient breaks
out in a superficial, patchy inflammation.

Illis observes, "The urine is often reddish-brown as a result of the presence of large quantities of porphyrins. There is a tendency for the skin lesions to ulcerate and these ulcers may attack cartilage and bone. Over a period of years structures such as nose, ears, eyelids and fingers undergo progressive mutilation."

Other effects of porphyria are pigmentation of the skin; and the teeth may be red or reddish-brown due to the deposit of porphyrins. As the reader may have noted, some of these medical symptoms are the classical signs by which the lycanthrope has been identified throughout the ages.

The wandering about at night, which the victim of porphyria would find more bearable than exposure to daylight; the excoriations and lesions to the skin of the face and hands, typical of the werewolf who had been bitten by wild animals; and possible nervous manifestations; all would have been enough, in medieval times, to condemn such a poor wretch to the execution block as a proven werewolf.

Significantly, Dr Illis postulates, "The nervous manifestations may be referable to any part of the nervous system, and include mental disorders, ranging from mild hysteria to manic-depressive psychoses and delirium. Epilepsy may occur."

The doctor says that there is an important geographic factor and such cases often occur, in Sweden and Switzerland, "in certain districts and especially along certain valleys. (Vannoti, 1954). This also reflects the hereditary factor in the development of the disease".

Dr Illis concludes, "It is possible, then, to paint a picture of a porphyric which, though not necessarily characteristic or typical, will fit with all the available evidence in the literature of porphyria; such a person, because of photosensitivity and the resultant disfigurement, may choose only to wander about at night.

"The pale, yellowish, excoriated skin may be explained by the haemolytic anaemia, jaundice and pruritis. These features, together with hypertrichosis and pigmentation, fit well with the descriptions, in older literature, of werwolves. The unhappy person may be mentally disturbed, and show some type or degree of abnormal behaviour.

"In ancient times this would be accentuated by the physical and social treatment he received from the other villagers, whose

By the light of the silvery moon—Lon Chaney and heroine Evelyn Ankers in a posed shot from Universal's *The Wolf Man*. The scene did not actually appear in the finished film

To the death—Henry Hull (right) as the lycanthropic Dr Glendon in the climactic fight with Dr Ogami (Warner Oland) from *The Werewolf of London* (1935)

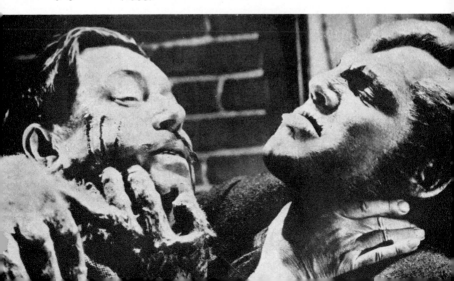

Lon Chaney as he appeared in his most famous screen role, that of
Lennie in the film version of Steinbeck's *Of Mice and Men*

instincts would be to explain the apparition in terms of witch-craft or Satanic possession."

The clinical behaviour of sufferers from porphyria as out-lined by Dr Illis in his original paper, exactly parallels those of the werewolf victims of which we have earlier spoken: the rough and broken skin; the yellowish and distorted features; even the hair, which might well have been the result of natural re-luctance to shave when suffering from such painful skin disorders; and the night wanderings. All these are the classic hallmarks of the werewolf of legend and of the medieval trials.

Add to this mental disorder and other disturbances, and the resultant confusion of such a poor wretch when hunted through the night; captured and possibly manhandled; and then finally brought before a magistrate or ecclesiastical commission. Small wonder that such "lycanthropes" were more than eager to confess to something they did not understand, even if only to alleviate their current sufferings.

What is the cause of this extreme form of porphyria and is it confined only to a comparatively few parts of the world, it might be asked. It is important to emphasize from the outset that the type of porphyria discussed by Dr Illis in his paper and which we are currently dealing with in this volume is an extremely rare condition and should not be confused with a common and widespread type which has nothing whatever to do with the subject of lycanthropy.

Dr Illis explains, "There are several types of porphyria and nearly all these types have a genetic basis. They are due to a metabolic disorder; or another way of describing them is that they are due to an inborn error of metabolism. One type of porphyria is relatively common and occurs in all countries, in-cluding Great Britain. This is *not* the type which has anything to do with the werewolf myth.

"I think this should be emphasized otherwise it would cause unnecessary suffering to people who have this type of porphyria. The type of porphyria which may possibly account for the origin of the werwolf myth is a *very rare* type of the disorder often known as congenital porphyria."

And Dr Illis asserts, "There are only about eighty cases re-ported in the world medical literature. It occurs in both sexes and there is no specific treatment. Death may occur at any age but if the patients live to maturity they usually exhibit severe scarring of the exposed parts of their body."

This is the type of porphyria which exhibits photosensitivity; haemolytic anaemia, which means the patient may have a greenish-yellow complexion with patches of excoriation; and the urine and teeth may be a pinkish-red colour.

Dr Illis concludes, "Porphyria has been reported in most countries, if not all countries in the world. Interestingly enough the only country which I definitely know does not have a werwolf myth is Ceylong where they have never heard of werwolves and where no doctor I met had ever seen a case of porphyria.

"Although reports of this disease have come from all over the world the disease certainly seems to occur in certain parts such as South Africa and South-eastern Europe."

I believe that with his original research and reasoned outline of symptom and effect, Dr Lee Illis has made an important and original contribution to our somewhat sketchy knowledge of a dark and mysterious legend of the world's primitive past.

In so doing he has let a little light into what has been a brutal and horrifying manifestation of man's inhumanity to man. He has not, of course, proved conclusively that *all* suspected lycanthropes were sufferers from a rare form of porphyria, neither has he sought to do so. The importance of Dr Illis' postulation is that *many* of the grotesque and horrifying holocausts of werewolf executions in medieval times may have been sparked off by the pathetic victims of a medical disorder which is still somewhat strange and bizarre to the modern layman, and for this insight we must be grateful.

It is time now to look at some almost equally strange byways of the werewolf legend: wolf-boys and their extraordinary rapport with savage beasts have been known since ancient times.

Now we shall examine another weird and tragic facet of the story of the lycanthrope, which deals not only with events in remote lands in ancient times but brings the story up to date, with many modern examples up to and including the late twentieth century.

NINE

WOLF-BOYS

So far in the sombre history of the werewolf we have dealt with the theme in legend; of how the legend became disseminated through the practices and traits of wolves themselves, in their age-old battle against mankind; and in the last chapter we have seen something of how unfortunate medical victims of porphyria could have become involved in the holocaust of judicial vengeance which spread throughout Europe in the Middle Ages.

But one of the most fascinating facets of the werewolf legend is that of the "wolf-boy", the child brought up among wolves as a wild beast himself and who had become so assimilated into the habits and practices of wild animals that he could no longer take his place among the family of fellow human beings.

The wolf-boy, as I observed in earlier chapters, was known from the beginning of time and Romulus and Remus were among the earliest recorded instances. But feral children themselves, though only peripheral to the legend of the werewolf, must have added a great deal to the lore surrounding this terrifying creature and for this reason alone it seemed apposite that the most famous instances of feral children should be touched upon in this book.

And here, we are dealing not with remote incidents in obscure parts of the world which happened many centuries ago. True, some of the most celebrated wolf-children were discovered in the eighteenth century and earlier, but there have been a number this century and the latest example of a child brought up as a wild beast occurred only in June 1973.

The world Press then widely reported the case of a boy discovered living with monkeys in the jungles of southern Ceylon (Sri Lanka) and whose behaviour was identical to that of the apes. Though this example is only remotely comparable with those cases of wolf-boys with which we shall be dealing in this chapter, it is a strange and vivid example of a variant history and worthy of passing mention.

One is inevitably reminded of Edgar Rice Burroughs' character Lord Greystoke, who became "Tarzan of the Apes", and this latest example is a vivid reminder that nature sometimes does imitate art; or did the prolific American author himself read of real-life examples of ape-boys before writing his *Tarzan* series, thus gaining a form of immortality?

The ape-boy in this recent instance was about twelve years old and was examined by medical and civil authorities when it was discovered that a woman was exhibiting him to the curious for money. She told the police that she had found the boy playing with monkeys.

The child, who was named 'Tissa', after a village with a long, almost unpronounceable name near which he was found, was unable to speak and barked and chattered like a monkey. He reclined in monkey-like postures and was unable to walk or stand without assistance. Normally he crawled on all fours. More significantly still, when offered plates of food he would first throw all the food on the ground before eating it.

A significant difference between the ape-boy and the wolf-boys we shall shortly be examining, is in the former's apparent adaptability. After a few weeks the ape-boy was eating with other children, wearing clothes and taking his food from a plate. Most of the wolf-boys in the literature on the subject had reverted to a wild state and were found to be completely ineducable.

A psychiatrist who examined the ape-boy said he might have been mentally retarded and so abandoned in the jungle by his parents. In that case he could have learned imitative behaviour from the monkeys in the jungle and so have survived.

More interesting, from the point of view of the legend of the werewolf, are the true wolf-boys, of whom there have been over fifty examples in recorded history. They seem to fall into two groups, the "lycanthrope", upon whom we shall be naturally concentrating; and the "savage boy", the victim of brutal and harsh upbringing, usually a timid child unable to cope with its circumstances. On the surface the case of the ape-boy reported would seem to fall into the second category.

The discovery of "wolf-boys" with all the savage traits of their wolf foster-parents would have immeasurably strengthened the werewolf legends among primitive peoples in European communities in the Middle Ages and onwards and such terrors lingered among simple folk well into the twentieth century.

It is easy to see why, for such tales always flourish where people live lonely, solitary lives; in vast, brooding solitudes such as the great stretches of forest land of Germany, France, Russia and Poland; and in primitive conditions where oil-lamps are the most sophisticated form of lighting and where water must be gathered from wells or from the edges of remote streams.

For just as the ghost flourished most strongly in the eighteenth and nineteenth centuries, particularly in the gaslit era of the '90s of last century; so did the vampire and the werewolf find their greatest days in more primitive eras of firelight, rushlight and torch.

The wolf-boy is unique in being a natural phenomenon but one central, I believe, to the dark history of the werewolf, and unusual in that the feral child has been known from earliest times up to the late twentieth century. Indeed, before this book is completed there might be as many as two or three more discovered in the forests of the Far East or in the jungles of Central Asia.

There is no suggestion, of course, that the wolf-boy is anything other than a freak of nature; but few would deny, I think, that his presence has added a great deal to the legend of the lycanthrope. Anyone who had seen such a child-savage, covered with cuts and sores; hair long and dishevelled; with filthy skin; animal-like posture; broken teeth and long, wolf-like fingernails; reeking breath; mouth bedabbled with blood from eating raw meat; and above all, with fierce, wolf-like howls and barks bursting from his mouth – could not have failed to be impressed with the dark horror of the situation.

The incidence of feral children in the remote places of the world over the past centuries has been remarkably high; as indicated, more than fifty from the fourteenth century to the present day, though there must have been many more instances unrecorded, particularly in earlier times. Indeed, it is no exaggeration to say that wolf-children, certainly wolf-boys must have existed since the earliest times of man's sojourn on this earth.

There are a number of required factors necessary to the

scientific mind to establish *homo ferus*, particularly in what I am styling the 'lycanthropic' version. He must be devoid of all that is normally thought of as 'human' attributes, such as affection, normal emotions and especially laughter; he must be mute, except when he growls, grunts or howls in his wolf-like outbursts; he should walk on all fours as a true quadruped. While incapable of living like a human being – he must exist like an animal and in particular eat like a brute beast – conversely, he must be able to survive entirely without human support.

In short, he must be of the beasts and an inhabitant of the jungle. These traits and others, less amiable perhaps, were all evinced to the full in the cases we shall be examining during the course of this chapter and the next.

Among them are Peter, the wild boy of Hanover; Victor, the wild boy of Aveyron; the celebrated Kaspar Hauser; and, a wild girl, Kamala, an Indian who was later brought up by a clergyman. Rousseau and Linnaeus were among the learned commentators who examined the enigma of the wild boy and the true example of the species, the lycanthropic version of *homo ferus*, is far from the noble savage of Rousseau's expectations.

Moreover, many of the stories which circulated about wild boys in past centuries were obvious concoctions and some of the genuine cases were encrusted with bizarre invention so that it was difficult for later investigators to come to any valid conclusions about a number of those cases recorded in earlier times. While it is true to say that many of the wolf-children were mentally retarded, it is equally certain that a number were intelligent, quick-witted and enterprising in their attempts to live wild and their success in surviving at all attests to this.

What is less obvious is whether those wolf-children who proved impervious to all civilizing influences were in fact mentally retarded or ordinarily intelligent children who had been among wild beasts so long that they had lost all normal human attributes and were unable afterwards to regain them. There seems to be evidence both for and against in some cases.

Certainly, a number of wild children discovered in modern times did prove amenable to more civilizing influences, but we do not know, of course, how long they had been in the wild; it might be they were merely re-acquiring knowledge once imparted in earlier years but which had become temporarily overlaid by the exigencies of two or three years of jungle life which had intervened.

And, we shall naturally be concentrating more closely on those examples of the 'lycanthropic' child, who behaved in a wolf-like manner and showed such bestial traits that people with whom he came in contact were as alarmed as they would have been at the sight of an actual beast; perhaps more so in noting a human being so transformed.

This is probably the explanation for a celebrated case of a "werewolf" which was discovered at a town near Strasbourg in Alsace as recently as 1925. The youth involved, aged about seventeen, displayed all the classic symptoms with which we have already become familiar and was put in medical care.

Or perhaps it was merely yet another example of an unfortunate sufferer from porphyria revealing the symptoms already so ably explained by Dr Illis? Certainly the youth concerned at Uttenheim was said to have howled like a wolf, to have been nocturnal in his habits and to have exhibited beast-like traits. Though the example mentioned occurred nearly fifty years ago, would today's medical authorities show any greater comprehension than those of their colleagues of half a century earlier – Dr Illis apart – one wonders? We turn now to specific cases.

As we have seen, muteness except when in distress, pain or hungry; incapable of communication with other human beings; a savage nature which would compel it to attack man or beast in search of food; the consumption of that food in its completely raw state; complete nudity, with a hairy skin much scarred and roughened by rocks and foliage; and, perhaps most important of all, the assumption of animal postures by running on all fours.

All these were the classic signs of the wolf-child, the lycanthrope, *homo ferus*; all these signs were present in full strength in one of the most remarkable examples of wolf-children ever recorded which took place several hundred years ago.

But first, we must set the stage for scenes which seem more like the wilder imaginings of Gothic romance than sober scientific fact. This is something which often confronts us in considering some of the more startling legends of mankind, of which the werewolf and the vampire are among the most potent, because

most legends have a basis in belief. This is a point made strongly
by the distinguished commentator Professor Lucien Malson, a
French scholar who has made a deep study of feral children.

He holds that all myth contains elements of truth and that one
should hesitate before rejecting a specific incident just because
part of it is obviously invented. This is sound advice and a pattern well worth observing in studying the history of the werewolf.

The threads of the werewolf and the vampire run back
through the fabric of human life until they are lost in the dim
distances of time. There have been many instances of wolf-
children and stories of them have been passed down verbally
by country people from generation to generation, embroidered
and embellished with wilder and still wilder imaginings until
the macabre detail has overloaded what was originally a
frightening and unusual, but certainly not a supernatural,
event.

Probably the earliest and certainly the most heavily documented instance of a wolf-boy occurred in the middle of the
fourteenth century with the advent of the creature who came to
be known as the Wolf Child of Hesse. Local people had for long
known that the woods near Hesse, a town in Germany not far
from Hanover, sheltered a shadowy being which had been
observed to run fleetly through the undergrowth whenever disturbed by man.

But it was not until 1344 that any real tangible proof of his
presence was obtained, first with authenticated sightings and
later with the capture of the strange, savage creature that was at
first regarded by local people with superstitious awe. The boy,
for such it proved to be, was running wild and when first seen
proceeded on all fours like a wolf. A number of people of both
sexes were involved in his capture and the boy was savage and
wild, being unable to speak, naked and, according to the contemporary reports, had been brought up by wolves.

Juvenis lupinus hessensis, as he came to be described in the
textbooks, had spent four years in a wild state, living in the
forest as an animal and eating his food raw. The boy, by all
accounts, had been discovered by wolves, who had dug a hole
for him and preserved his life by protecting him with their
bodies.

Some even said they had carpeted the hole with leaves to
make him a sort of nest and by this means and their animal

heat had preserved him through the hardest winters. As we have seen, this is not beyond the bounds of possibility, and is corroborated by other stories of feral children of the period.

The boy, who appears not to have been given a name, was about eight years of age and had become so used to moving on all fours that boards had to be strapped to his legs to enable him to hold himself upright and walk in a human posture. It took the unfortunate child a long time to learn to walk as his fellows and he became famous in his own time, being brought to England and presented at court.

He could only grunt and make animal noises, ate raw food and, if truth were known, was probably happier in the wild state to which he had been reduced. The celebrated case of the Wolf Child of Hesse was commented on by Linnaeus and Rousseau, among other learned authorities.

Another wolf-child was discovered around the same time, in a thickly forested area of Bavaria. Known as the Wolf-Child of Wetteravia, his case had a great similarity to that of the Hesse boy, though his circumstances would appear to be even more hopeless, he being over twelve years old when discovered.

These two cases and those even earlier suffer from the disadvantage that no studies in depth on them were made by learned persons until the mid and late eighteenth century; that is, until more than four hundred years had passed.

Even more wild in their demeanour were three bear children which were discovered in Lithuania at different stages in time in the seventeenth century. The boys were savage and uncontrollable, fought their captors, lived on grass and raw vegetables. The so-called 'calf-child' of Bavaria was even said to have fought dogs with his teeth. Some of these children adjusted to society and one even learned rudimentary speech but for the most part they were never able to achieve status as normal human beings though, of course, they had made remarkable progress from their condition when first found in the forest.

More germane to the theme of this book were later wild children, including the famous cases of Peter of Hanover and the Wild Boy of Aveyron. It should perhaps at this stage be emphasized that many commentators, notably those of our present day seem to favour the theory that so-called wolf children are suffering from mental backwardness and are otherwise retarded.

It is this, and not their environment, which causes them to remain in a semi-wild state when caught, to be almost ineducable and to remain incapable of speech, the arguments run. This is not the view of so distinguished an authority as Professor Malson who reasons that such a position is contrary to all scientific evidence.

He says that one should not be surprised that a non-human environment produces non-human children. This is precisely the view of Jean Itard, the heroic pioneer teacher and psychologist, who laboured for years in the early nineteenth century to communicate with and educate Victor of Aveyron

TEN

"THE FANTASTIC PEOPLE"

Before we turn to the most famous cases, we will briefly examine those examples of wolf-boys which occurred over wide intervals of time in places as far apart as Germany, Russia and India. One of the most extraordinary instances of *homo ferus* occurred at a place called Overdyke in Holland, which was first reported in 1863.

This wolf-child, a boy whose age was not determined, was discovered in a savage state. His most remarkable habit was that of eating birds. To do this he would imitate bird-calls, scale trees and subsist either on the eggs or eat raw any young birds or adult birds he was able to catch.

India seems to have been a favourite place for wolf-children, perhaps because the inhabitants in their wretchedness were more prone to abandon young children in the jungle, where they ran wild and adapted themselves to a primitive existence. No less than sixteen wolf-children of both sexes were reported between the years 1843 and 1933, some of them by a Major-General Sleeman. Other army officers also reported a number of cases, which included so-called panther-children and leopard-children but some of these stories were undoubtedly apocryphal.

But there were a number of Indian cases which are well attested and like the tree-climbing wolf-boy already cited, it proved almost impossible to break them of their ingrained jungle habits. Which is not surprising, really, when one considers that some of them had spent up to ten years and more in the wild.

Valentin Ball first reported in detail the cases of Indian wolf-children in his *Jungle Life in India*, published in London in 1880. Though Ball obtained his accounts at second-hand there is little doubt in these instances. The first wolf-child, Dina Sanichar, was captured by villagers near a place called Mynepuri in 1872. He was apparently about six years old and bore all the classic signs of *homo ferus*.

He was naked and savage, mute – apart from the ability to utter guttural growls – and like an animal, had sharpened his teeth to razor-like edges by the constant gnawing of bones. It was, of course, impossible to determine just how long he had been in the jungle, but he was obviously easily able to survive in the wild, as his physical vigour and physique testified. He ran on all fours like the other children cited and fiercely resisted all attempts to make him wear clothing.

Unlike many other wolf-children Dina survived for two decades in human company. Though there was no evidence that he was in any way mentally retarded his progress during that twenty years bears out Professor Malson's thesis. For despite the most patient teaching his only achievements during that long space of time were to learn to dress himself, to stand upright – though he never found this easy – and to take care of his own eating utensils.

Ball also cited another wolf-boy, this time from Lucknow, a child of ten, who was discovered two years later than Dina. He was taken in by an orphanage at Sekandra but despite extensive efforts at re-educating him, his achievements were, if anything, even less impressive than those of the first boy, though he did learn the dubious distinction of smoking cigarettes. Both children remained dumb to the end of their lives.

These were some of the classic examples of the wolf-child, which may have helped to keep alive the legend of the werewolf over the past hundred years. India was again the scene for four more cases of wolf-children between 1893 and 1898 but the two most famous examples were much nearer to our own time, those of Kamala and Amala, two wolf-girls, who were discovered by an Indian cleric in 1920.

Dr J. A. Singh was the rector of the Midnapore orphanage and he wrote a long and detailed report of his observations of the two wolf-girls in his care, the entries being made over a lengthy span of time, so that there is little doubt of the truth of his observations, which were well attested by other witnesses. It was in October of 1920 when this reverend gentleman was preaching in a district known as Godamuri, that he was approached by local villagers who excitedly told him that there were 'fantastic people' living in the jungle round about.

In a scene more reminiscent of Gothic romance than reality, the doctor was taken to a remote spot in the forest and there, as dusk fell, he and the villagers saw a family of wolves emerging from a hole in a bank. They were headed by three fully-grown wolves, followed by two cubs and then, according to the terrified villagers, two 'monsters'. These were strange-looking animals, which the Rector was unable to place.

They walked on all fours and their long and matted hair hid their faces. In addition the dusk gave their shapes an indefinite outline. The 'monsters' jumped out of the cave lair last and it was all Dr Singh could do to prevent his companions from shooting at them with their ancient rifles. The 'monsters' had inspired such terror that he had to visit a village some miles away to ask for volunteers to capture the strange creatures he had seen.

On his return to the wolf-lair a week or so later two of the wolves ran off but a she-wolf, guarding the cave-entrance had to be shot. Huddled at the back of the cave the Rev. Singh and his companions were astonished to find two cubs and two human children. The latter were naked and covered with sores and bruises but, extraordinarily, the children showed more aggressive spirit than their wolf-cub companions, and prepared to defend their territory vigorously.

The two youngsters were removed from the lair, but were unfortunately given in the first instance to local villagers to care for. These wretched people abandoned the children at the first opportunity and Dr Singh found them some days later almost dead from starvation. They were tended and force-fed with milk and other nourishing foods and taken in the doctor's ox-cart to the Midnapore orphanage in November 1920.

Incredibly, the younger of the two girls, Amala, was only about eighteen months old and the elder, Kamala – they were so christened by Dr Singh – about eight years old. Both had the skin of their bodies heavily scored and calloused, their tongues protruded from their mouths like wild animals and they bared their teeth like wolves and panted like dogs in order to cool themselves.

Even more astonishing facts were to emerge later. The children were unable to see during the day and spent their time on all fours in shady corners, or facing walls. At night-time they howled and raged about in their efforts to escape captivity. In all they appeared to sleep only five or six hours out of the twenty-four; they ate nothing but raw meat and lapped up liquid in a "four-legged" position.

The two girls crawled on their knees and elbows when in confined spaces but when they wished to run crouched on their hands and feet, when they were able to proceed at quite a fast pace. They snarled at all human beings and arched their backs like wolves at the approach of what they considered to be danger. They 'hunted' by chasing chicken and other domestic stock and also rooted about the yard for scraps of offal and entrails, which they devoured greedily.

But the two wolf-children were not to survive together long in the supposedly more beneficial atmosphere of "civilization". The younger girl, Amala, lived for less than a year in captivity, dying of nephritis and oedema in September 1921. Like her wolf 'sister' she had been unable to do more than growl or make primitive noises. Though Kamala lived to be about sixteen or seventeen years old – that is, for something like nine years in captivity – she too never learned to talk properly, though some human attributes were gradually inculcated.

She took years to learn to walk, though until the end of her short life, she never managed to throw off a wolf-like gait. She learned to wash and to use a glass for drinking and even a few words of speech. But she still ate raw meat and offal until 1926 and avoided all dogs. The fact that she acquired rudimentary speech shows that she had no mental defects at birth and that her wolf-like traits were entirely absorbed from her wild foster-parents, the wolves.

Small wonder that the simple Indian peasants had been terrified by the 'monsters' in the cave even in the 1920s; fear of the werewolf as of the wolf is one of the oldest primal instincts of mankind; as of all manifestations of the bizarre or of the unknown. The story of Kamala and Amala is yet one more strand, albeit a natural one, in the dark story of the werewolf.

With Kamala's death in November 1929 of the same disease as her sister, nephritis, ended one of the strangest true stories of modern times though speculation and study of the two wolf-children and their dark history has continued to this day. Why such children should not have been instantly devoured by the wolf family is still a matter of mystery, and indeed the whole of the circumstances surrounding the history of wolf-children remains shrouded in obscurity.

None more so than two of the most bizarre examples of the feral child, the enigmatic Kasper Hauser and Victor, the wild boy of Aveyron.

We have so far avoided in this necessarily brief survey of feral children, the so-called baboon-child, the leopard-child, the gazelle-child and so on, not because their incidence is rare or because their circumstances are far-fetched; on the contrary, such cases have been frequent and well authenticated and, as we have seen, the latest of them occurred only in 1973.

The reason they have been but sparingly evoked is because the circumstances are roughly similar in each case and a complete listing would have made for tedious repetition. Also, cases other than wolf-children would have been outside the terms of reference of this study in that the wolf-child has strengthened and added to the legend of the werewolf.

One might then ask why Kaspar Hauser and Victor of Aveyron are cited as their cases break some of the self-imposed rules I have laid down for the true wolf-child. But their tales exhibit all those elements of strangeness and mystery that surround the werewolf itself as well as that of the feral child and my excuse, if excuse were needed, is that their case-histories have been cited by learned authorities in the past as those of the true wolf-boy.

That of Kaspar Hauser is possibly one of the strangest ever recorded and for this reason alone is worthy of listing alongside other authenticated reports of wolf-children. It began in Nuremburg, Germany, in 1828, a period close enough to our own to receive reliable documentation as was the case some thirty years earlier with Victor of Aveyron.

These two most remarkable instances of feral children are richly documented and there are striking parallels between them; neither of the two boys could recognize their own reflections in the mirror and both found bright light oppressive.

But Kaspar's was perhaps the more sensational appearance of the two for he, alone among a large number of reported cases, was first seen, not in a state of nature but fully clothed and unlike those of the other children his bizarre end and the enigmatic circumstances surrounding his appearance and disappearance from the stage of life, have combined to make him a figure which arouses considerable controversy.

He, together with Victor and a handful of others, alone developed the ability to communicate with fellow human beings and he alone emerged from nowhere at the comparatively advanced age of seventeen.

Learned scholars have argued that abandoned children are unlikely to survive long in the wild; that hunger, cold and lack of human company would soon assure their deaths; that a diet of raw food would be more than likely to hasten early mortality; and that, above all, the incompatibility between animals and humans would prevent wolves from mothering human children.

Other equally learned opinion is of the opposite persuasion; that the human child is infinitely adaptable; that diverse animals such as dogs, cats, birds and mice learn to live together in harmony. That savage animals can and do accept human company is indisputable. But there is so much authentic material regarding the feral-children which have been discovered since the mid and late eighteenth century, that the provenance of wolf-children and their upbringing in the wild is now beyond dispute one would have thought.

Certainly the remarkable young man walking along a road in Germany in 1828 became a legend in his own life-time and one of a handful of feral-children whose circumstances are beyond doubt. The story began at about five in the afternoon when a man who was sitting outside his home on a street in Nuremburg called the Unschlittplatz, suddenly noticed a curious sight. It was that of a young man who was staggering along dressed in a bizarre fashion, which instantly attracted the citizen's attention.

The youth wore, among other things, top-boots with horse-shoes which clicked along the paving as he walked; a felt hat to which was attached a picture of Munich and coarse clothes.

When questioned he was unable to speak but produced a letter which was addressed to a captain commanding a cavalry squadron of the Nuremburg Regiment, stationed in the city. The boy was taken to the barracks where the letter, on examination, was found to contain the information that the boy's name was Kaspar Hauser. The document was apparently from his mother and said the boy was born on 30th April 1812, and that when he was seventeen he should be taken to Nuremburg, where his father had formerly served in the cavalry.

Kaspar Hauser was given a bed in some stables and when, next day, he appeared at the police station, where he was lodged for some time in a cell, he was able to write his name when offered a pen. A great difference already, one might think, from the previous accounts of wolf-boys. But a strangeness was immediately noticed about him, which set him apart from other young people of his age.

He had the mind of a child of only about two years old; he spent most of his time sitting on the ground; slept as dusk approached but awoke with the onset of dawn; and could use his hands for only one purpose, that of picking up objects between his thumb and index finger. It was as though he had never been taught to do the elementary things which are natural to all young children under parental guidance.

Other things set him apart from the run of humanity too. He appeared uninterested in the life around him and spent long hours of each day in sitting on the ground with his feet spread out in front of him, staring into nothingness. He was kept in his cell for observation, while inquiries were made about him, and though the police authorities said Kaspar would sometimes play with other children, his movements seemed hesitant and unco-ordinated and he would eat little other than bread and water.

In view of the cases of the other feral children we have studied, he differed from them in one important instance; he would not eat meat at all and spat it out whenever it was offered to him. He was able to utter only a jumble of sounds and appeared brutish and sullen in aspect.

He cried, shouted, laughed and displayed extreme emotion for no apparent reason and was frequently frightened by incidents which had no menacing aspects or, even more strangely, for no reason at all. The boy was an enigma and his case rapidly grew beyond the comprehension of the simple guardians who were first entrusted with his care.

He had various cuts and scars on his body and arms and complained constantly of severe headaches. An even stranger aspect was that, as already indicated, he could write his signature and he could also form the letters of the alphabet with some difficulty, when given a pen. A lawyer, Dr Von

Feuerbach, who was formerly president of the Ansbach Appeal Court, was one of the first to see the boy and he was also the first to write a celebrated account of the strange visitor, which was first published in 1832.

"He resembled a creature from another planet," Von Feuerbach was to write percipiently of Nuremburg's bizarre visitor. But the boy's plight had aroused the interest of a Dr Daumer, a local practitioner, who took the lad into his own home where he rapidly settled in and after some months lost some of his more brutish characteristics.

Like most other examples of *homo ferus* he displayed little or no sexual appetite and took the greatest interest in food and drink i.e. in the basic wants of life. Not surprisingly and again like most of the other examples cited, he evinced great sympathy with animals; in Kaspar's case he developed a great fondness for horses and spent hours alone with them, being apparently completely happy on these occasions.

Some authorities have maintained that all wolf-children were hairy; in actual fact few appeared to have been so and Kaspar himself was a fairly normal young man from the physical aspect. Dr Daumer found that he soon gained strength; learned his way about the house; and became less emotional. Though he learned how to sleep in a bed he was still terrified of noises, colours, light and anything unusual. He appeared unable to make out distances and often felt ill for no discernible reason. But he did learn to draw and make sketches, an almost unique attribute among feral-children, which seems to indicate that he was abandoned fairly late in his development.

Mirrors confused him and he invariably looked behind them to see who was staring at him; he remained able to see in the dark but, like the vampire of legend, could not abide the sunlight, staying indoors or in shadow whenever possible. Could this be perhaps because he had been confined in a cellar or the interior of a house for long periods during his early life? We shall never know and all speculation is useless now, not only because of the distance in time, but because Kaspar's life was terminated under mysterious circumstances, long before his story would normally have been done.

Kaspar was eventually put to school and did learn to speak, though his grammar was imperfect and elementary; his memory slowly came back, like the lifting of a curtain and he was able to tell friends that he had arrived on this planet in the city of Nuremburg. He maintained he had been drugged with opium and had been imprisoned for some while. In the manner of the best classic detective fiction he said that a dark figure brought him food and stood behind him sometimes.

Tragically for the young man, Nuremburg began to buzz with gossip when this stage in Kaspar's education was reached and soon stories were bruited abroad that Kaspar was about to reveal the identity of the mysterious "man" who had imprisoned him. The entire bizarre affair of Kaspar culminated in a Grand Guignol finale when the unfortunate youth was attacked by a vicious intruder when he was alone in the doctor's house in mid-October, 1829.

Dr Daumer's sister discovered a trail of blood on the stairs at midnight and after a search, the horrified household discovered Kaspar in a gravely injured condition in the cellar. He had been brutally attacked and a blow on the temple put him in a coma for forty-eight hours. He could only mutter brokenly "Man", when he was found and this he continued to repeat.

Feuerbach's own narrative of the extraordinary story of Kaspar Hauser hinted that the "man" in question had been seen in Nuremburg and identified. If this was so it must have sealed the wolf-boy's doom, though it was almost four years before the sinister figure of the stranger struck again. Kaspar took over a month to recover from the first attack and his terror and the awful atmosphere surrounding the incident was gradually forgotten.

The tale of Kaspar came to its horrifying and shadowy end in a park in Ansbach in the spring of 1833. Kaspar was staying with Dr Von Feuerbach at the time and had gone for a walk in the park when he was attacked by the mysterious "Man" and stabbed with a knife, dying a day later. Some time afterwards a monument was erected on the spot, bearing the melancholy legend that "one unknown was murdered by another" there, an inscription that must be unique in necrology.

As the years passed many wild stories about Kaspar and his mysterious life and death were circulated on a world scale; among them was the fable that the boy had been the son of the Empress Josephine's niece, Stephanie Beauharnais who married Prince Charles of Baden at the behest of Napoleon. Kaspar had been put in the charge of a gamekeeper (by inference, the

"Man"), so that the crown would revert to the children of a morganatic line.

It makes a fine Gothic fable which we need not take too seriously, and it is certain that the truth will never be known. What is certain is that Kaspar Hauser, whatever his origin and the complex reasons behind his brutal and lonely death, was a wolf-boy who was a unique example of the genre, both in his circumstances and in the manner of his life and death.

As such his case cannot but have added to the legends surrounding both wolf-boy and werewolf. It is time now to turn to the last example in this series, Victor, the wild boy of Aveyron.

ELEVEN

THE SENSES AND THE HEART

The case of Victor of Aveyron comes before that of Kaspar Hauser chronologically and is seemingly much more straight-forward. It too contains some unique circumstances and Victor and his background have certainly received more detailed study and examination over a long period of years than any other known feral child. His story also began in the classic manner of all the other wolf-children we have examined, with the single exception of Kaspar.

It was in 1797, thirty-two years before the German boy's strange appearance in Nuremburg, that the villagers of a wild and remote region of the Tarn Department of southern France, first became aware of a strange and wild figure which flitted through the thicker fastnesses of those lonely and savage woodlands.

Unlike all the other reported cases of wolf-boys, the child who came to be known as Victor was first captured on two occasions but each time escaped and it was not until 1800 that he was finally brought under civilizing influences.

Villagers had been frightened at glimpsing the unkempt and naked figure of a 'wild man' in the forest, but despite numerous sightings they were unable to establish close contact.

It was in April of 1797 that the boy, who was then about nine years old, was seen playing near a small village called La Bassine. He was chased and captured by local villagers but the shed in which he was confined was evidently far from secure and Victor again took to the forest and was not observed for a long time.

In fact it was over fifteen months before he was again seen closely but contact was retained and he was then sighted in a tree by a party of hunters. This was in July 1798 and despite his agility and efforts to elude his pursuers, he was captured and taken to a house in a nearby village. There was a high degree of incompetence on the part of these simple folk because it took Victor only a week to escape once again, on this occasion from the house of a widow with whom he had been lodged.

This time, naked and alone, he spent the bitterly cold months of the winter hiding out in the woods, which testifies to the child's hardiness. In fact he seems to have regained some of prehistoric man's toughness and ability to survive without adequate clothing under extreme climatic conditions.

He appeared to favour a known geographical location because he reappeared only a short distance from La Bassine on the road to the village on 9th January 1800, when he was immediately seized and held by a group of villagers in the garden of a man named Vidal. Victor was naked, unkempt, covered with cuts and sores and extremely frightened at the situation in which he now found himself.

The following day he was conveyed to a hospital in a place called Saint-Affrique, where he was medically examined and cared for. The first report on Victor, as he came to be called, was made by a naturalist called Pierre-Joseph Bonnaterre, who examined the wolf-child at Rodez. Bonnaterre later wrote a detailed account of Victor and his conclusions were published in Paris that same year of 1800 as "Notice Historique sur le Sauvage de l'Aveyron", which created a great deal of attention among medical men and naturalists.

Victor proved perhaps the strangest of all wolf-children which were subjected to long examination under controlled conditions. Like many other such children he became angry for no apparent reason; slept when dusk fell and awoke at daybreak; and was unable to understand that his image in the mirror represented himself.

But unlike most of the other children, he suffered convulsions and his skin was so insensitive to pain that he was able to bear handling burning billets of wood direct from the fire without apparent ill effect. His sense of smell was peculiar also and he was unable to detect some odours even when substances were placed directly beneath his nostrils.

His hearing was equally strange. In controlled experiments he evinced no sign of surprise or agitation even when a gun was fired close behind him, though he would whirl around at very slight sounds, such as the footfall of a person behind him. But he resembled his fellow unfortunates in his dislike of sleeping in a bed and, like the others, he could tolerate immense discomfort.

Among these attributes, as might be imagined, was indifference to extreme cold; as we have seen, he spent the winters naked in the woods. He preferred eating the raw products of the earth, such as berries and chestnuts and showed a marked aversion to more sophisticated diet. He also tried constantly to escape but his captors were on guard now and his attempts were frustrated.

The boy was taken to Paris where he was examined by Dr Pinel, a well-known psychologist of the time, who categorically pronounced that Victor was an idiot and not merely a deprived boy.

Then began one of the great epics of psychological medicine. A young doctor named Jean Marc Itard, who was only twenty-five years old when he came into contact with Victor, had been appointed in 1800 to the post of chief physician to the Imperial Institute for the Deaf and Dumb in Paris.

Itard examined the boy, whose case had by this time become famous and disagreed with the demi-god Pinel, holding that Victor was only an idiot inasmuch as he had been culturally deprived by his savage upbringing. This young doctor's heroic efforts to communicate with and educate the wolf-boy of Aveyron lie outside the scope of this book. The interested reader is advised to turn to Itard's own account.

The French film director François Truffaut made a strange and moving film about Itard's efforts to educate Victor in *L'Enfant Sauvage* (1969), in which he himself played Itard; the film is of great interest, particularly in the intense performance he elicited from a young gipsy boy, Jean-Pierre Cargol, who played Victor.

In all Itard spent some six or more years of patient and persistent struggle in attempting to bring Victor, the poor savage of Aveyron, back into something resembling a human state. His pioneer efforts, which were notable for humanity, understanding and skilled knowledge of his patient's needs, were rewarded with a marked improvement in Victor's condition, though he was never to be a member of the human race as it is normally understood.

But Itard, who was to die prematurely in 1838 at the age of sixty-four, ten years after Victor's own death at the age of forty, had disproved the distinguished Pinel; Victor was not a congenital idiot but only a deprived child and though Itard was not able to wipe away the years of savagery, at least he was able to enrich the boy's life and in so doing to reveal himself as a giant among medical men and a pioneer psychologist.

He first came in contact with Victor after Pinel's examination and at a time when the boy was causing considerable excitement among medical and scientific circles. Victor was brought to the Institute at a particularly difficult period, during which he had convulsive fits and was in a dangerously excitable mood which impelled him to run away at the earliest opportunity. Itard, who was perhaps to devote more close study to Victor than had been invested by one human being in another up to that time, noted a number of strange things about the boy at that first meeting.

In addition to those traits already mentioned, Victor spent long periods looking at himself in the placid waters of a pond; he spent equally long hours gazing in fascination at the moon at night; he was not interested in other children or in their play; and he more than once set fire to wooden toys which were given him by the well-meaning.

As we have noted, he preferred a raw diet akin to that he had survived on in the wild and he was unable to concentrate; more peculiarly he seemed unable to distinguish music or the human voice from other sounds and he could not carry out the most simple movements or tasks.

In that respect he was more helpless in sophisticated surroundings than a monkey would be. He could only grunt like an animal. Perhaps the weirdest thing of all, he could never smile, being able only to make a curious contortion of his face, like a rictus.

Victor was the classic example of a true wolf-boy and was never able to speak, despite the most heroic efforts by Dr Itard to communicate with and educate him, over the next few years. Itard's patience must have been tremendous; he christened the boy Victor because O appeared to be the only vowel which interested him during the doctor's phonetic experiments and eventually Victor learned to recognize a number of words.

Apparently his greatest intellectual achievement during all

this time was his flash of inspiration in creating a pencil-holder from an old skewer; his greatest recreation seemed to be in repetitious domestic tasks such as chopping wood. He would spend hours on the latter occupation, never tiring of the chore and even seeming to derive pleasure from it.

It took the doctor years of unremitting, patient work to rid the boy of his wildness and his published observations over six long years bear witness to a remarkable man's genius in his chosen field. The remainder of the Victor of Aveyron story is, however fascinating, really outside the general terms of this study. It may be briefly told.

Even after three years the boy pined for the freedom of the wild and when taken on walks in Paris would break away to climb trees and he several times attempted to escape from captivity. He got as far north as the area of Senlis but was re-captured by the police. On this occasion he fainted with emotion on seeing his governess, Madame Guerin, to whom he had become deeply attached.

It may be felt that with this background, Victor's progress and gradual weaning from the wild state was no less remarkable than that of the efforts of his teacher. Over the years he learned to distinguish objects and articles; gradually learned to read and write and within a year it was obvious that Pinel's theory that Victor was a cretin was not only untenable but ridiculous.

As indicated Victor never learned to talk but his story was a comparatively happy one compared to many of the cases we have examined; moreover, a benevolent government and, one may feel, remarkably enlightened for the time, paid an allow-ance to Madame Guerin for looking after Victor. He was well cared for and lived at an annexe of the Paris Institute for the Deaf and Dumb until he died at the comparatively advanced age of forty in 1828.

One says advanced advisedly, bearing in mind the average lifespan of individuals in the early nineteenth century and the survival rate of feral children. Jean Itard himself became em-bittered at attacks by medical men of the day who misdescribed his pioneering work and continued to class Victor as a con-genital idiot. He was angry too at those who had lost interest in the case and refused to help.

Let Jean Itard himself have the last word. Today, a more enlightened general public would agree with him when he observes in one of his numerous reports on the young savage, printed at intervals in the early nineteenth century, "If there exists in mankind a relationship between the needs of the senses and the emotions of the heart, then this harmony and sympathy is, like most great and noble passions, the fortunate fruit of man's education."

TWELVE

FULL CIRCLE

With the history of the feral children the werewolf theme has come full circle. The wolf, the werewolf, the victim of the lycanthrope disease and the wolf-child are firmly linked in both life and legend and I have tried to make something of their history and relevance clear.

The wolf itself, savage, unreliable; sharp-fanged and red-eyed; slinking through the shadows of the night, was feared by primitive man as he is still feared by those living on the more remote fringes of the world. The wolf has not gained his reputation through gentleness and his bloody deeds over the past centuries and the human lives cruelly taken have earned him a dark place both in natural history and in folklore.

The terror of the wolf was transferred to an even more fright-ful beast in medieval and earlier times; the were-creature, the man or woman transformed into the semblance of a wolf which ran through the night with the blood-lust on it, rending and tearing, bringing death and horror to anyone in its path. That many of the lycanthropes were unwitting victims of a curse which transformed them against their will, tinged their deeds with a peculiar thrill of terror.

The blood-baths of Central and Eastern Europe, as we have seen in the course of this study, held a peculiar appeal for the righteous and in a primitive and superstitious age neighbour denounced neighbour; husband wife; wife husband; while that most odious of creatures, the public informer, assumed an important role.

In earlier times there was little clear distinction in people's minds between the wolf itself and the werewolf, so fearful was the terror that they both inspired. The position is admirably summed up in Kramer and Sprenger's classic study of witch-craft, *Malleus Maleficarum*, mentioned earlier.

On the point they say, "Question Ten deals with whether or not witches can by glamour change men into beasts, and with the question of Lycanthropy – whether ravening wolves are true wolves, or wolves possessed by devils. They may be either. But it is argued in another way, it may be an illusion caused by witches."

We have observed something of the agony of the victim of lycanthropy and the pitiless way in which innocent and guilty alike were hounded in the mass-frenzy of trials and denouncements. And we have followed the dark history of individual cases in which the lycanthrope was betrayed to justice, either by a tell-tale wound or some other piece of incriminating evidence.

Unlike the twin-demon of the vampire, the true werewolf was not something which returned after death but a living being doomed by his curse to change form at the time of full-moon, until the stake or the gallows or, most merciful of all, a silver bullet aimed at the heart, put him out of his agony.

From the legend of the true werewolf it was but a short step to the true lycanthrope; the victim of an actual disease which may have doomed many innocent people in medieval times. Dr Lee Illis' theory of a rare form of porphyria seems to me to be an ingenious and thoroughly convincing hypothesis to account for *some* of the suspected werewolf-victims whose arrest and non-recognition as genuine medical cases may well have sparked off mass hysteria among the legal and civil authorities of the time.

Dr Illis emphasizes that the type of porphyria with which his thesis was concerned is a rare and unusual form of the disease and not that of the common and more widely distributed species.

As he says, "Congenital porphyria is a rare disease, due to a recessive gene, in which there is an inability to convert porphobilinogen to porphyrin in the bone marrow."

The condition is hereditary and uncommon, though it is found in many parts of the world. In the course of the disease, which is not curable, though it can be arrested by treatment with modern drugs, the teeth of the victim may turn red or reddish brown; skin lesions form and ulcerate and mutilation of nose, ears, eyelids and fingers takes place.

The disturbance in the body metabolism also results in

severe photo-sensitivity in which the victim is unable to bear the action of light upon his skin and for this reason prefers to wander about in the dark.

Dr Illis argues skilfully that such victims of porphyria in medieval times may have been brought before the authorities, when they may well have been taken for werewolves. Their preference for the dark of the night; the sores and lesions – so like those of the savage boys brought up among wolves; the tendency to mental disturbance which would have led them to confused replies when being questioned; and the strange aspect of the reddened teeth – these and other clinical symptoms would only have branded them as lycanthropes.

Their doom would inevitably have led to a whole district falling beneath a cloud and thus to an orgy of denunciations and a corresponding blood-bath in which swift trials and summary "justice" by sword and stake would have been the corollary. As will be seen in the illustrations of porphyric patients in this book – both of which originally appeared in support of Dr Illis's thesis – even a modern observer faced with such a person in a wild and remote spot might be mistaken for supposing that something bizarre and unnatural was involved – as indeed it is, from a purely medical point of view.

It has been suggested that the wretchedness of life in earlier times, particularly in the Middle Ages, and the novelty of the trials and denunciations, may have led people into a sort of auto-suggestive and hallucinatory madness in which they contributed to the chaos in order to escape from the drabness and sordid animalism of their own surroundings. There is a great deal in this and it is undoubtedly true that such conditions are always fertile breeding ground for revolution.

Certainly, in medieval times, there would have been little chance for wretched peasants in revolutionary activity; faced with the most rigid caste and social system the world has ever known and up against the overwhelming might of steel-clad men of the temporal authority and correspondingly steel-hearted men in judicial office.

So the witch-hunts and trials, with their orgy of self-confession and denunciation, may have been the result of an explosion against wretchedness. In these circumstances and in these narrow, cramped surroundings of medievalism, the thesis of

Dr Illis seems eminently apposite. The victim of hereditary disease such as the rare brand of porphyria we have been discussing, instead of receiving medical assistance, was awarded a death sentence at the hands of a heartless and merciless judiciary.

Together with the criminal, the suspected werewolf and the lycanthrope, the victim of porphyria found himself at the bar of a tribunal from which there was no acquittal; the morbid evidence of disease had acquired the trappings of the lycanthrope. The beast-victim was persecuted through clinical symptoms and the patient, ignorant and unknowing, found himself both cause and effect of a terror which was not to be seen again until the eighteenth century witch-trials of New England.

With such scenes, which are better left to the imagination than description, the curse of the werewolf reached its highest peak; these were truly the Dark Ages and mercifully, their like has not been seen again.

And finally, as another strand in the pattern, we have the feral children; the wolf-boys and girls, reared in primitive circumstances by the beasts of the forest and jungle. We do not know how they were treated in earlier times, particularly in the more primitive eras of Continental Europe, though we can surely guess.

But children such as Kaspar Hauser and Victor of Aveyron, tragic though their circumstances might be, were surely fortunate in living in more enlightened times, when the great age of scientific medicine was just beginning. The peasantry, among whom they were first discovered, we may be sure, would have had terrified reactions and would have grouped them instinctively with the werewolf of the lonely forest, a monster with which their forebears had been familiar for centuries.

So that the wolf-child, though a medical phenomenon, is part of the werewolf legend too and like his predecessor ran naked and savage through the wild places of the earth. Fortunate though, in that he had a Jean Itard or a Dr Singh to give him comfort and loving care.

Cut off as he was from all humankind and brought up among the savage beasts of the forest, the wolf-child has a special place in the history and the literature of lycanthropy. Though the scientist, the psychologist and the medical worker would regard

him as a medical case-history only and in no way to be compared with the lycanthrope, it is surely not beside the point to
regard him as yet another facet of the wolf/man legend.

The savage boy was a fearful sight; he fought and struggled
for his freedom and did not hesitate to attack those – human or
animal – who disturbed him in the forest; and like the true
werewolf, he had an affinity with the moon. He would howl
and become restless at night and in at least one case, that of
Victor, would stare at the moon for hours on end. For the
moon had a terrible and startling effect on the werewolf.

It was at the full of the moon that the curse of the werewolf
came upon the victim/monster and the man-beast would then
undergo his terrible metamorphosis and, casting off his clothes,
would run baying through the night to rend and tear his
unfortunate victim.

Now it is time to leave the wolf, the werewolf, the medical
victim; and the wolf-boy and turn to their strange, magical
manifestations in the world's literature.

Here we shall find some bizarre and classic examples of
lycanthropy, though hardly more extraordinary than their
models on the night-side of reality. We shall really be meeting
their mirror-image again, transmuted by art, and in a slightly
different form.

Seventeenth-century view—the head of a werewolf from an ancient engraving by the French artist Jacques Callot of Nancy. Callot's fanciful interpretation has added horns and a goat-like aspect to the legendary monster

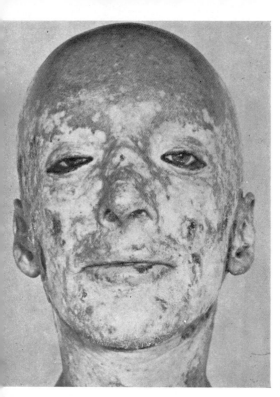

'The Werewolf Disease'. The victim of an extremely rare type of porphyria. These photographs show the classic scarring and lesions to the face and hands

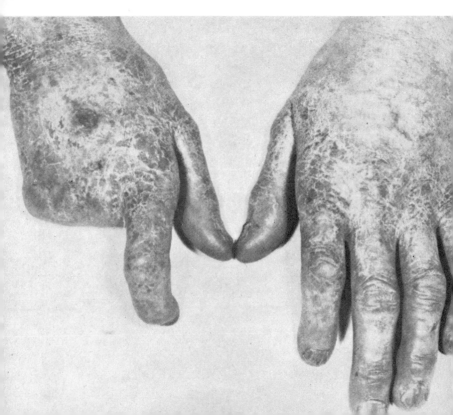

In Art: Literature

THIRTEEN

ENTER THE WEREWOLF

The werewolf theme was but sparingly evoked in fiction before the advent of the nineteenth century. Indeed, like the vampire, apart from fleeting evocations in poetry, it was almost non-existent.

There were, it is true, brief references to the phenomenon in medieval times, particularly in French romance, e.g. *William and the Werewolf* of the fourteenth century. And the lycanthrope was occasionally utilized for episodes in longer novels, as in the early nineteenth century. One of the best-known examples is that by the indefatigable Charles Maturin (1782–1824), whose almost indigestible Gothic masterpieces reached their peak in his *Melmoth the Wanderer*, published in 1820, whose wandering narrative and immense length sorely tries the patience of the modern reader.

In his *The Albigenses*, published in the year of his death, Maturin tried his hand at a werewolf episode but, like much of his outdated fiction, it was but another undigested gobbet of macabre information, thrown into the main body of the novel to make weight. This is no doubt one of the main reasons why the good cleric is so little read today, while the polished tales of his fellow countryman Sheridan Le Fanu seem only to become more powerful with the passing of time.

The main theme of *The Albigenses* need not concern us here and its only interest to this study is the author's inclusion of a hairy werewolf figure in the castle dungeon of the hero, Sir Paladour, which appears screaming and gibbering before the master of the house. The episode is a ridiculous one, typical of Maturin and, one suspects, merely brought in because the author wished to seem in the fashion of the time.

Many of the lesser writers of the nineteenth century also employed the slinking, bestial figure of the lycanthrope but most of

them failed to raise a shudder in the breasts of their unsophisticated audiences. One such was a writer named N.
Weber who was early on the scene with a novel containing
werewolf episodes, *The Tribunal of Blood*, which was issued as a
part-publication in 1806.

There were more worthwhile essays in the genre, from such
skilled pens as those of the author of *Midshipman Easy*, Captain
Marryat, but these will be dealt with when we come to consider the short story form. Even Alexandre Dumas brought the
lycanthrope theme into his fiction though, like others before
him, he did not think enough of it to embellish the legend and
flesh it out for the main subject of a full-length novel.

In his little-known *The Wolf Leader*, published in Paris in
1857 he utilizes the Faust motif by having his peasant hero
make a pact with the devil, who appears in the guise of a
black wolf. The novel is mainly concerned with devil-worship
and so is somewhat marginal to the lycanthropic genre.

Of more than passing interest is another of the works issued
in weekly parts, which were so beloved of the early nineteenth
century. This is *Hugues, The Wer-wolf* by a prolific writer called
Sutherland Menzies, who set his tale in the Weald of Kent; to
prove the authenticity of his location he even includes scholarly
footnotes from Hasted's *Kent*!

But the tale is vivid and exciting and, interestingly for modern
readers sated with the remote fastnesses of Eastern Europe or
the Black Forest of Germany, takes place in the area between
Ashford and Canterbury, then at the time of the story – 1838 –
remote and Arcadian, but now so sadly defaced by light
industry and cut up by motorways and fly-over bridges.

The story concerns a community of woodcutters involved in
lycanthropy and Menzies could claim to be the poor man's
Walter Scott in his use of dialect and rural locations. Unfortunately, the lycanthropic goings-on are described in such a
limp manner that the book is put out of court and despite its
interest remains only a marginal essay in the genre.

It remained for a more prolific writer and one capable of
sustained invention to put the werewolf theme firmly on the
nineteenth-century literary map in the full-length form. This
honour fell to George W. M. Reynolds.

Strangely enough, Reynolds' massive novel *Wagner, the Wehr-*

Wolf, was published in the same year as Menzies' work – 1857 – but rapidly outstripped the latter in its invention and story-telling ability. This was hardly surprising as Reynolds, together with Prest, was one of a handful of outstanding writers of 'penny dreadfuls' whose Balzac-like endeavours – though without the Frenchman's genius – turned out 800 and 1,000 page novels with stupefying facility. These were mainly published by a celebrated London character of the day, Edward Lloyd of Salisbury Square, Fleet Street, who flourished on the profits of these early part-publications.

Wagner, the Wehr-Wolf first appeared in weekly penny numbers or monthly sixpenny parts for Lloyd, but was printed by John Dicks of Wellington Street North, Strand. It was described as "A Romance by George W. M. Reynolds", and went on to describe him as the author of numerous books including, "The Mysteries of London", "The Necromancer", "Robert Macaire", "Pope Joan", etc.

It ran to no less than seventy-seven chapters but because of the large format of the page and the tiny type used, its 192 pages as a bound book would make at least 600 for a normal volume published today in modern type-face. The undistinguished illustrations by Henry Anelay are typical of the period, though some of them vividly capture Reynolds' racy prose.

The chapter headings too are set out in the florid manner so dear to this style of Victorian writer. To take only two examples, those of the first and last chapters yield, "The death-bed – the oath – the last injunctions" and "The Grand Vizier of Florence".

The book is nowhere as well written as "Varney the Vampire", by Reynolds' colleague Thomas Preskett Prest; both men flourished at the same time, both shared the same publisher and while Reynolds enjoyed a huge success among his mid-Victorian audience, it was not on quite so lavish a scale as Prest's.

For that reason and also for the better one that his writing lacks the vividness and sparkle of Prest at his best, Reynolds' name is little known today, even to the scholar and the lover of the bizarre. Apart from its great length, *Wagner*'s long diversions and sprawling asides make it little suited to modern taste, even for those who enjoy the Gothic, and undoubtedly that is the principal reason why such works have never been re-printed *in toto* in modern times.

Yet Reynolds' work might still survive if an editor were to undertake the onerous task of compression and excision, for there are some splendid sequences; the illustrations also, though generally insipid, show similar peaks, one of them de-picting Wagner in his lupine guise, running amok among a procession of shaven-headed priests in a churchyard.

Something of Reynolds' former popularity can be glimpsed in such scenes as he gives us in the opening passages of *Wagner*. Here are his first few sentences from the Prologue in their entirety.

It was the month of January, 1516. The night was dark and tempestuous; the thunder growled around; – the lightning flashed at short intervals – and the wind swept furiously along, in sudden and fitful gusts.

The streams of the great Black Forest of Germany babbled in playful melody no more but rushed on with deafening din, mingling their torrent-roar with the wind creaking in the huge oaks, the rustling of the firs, the howling of the affrighted wolves and the hollow voices of the storm.

The dark black clouds were driven restlessly athwart the sky; and when the vivid lightning gleamed forth with rapid and electric glare, it seemed *as if dark jaws* of some hideous monster floating high above ground, opened to vomit flame.

And as the abrupt but furious gusts of wind swept through the forest they raised strange echoes – as if the impervious mazes of that mighty wood were the abode of hideous fiends and evil spirits, who responded in grisly moan and lamentations, to the fearful din of the tempest.

It was indeed an appalling sight!

An old – old man sat in his little cottage on the verge of the Black Forest. He had numbered ninety years; – his head was completely bald – his mouth was toothless – his long beard was white as snow – and his limbs were feeble and trembling.

In such a manner does Reynolds introduce his principal character and the hero of this enormously long and involved novel, *Wagner*. And yet, for all its repetition and wearisome use of adjective and hyperbole, something of Reynolds' popularity can be glimpsed and it is not difficult for the modern reader to catch glimpses of the unflagging zest for narrative which cap-tured his simple audiences in that gaslit Victorian era.

Like most other novelists of that time Reynolds knew how to hold and immerse the reader in his involved plots; he was a true professional in that respect and he hits the target again and again in episodes and passages that are shrewdly designed to become best-selling prose.

Wagner, like Goethe's Faust is offered a bargain by the Devil in disguise; in this case a handsome stranger; as Reynolds describes him, a tall man of forty with long hair and blue eyes – unknowingly he strikes a twentieth-century note here, as his description fits a modern drop-out. The stranger seeks shelter in Wagner's forest home at the height of the storm in the best tradition of this type of fiction.

In the long conversation which follows he tells the old man that inevitably his days are numbered and that once he has died the wolves of the forest will break into his house and "mangle your corpse!"

This kindly prediction is hardly one likely to endear the stranger to the old man but Wagner, instead of taking offence, becomes terrified, as well he might. In his understandable agitation he questions the stranger further, who makes him an extraordinary offer. In return for being made "young, handsome and wealthy", he must agree to two conditions.

The first is that Wagner must accompany the stranger on all his wanderings throughout the earth – which will, of course, give Reynolds scope for those 'exotic' and fantastic touches so beloved of the writers of this period – for a space of eighteen months.

The second – and more sinister – is that he must prey upon the human race which, the stranger assures him, "I hate, because of all the world, I am so deeply, so terribly accurst!"

When Wagner inquires more closely into the stranger's terms he sees into what abyss he must plunge in order to attain youth, wealth and good looks.

Says the stranger, "Knowest thou not that there is a belief in many parts of our native land that at particular seasons certain doomed men throw off their human shape and take that of ravenous wolves?"

Wagner replies, "Yes – yes – yes – I have indeed heard of those strange legends in which the wehr-wolf is represented in such appalling colours!"

And a terrible suspicion passes across his mind. " 'Tis said that at sunset on the last day of every month, the mortal to whom belongs the destiny of the wehr-wolf must change his natural form for that of the savage animal – in which horrific shape he must remain when the morrow's sun dawns upon the earth.''

This Faust-like opening, which promises so much, is somewhat dissipated by the welter of purple prose which follows, though there are peaks in the writing which carry the reader along in quite an exciting manner. It was this vitality and unflagging enthusiasm for the genre which evidently sustained Reynolds as a master in his chosen field and which in large measure accounted for his enormous popularity and that of his peers.

There are so many diversions and sub-plots in the fashion of the day that the modern reader's patience would be overtaxed long before the opening chapters were concluded. So it would be tedious in the extreme to detail Wagner's adventures in the werewolf guise, though we shall be sampling a specimen chapter at a later stage, in order to capture the full flavour of Reynolds at his best.

As literature, *Wagner, the Wehr-Wolf* is a non-starter; as Victorian melodrama with all the stops out it can be highly diverting.

Unlike Prest, Reynolds does not seem to have made a very deep study of his chosen subject but he more than makes up for his lack of detailed expertise with his inexhaustible energy. He is a shadowy figure, even in the literature of the time, and if he survives at all it will be in extract form in the compilations which publishers are increasingly fond of issuing at the present moment.

That there is gold to be extracted is undeniable, but for every genuine shudder the researcher must be prepared to wade through miles of turgid and vapid 'romanticism'. Reynolds is naïve too, but even this has a charm of its own at this distance in time. For example, later in the book, when he switches the scene to Florence, he observes, "The Count had been ill for some weeks at the time when this chapter opens".

The story proceeds with vast digressions, lapses in time and with much romantic embellishment, the whole padding out what would have been a more impressive story left unadorned. The best example of the method, as I have already indicated, is

Maturin's *Melmoth*. Though this has been re-issued in paperback in modern times, it is well-nigh unreadable for this
reason, one of the major faults of Victorian popular literature.

But then, of course, the reader of those days, with no radio,
TV or cinema and long, candle-lit evenings to get through,
had little else to do but read for pleasure, and authors were
expected to provide vast gobbets of material for this captive
audience. Even Dickens had to resort to padding for publication in weekly parts.

Reynolds is only following the popular trend in his excur-
sions to such places as Italy and Constantinople, locations of
which he knew little himself, and his hero, Wagner, in the
guise of a young man, enjoys life and woos rich and beautiful
women. But he cannot throw off the taint of the werewolf and
he returns to his lupine shape on occasion with inconvenient
and sometimes tragic consequences.

In the manner of a far more celebrated monster some forty
years later – Bram Stoker's Dracula – he eventually meets his
end by dissolving away. In a striking and impressive scene he
reverts to an incredibly old man and collapses and dies as the
ancient of the Prologue.

Like most of the were-creatures we shall be examining in the
fiction field, he was more victim than monster and the Victorian
reader must have felt a stab of pity at his dissolution. Like the
werewolf of legend, he bitterly regretted his state.

In the finale which really brings this long and sometimes
exasperating book to a close, Wagner kneels before a closet for
a shock finish which must have greatly impressed the contemporary reader. As the doors open two skeletons are revealed
suspended in the interior.

Reynolds continues, "There – even there, as he kneels –
and even now, as his looks remain bent upon the ghastly
skeletons which seem to grin with their fleshless mouths and to
look forth with their eyeless sockets – yes – even there and even
now – is an awful and a frightful change taking place in him
whom Nisida loves so well – for his limbs rapidly lose their
vigour and his form its uprightness – his eyes, bright and gifted
with the sight of an eagle, grow dim and failing – the hair disappears from the crown of his head, leaving it completely bald –
his brow and his cheeks shrivel up into countless wrinkles – his
beard becomes long, flowing and white as threads of silver –

his mouth falls in, brilliant teeth sustaining the lips no more –
and with the hollow moan of an old, old man, whose years are
verging fast towards a century, the dying Wagner sinks upon
the floor!''

The contemporary reader must have been almost as stupefied
at such a sentence as the unfortunate heroine at the dissolution
of her lover.

"Merciful God!" cries Nisida, not surprisingly, and she
"Likewise falls down, her heart-strings cracking with burning
grief".

Even so, Reynolds is not yet done and he goes on for another
fifty pages or so of explanatory material, before the book comes
to an end. But as I have indicated, this novel, despite all its
turgidity and length, does have style and vitality and *Wagner
the Wehr-Wolf* was the only major work of fiction on the theme
of lycanthropy, in my view – until the advent of a modern
classic almost a hundred years later, leaving aside some notable
and honourable examples in the shorter form which we shall be
discussing in due course.

Wagner does have moments of great horror, and we shall
concentrate on some of the highlights of this long-forgotten
shocker in the next chapter.

FOURTEEN

THE WEHR-WOLF ATTACKS

When reading such works as Victorian Gothic novels one must accept the dross with the gold. George Reynolds could write excitingly and convincingly, most probably when he was forgetting that he had to earn his bread and butter. Then his narrative flowed smoothly and the purple prose seems apposite to its purpose; namely to rivet and thrill the contemporary reader. Even today, there is much that is entertaining and exciting in his racy narrative.

One of the best chapters of *Wagner* is the scene where the hero is awaiting execution for his crimes and unexpectedly metamorphoses back into his bestial shape, to the consternation and horror of his judges. Here is Chapter Thirty-nine in its entirety.

It was the last day of the month; and the hour of sunset was approaching. Great was the sensation that prevailed throughout the city of Florence. Rumour had industriously spread and with equal assiduity exaggerated the particulars of Fernand Wagner's trial; and the belief that a man, on whom the horrible destiny of a wehr-wolf had been entailed, was about to suffer the extreme penalty of the law, was generally prevalent.

The great square of the Ducal palace, where the scaffold was erected, was crowded with the Florentine populace; and the windows were literally alive with human faces.

Various were the emotions and feelings which influenced that mass of spectators. The credulous and superstitious – forming more than nine-tenths of the whole multitude – shook their heads and communed among themselves in subdued whispers on the profane rashness of the Chief Judge who dared to doubt the existence of such a being as a Wehr-Wolf.

The few who shared the scepticism of the judge, applauded that high functionary for his courage in venturing so bold a stroke in order to destroy what they deemed to be an idle superstition.

But the great mass were dominated by a profound and indeed

most painful sensation of awe; curiosity induced them to remain, though their misgivings prompted them to fly from the spot which had been fixed for the execution.

The flowers of Florentine loveliness – and never in any area did the republic boast so much female beauty – were present; but bright eyes flashed forth uneasy glances and snowy bosoms beat with alarms and fair hands trembled in the lovers' pressure.

In the midst of the square was raised a high platform covered with black cloth; and presenting an appearance so ominous and sinister that it was but little calculated to raise the spirits of the timid.

On the scaffold was a huge block; and near the block stood the headsman carelessly leaning on his axe, the steel of which was polished and bright as silver.

A few minutes before the hour of sunset the Chief Judge, the Procurator Fiscal, the two Assistant Judges, and the Lieutenant of Sbirri and several subordinate police officers were repairing in procession along the corridor leading to the doomed prisoner's cell.

The Chief Judge alone was dignified in manner and he alone wore the demeanour denoting resolution and at the same time complete self-possession. Those who accompanied him were without a single exception prey to the most lively fear; and it was evident that had they dared to absent themselves they would not have been present on this occasion. At length the door of the prisoner's cell was reached; and there the procession halted.

"The moment is now at hand," said the Chief Judge, "when the monstrous and ridiculous superstition imported into our country from the cradle and nurse of preposterous legends – Germany shall be annihilated for ever.

"This knave who is about to suffer has doubtless propagated the report of his lupine destiny in order to inspire terror and thus prosecute his career of crime and infamy with the greater security from chance of molestation. For this end he feigned the figure which appalled so many of you in the Judgment Hall but which, believe me my friends, he did not always believe destined to retain its sable covering.

"Well did he know that the curiosity of a servant or a friend would obtain a peep beneath the mystic veil; and he calculated that the terror with which he stood to invest himself would be enhanced by the rumour and representations spread by those who thus perpetrated into his feigned secrets.

"But let us not waste that time which now verges towards the crisis whereby doubt would be dispelled and the ridiculous superstition destroyed for ever."

At this moment a loud – a piercing – and an agonizing cry

burst from the interior of the cell.

"The knave has overheard me and would fain strike terror to your hearts," exclaimed the Chief Judge; then, in a still louder tone he commanded the turnkey to open the door of the dungeon.

But when the man approached so strong – so appalling were the sounds which came from the interior of the cell that he threw down the key in despair and rushed from the dreaded vicinity.

"My Lord, I implore you to pause!" said the Procurator Fiscal, trembling from head to foot.

"Would you have me render myself ridiculous in the eyes of all Florence?" demanded the Chief Judge sternly.

Yet so strong were now the noises which came from the interior of the dungeon – so piercing the cries of agony – so violent the rustling and tossing on the stone floor that for the first time this bold functionary entertained a misgiving as if indeed he had gone too far.

But to retreat was impossible and with desperate resolution the Chief Judge picked up the key and thrust it into the lock.

His assistants, the Procurator Fiscal and the Sbirri drew back with instinctive horror as the boards groaned and the ironwork which held them; the chain fell with a dismal clanking sound; and as the door was opened a horrible monster burst forth from the dungeon with a terrific howl.

Yells and cries of despair reverberated through the long corridor; and these sounds were for an instant broken by that of the falling of a heavy body.

'Twas the Chief Judge – hurled down and dashed violently against the rough uneven masonry by the mad careering of the wehr-wolf as the monster burst from his cell.

On – on he sped with the velocity of lightning along the corridor – giving vent to howls of the most hideous description. Fainting with terror, the Assistant Judges, the Procurator Fiscal and the Sbirri were for a few moments so overcome by the appalling scene they had just witnessed that no-one thought of rescuing the Chief Judge, who lay motionless on the pavement.

But at length some of the police officers so far recovered themselves as to devote attention to that high functionary; it was, however, too late – his skull was fractured by the violence with which he had been dashed against the rough wall – and his brains were scattered on the pavement.

Those who now bent over his disfigured corpse received looks of unutterable horror. In the meantime the wehr-wolf had cleared the corridor – rapid as an arrow shot from the bow – he sprang bounding up a flight of steep stone steps as if an elastic art bore him on – and rushing through the open door burst suddenly upon the crowd that was so anxiously waiting to behold the procession issue thence!

Terrific was the yell that the multitude sent forth – a yell formed of a thousand combined voices – so long – so loud and so wildly agonizing that never had the welkin rung with so appalling an ebullition of human misery before!

Madly rushed the wolf midst the people – dashing them aside – overturning them – hurling them down – bursting through the mass too dense to clear a passage of its own accord – and making the scene of horror more horrible still by mingling the hideous howling with the cries – the shrieks – the screams that escaped from a thousand tongues.

No pen can describe the awful scene of confusion and death which now took place. Swayed by no panic fear but influenced by terrors of dreadful reality the people exerted all their efforts to escape from that spot; and thus the stronger, crushing, pushing, crowding, fighting and all the oscillations of that multitude set in motion by the distant alarms were succeeded by the most fatal results.

Women were thrown down and trampled to death – strong men were scarcely able to maintain their footing – females were literally suffocated in the pressure of the crowd and mothers with young children in their arms excited no sympathy.

Never was the perfidy of human nature so strikingly displayed than on this occasion; no-one bestowed a thought upon his neighbour – the chivalrous Florentine citizen dashed aside the weak and helpless female who barred his way with as little re-morse as if she were not a thing of flesh and blood – and even husbands fled their wives, lovers abandoned their mistresses and parents waited not an instant to succour their daughters.

Oh! It was a terrible thing to contemplate – that dense mass oscillating furiously like the waves of the sea – sending up to heaven such appalling sounds of misery – rushing furiously to-wards the avenues of egress – falling back baffled and crushed in the struggle where only the very strongest prevailed – labouring to escape from death and fighting for life – fluctuating and rushing of maddened excitement like the heaving ocean – Oh! all this wrought a dreadful sublimity with those cries of agony and that riot of desperation.

And all this while the wolf pursued its furious career amid the mortal volcano of a people thrown into horrible disorder – pursued its way with savage howls, glaring eyes and foaming mouth – the only living being there that was infuriate and not alarmed – battling to escape and yet unhurt!

As the whirlpool suddenly strikes a gallant ship – makes her undulate and rock fearfully in a few moments and then swallows her altogether – so was the scaffold in the midst of the square shaken to its very basis for a little space and then hurled down – disappearing altogether amid the living vortex.

On the balconies and at the windows overlooking the square the awful excitement spread like wildfire; and a real panic prevailed amongst those who were at last beyond the reach of danger. But horror paralysed the power of sober reflection; the hideous spectacle of volumes of human beings battling – and roaring – and rushing and yelling in terrific frenzy produced a kindred effect and spread a wild delirium among the spectators at those balconies and those windows.

At length in the square below the crowds began to pour forth from the gates – for the wehr-wolf had by this time cleared himself a passage and escaped from the midst of that living ocean so fearfully agitated by the storms of fear!

But even when the means of egress were thus obtained the most frightful disorder prevailed – the people remaining in heaps upon heaps – while infuriate and agile men ran on the tops of the recumbent masses in their delirium as if in abandoned insanity.

On – on sped the wehr-wolf, dashing like a whirlwind through the streets leading to the open country – the white flakes of foam flying from his mouth like spray from the prow of a vessel – and every fibre of his frame vibrating as if in agony.

And oh! what dismay – what terror did that monster spread in the thoroughfares through which he passed. How wildly – how madly flew the men and women from his path – how piteously screamed the children at the house doors in the poor neighbourhoods! But as if sated with the destruction already wrought in the great square of the Palace the wolf dealt death no more in the precincts of the city and as if lashed on by invisible demons his aim – or his instinct was to escape.

The streets are threaded – the suburbs of the city are passed – and open country is gained; and now along the banks of the Arno rushes the monster – by the margin of that pure stream in whose enchanting vale a soft twilight lends a more delicate charm.

On the verge of a grove with its full budding branches all impatient with the spring, a lover and his mistress were murmuring fond farewells to each other.

The handsome youth pressed the maid's fair hand and said, "Tomorrow, beloved, we'll be united, and again to your parents' cot and renewed happiness."

The youth stopped and the maiden clung to him in speechless terror for an ominous sound as of a rushing commotion – and then a terrific howl burst upon their ears. No time had they for flight – not a moment even to collect their scattered thoughts.

The infuriate wolf came bounding over the green sward; the youth uttered a wild and fearful cry – a scream of agony burst from the lips of the maiden as she was dashed from her lover's arms – and in another moment the monster had swept by.

But what misery – what desolation had his passage wrought; though unhurt by his glistening fangs – though unwounded by his sharp claws – yet the maiden – an instant before so enchanting in her beauty and so happy in her love – lay stretched on the cold turf, the chords of life snapped suddenly by that transition of perfect bliss to the most appalling terror!

And still the wolf rushed madly and wildly on.

It was an hour past sunrise and from a grove in the immediate neighbourhood of Leghorn a man came forth; his countenance though wondrously handsome was deadly pale; traces of mental horror and anguish remained on those classically chiselled features and in those fine eloquent eyes.

His garments were soiled, bloodstained and torn. This was Fernand Wagner. He entered the city of Leghorn and purchased a change of attire for which he paid from a purse well filled with gold. He then repaired to a hostel or public tavern where he attended to the duties of the toilette and afterwards the refreshment of which he appeared to stand so much in need.

By this time his countenance was again composed; and the change which new attire and copious ablutions had made in his appearance were so great that no-one who had seen him issue from the grove and beheld him now would have believed in the identity of person.

Quitting the hostel he repaired to the port where he instituted inquiries relative to a particular vessel which he described and which had sailed from Leghorn upwards of a fortnight previously.

He soon obtained the information which he sought; and an old sailor, the same to whom he had previously addressed himself not only hinted that the vessel in question was suspected when in the harbour to be of a piratical character but also declared that he himself had seen a lady conveyed on board during the night preceding the departure of the ship. Further inquiries convinced Wagner that the lady spoken of had been carried by force and against her will to the corsair-vessel; and he was now certain that the demon had not deceived him – that he had indeed obtained a trace of his lost Nisida!

His mind was immediately resolved on how to act; and his measures were as speedily taken. Guided by the advice of the old sailor from whom he had gleaned the information he sought he was

The strangest case of a feral child on record. The enigmatic Kaspar Hauser, from an artist's impression of about 1830

Wolf boy—a feral child, unable to stand upright, who was discovered in the jungles of Sri Lanka (Ceylon) in the early 1970s

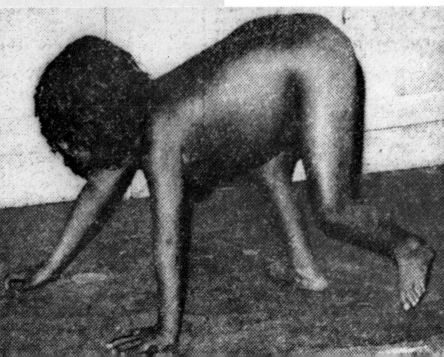

L'enfant Sauvage, François Truffaut's 1969 moving film study of the real-life feral child, Victor of Aveyron. Left, the director as actor: Truffaut himself as Dr Jean Itard with the young gipsy boy, Jean-Pierre Cargol, as Victor

able to purchase a fine vessel and equip her for sea within the space of a few days.

He lavished his gold with no niggard hand and gold is a wondrous talisman to remove obstacles and facilitate human designs. In a word on the sixth morning after his arrival at Leghorn Fernand Wagner embarked on board his ship which was manned with a gallant crew and carried ten pieces of ordnance.

A favouring breeze prevailed all the time; and the gallant bark set sail for the Levant.

So, in this lively, vigorous and romantic fashion George Reynolds launched the first major essay into the fictional field of the werewolf; one that was to stand for a good many years until more skilled and subtle pens took up the theme.

FIFTEEN

SOME MINOR BEASTS

The whole of werewolf fiction of any importance can be contained within the comparatively brief span of the past hundred and fifty years and during that period relatively few works of lasting quality have been produced. We shall be looking at most of those of any value in the course of this book. The werewolf theme has not been nearly so popular as that of the vampire and there is an important reason for this. The physical change of a human being, in any art form, has to be carefully treated if the ridiculous is to be avoided; for this reason if for no other the writer in particular must be subtle and his effects shaded if he is not to topple over into the ludicrous. Stevenson recognized this when writing *Dr Jekyll and Mr Hyde* and the metamorphosis of the 'good' Dr Jekyll into the 'evil' Mr Hyde was described in such a way as not to strain the reader's credibility in this beautifully realized novella.

Hyde's bestiality is suggested in telling detail rather than in long descriptions of hairy flesh and blazing eyes; some of the personifications of Hyde in the cinema, such as that by John Barrymore, who used little make-up, and that of Spencer Tracy in the 1940s, have been subtle indeed and far more powerful as a result.

The theme of lycanthropy contained this major difficulty which was never entirely overcome in the cinematic evocations of the were-monster; and the crudely stated effects, both in films and in many of the literary essays devoted to the subject have meant that there have been few works which can truly be described as classics in the field. There are none in the cinema, though one or two made a decent stab at it; literature has been more fortunate in that the writer has more technical equipment at his command and the reader's own imagination on which to work.

There have been successes, as I will endeavour to indicate, in the short form, but the novel is a different matter; the sustained narrative in any field is difficult enough of achievement but the novel of terror sets an almost impossible task. In the field of the vampire *Dracula* fell into this trap; though there are genuine peaks of terror, there are deserts of boredom for the reader to wade through.

The sustaining of terror, as all the masters of the genre from Edgar Allan Poe onwards realized, can only be achieved for very short stretches; the finest practitioners of the form not only took this into account but made sure there were no flat patches in their short stories. Therefore the surrounding passages which bolstered and set the stage for the peaks of terror were almost entirely devoted to atmosphere and suggestion.

From the ordinary to the extraordinary but in subtle stages through carefully chosen detail; there is certainly something of this in the literature of lycanthropy in the shorter form; practically nothing in the field of the novel, though one work, which we shall be examining at length, almost succeeds. Better written than *Dracula* and sparing in its effects, it has been unjustly neglected.

But before we turn to a full-length study of this outstanding novel, we must examine some of the longer essays in the lycanthropic genre which, if not among the more distinguished flights of imaginative fantasy, are at least worth some attention. And in recapturing, here and there, an ancient thrill we may serve to introduce new generations in turn to works which have too long remained hidden on dusty shelves. Certainly, publishers today are becoming more enterprising and imaginative in their turn. The weavers of terror in the Victorian fiction-factory may yet come to new popularity in the paperback field. Many of them were master craftsmen and their carefully wrought fantasies pay homage to one of the most terrifying and potent beasts of fact and legend, the werewolf.

Mist writhes over the surface of the marsh and through the wavering whiteness the filigree-work of dark branches stands out stark and ugly. The piercing cries of a few birds break the silence; the occasional snapping of a twig, the soft lap of water and the faint murmur of wind are the only other sounds that meet the ear.

Wings scatter somewhere in the marsh as footsteps approach; a large body of people is on the move. The baying of dogs is heard and the wavering outlines of men appear through the mist. Many men, carrying rifles over their arms, while others have heavy sticks. The dogs strain uneasily at the leashes and their mournful barking adds a melancholy dimension to the scene, while their large eyes look unseeingly into the shroud of whiteness which swirls across the swamp.

The men confer briefly as they stand on a knoll near the edge of the water, while the dogs mill aimlessly around, apparently oblivious of the curses of their handlers. The leader of the hunters, a tall, broad-shouldered man with a unique air of authority, points to the north. The other men, dressed like him in thick jackets and wearing gaiters, cluster around as he gives his instructions.

Moisture clings in droplets to the rims of their broad-brimmed hats, the bands decorated with the bright feathers of game-birds. Then the group dissolves as they stream away in the direction indicated by the tall man. The dogs follow, their excited barking muffled by the mist. Silence once again descends until there is nothing but the brittle chatter of birds and the faint slap of water against the reedy marsh.

Then, after more than a quarter of an hour has elapsed, there is a stirring in the grasses and a low moaning borne on the wind. A figure emerges from the marsh and pauses diffidently, before stepping on to the firm shore. The hunched form gazes anxiously through the gloom as it slinks forward, bent toward the ground. It is shaped like a man and yet is not a man. Naked and shivering, the body disfigured with cuts and sores, the creature is covered with coarse, bristling fur, now coated with mud and glistening with globules of water.

It walks half upright, its square feet like that of an animal and armed with strong black claws which sink like hooks into the ground. A low moaning noise from down in its throat sends birds up from the reed-edged marsh, as the creature takes its bearings. Then it sets out at a whimpering rush through the forest to a grove of oaks about a hundred yards away.

The face, half-seen through the mist, is like something out of a canvas by Goya. Covered with thick black hair from which two red eyes burn like banked-down furnaces; the nose is squat and reminiscent of a gorilla and the wet, broad nostrils sniff the air as it moves its head from side to side. The ears are long and covered with thick fur and they are as busy assessing every chance noise as the nostrils with the acrid stench of the swamplands.

The mouth is wide, the thick red lips parting every few seconds to emit a stream of saliva through the crooked, yellow teeth. These resemble those of an old and savage animal; strong, squat and razor-sharp they are equipped to tear flesh and bone and sinew. And yet the monster, for all its size and strength is a pathetic sight; it whimpers miserably to itself as it comes at last within the grove of oaks.

Then, emitting one long-drawn out howl of rage and agony the beast throws itself to the ground, its form racked by sobs. Half an hour passes; the mist writhes from the marshes and in the far distance an occasional gun fires. The voices of the hounds are heard baying down the wind. In the grove the tall, powerful figure of a man stirs. He looks round hastily, scrabbles furiously in the bole of a hollowed-out tree. Shivering with cold and pain he hurriedly draws on his clothes. Despite the weather his face is a beaded mask of perspiration and of a deathly white pallor.

He makes a rapid toilet with the aid of a small hand-mirror he draws from an inner pocket. Smoothing his rumpled hair he at last decides that he is fit to mingle with his fellow men. He thrusts his hand within the tree-bole and picks up his fowling piece. Something gleams dully on the palm of his hand. It is a strange scar, a blackened, mis-shapen thing making the pattern of a five-pointed star; the pentagram – the mark of the beast.

The hunter glances at it guiltily and quickly draws on a pair of chamois-leather gloves. A crackling sounds in the under-growth as he shoulders his gun and walks confidently across the undulating ground. The hounds burst forth from cover and bark excitedly; figures emerge and wave.

"Come along, Hans, we've lost the trail," calls their leader impatiently. "If you had kept up we might have retained contact."

Hans nods absently and rejoins the group. They move off, an excited crowd of muscular young men, flushed with the thrill of the chase. The fog swallows up their figures; the reeds sway in the quickening breeze and the forest is once again given over to the peace and tranquillity of the natural order of things.

This was the were-creature, the man-beast so beloved of the fiction writers of the late Victorian and early Edwardian period. It may stand for twenty or thirty longer pieces in the fictional mould which thrilled less sophisticated palates in that gaslit era. For all had a similar climactic scene in which the beast/man legend was fused in stories by gifted pens, or by others more clumsy and unable to convey the theme adequately.

But all had a standard incident in which the reader was made aware that the villain or, perhaps the hero, was not what he seemed to be. It would be tedious to attempt to notice all these longer stories, many of which simply repeated incidents in different guises, which had already been dealt with by more talented writers. I am attempting to be selective here, for the choice is wide; otherwise this study would become a catalogue.

Something of the possibilities of the genre in the fictional field have been glimpsed in *Wagner*, the creation of George Reynolds, probably the first super-beast in the field, the fore-runner of a gallery of cursed beings whose fate it was to roam the night and be hunted down mercilessly by their fellow men, whose ways they had temporarily forsaken.

Yet should not the true monster really be the citizenry at large, the peasants, neighbours and townsfolk who so gullibly gave the innocent man to the gallows, the branding-iron and the rack? For there were days when thousands perished at the stake for no other reason than that they had strange looks, that their fingers were long and crooked; or that hair grew out of their ears. The blood of the innocent must surely be laid at the door of those who denounced their neighbours.

However, we should not forget that terror is a hard task-master and the man who so eagerly consigned his fellow to the flame was perhaps thereby ensuring his own survival in the day when the magistracy, the judiciary and the military were more concerned with the totals they successfully hanged or burned, rather than in the workings of justice.

For there was no justice. The very word is an abstraction which it is not possible always to ensure even in the more compara-tively enlightened days of the late twentieth century. How so should it be ensured in a period when men lived at a brutish level and it was difficult enough to survive even without man's inter-ference? It is easy to be severe at this distance in time; but if we cannot always forgive at least we should strive to understand.

Forgiveness is not a quality which often finds its way into werewolf fiction; where it is found it gives an extra dimension to the story and paints in even more tragic colours the werewolf's plight.

Something of this melancholy essence was captured by the writers of the Victorian age who tried their hand at lycanthropic fiction in the longer form; they used the broader canvas to sketch in the moral dilemma of their monster-victims. This quality was not absent from a comparatively primitive piece of fiction such as *Wagner* and as more sophisticated writers took over this dimension of pity added, if anything, greater terror to their plots.

As the nineteenth century advanced an avalanche of werewolf material appeared; although some of the literature germane to the theme appeared from such distinguished pens as those of Algernon Blackwood, much of what was described as werewolf fiction was dross and may quickly be passed over.

It was not until the Edwardian age began – and I am still discussing the longer form – that a more subtle and worthwhile type of literature began to appear. One of the key works of this period, which attempted to re-animate the rich flowering of the Gothic-style novel of terror of the early nineteenth century, was that of a strange and elusive writer, Gerald Bliss, whose *The Door of the Unreal* was a lycanthropic novel of great power and tension.

It told of a young man cursed with the mark of the beast and in working out the story Bliss, a contemporary of Blackwood, Arthur Machen and Conan Doyle, cloaked his purposes in subtle and invigorating prose. The book appeared about 1905 and while perhaps influenced by Stoker's *Dracula* of a decade earlier, avoids most of its crudities and pitfalls.

Many of the so-called 'werewolf' novels were turgidly written and disappointing in the extreme and others, while hailed as being germane to lycanthropy are often entirely outside the genre or have only tenuous connections, such as those which contain only a single scene taking up perhaps a page or two. Such was the case with William Beckford's famous Gothic novel *Vathek* which first appeared in France in 1787 and only later in England; a splendid example of the genre, *Vathek*, subtitled an 'Arabian tale' was later said to be a 'werewolf' story, presumably on the slender basis that in one scene a caravan is menaced by wolves and other savage beasts!

Similarly, such a splendid novel as David Garnett's celebrated *Lady into Fox*, first published in 1922, has been invoked by those wishing to display their erudition; and even the many examples of cat-stories, such as those by Poe and Algernon Blackwood, have been made to serve their turn in article and thesis.

Interesting as many of them are, they are completely wide of such a study, which is why examples of the true werewolf novel which convinces both in atmosphere and terror are comparatively rare.

One of those worthy of note is by Frank Norris, prolific turn-of-the-century novelist whose most famous work was *McTeague*, a story of man's degradation in his love for gold, which was made into an even more distinguished film *Greed*, by the genius of Erich von Stroheim.

Vandover and the Brute, though not a true werewolf tale, has the hero metamorphosed into a wolf in all but form; his hero has a mental change in which he imagines himself to be turned into a brute beast and rolling horribly on the floor, snaps and foams in savage abandon.

Norris' book is a fascinating clinical study of a mind deranged and is totally convincing within its own terms of reference; an unusual and refreshing slant and something different from the 'normal' novel of lycanthropy.

Those more interested in the medical aspects of the condition, both physically and mentally, such as evinced in the 'werewolf disease' of medieval times, which we have already examined, are directed to such brilliant clinical studies as Frank Hamel's *Human Animals*, which was first published in 1915; and to Robert Eisler's more recent study *Man into Wolf* (1947).

The man-wolf theme in fiction has been epitomized in more recent times by the German novelist Herman Hesse, whose massive novel *Steppenwolf*, which appeared in the late '60s, has become a cult-book in much the same way as J. R. R. Tolkien's *Lord of the Rings* captured the imagination of the student generation.

The English novel of terror, of which the werewolf was but one strand, fell into disrepute in the '20s, though it was kept alive to a certain extent in countries like America, where the pulp novel and the anthology of long-short-stories flourished.

A rare humorous novel of lycanthropy was Ewart C. Jones' *How Now, Brown Cow* which appeared in 1947. Other novels in the genre worth mentioning include Franklin Gregory's *The White Wolf* (1941); and Jack Williamson's *Darker than you Think* (1948) of the more modern stories; and in earlier times Robert W. Service's *The House of Fear* (1927); Alfred H. Bill's *The Wolf in the Garden* (1931); Jessie Douglas Kerruish's well-known *The Undying Monster* (1936) and Arlton Eadie's *The Wolf-girl of Josselin* (1938). All had commendable moments and such magazines as the celebrated *Weird Tales* did a great deal to keep the genre alive.

But works of high quality in the longer form were few indeed and though such gifted writers as Blackwood and Arthur Machen went on producing first-rate work in isolation, the '30s and '40s were fairly lean years for the genre.

Oddly enough an outstanding novel surfaced briefly in the '30s and then became almost lost for something like three decades. The time was long overdue for a work in the full-length form which would do for the werewolf theme what Bram Stoker's *Dracula* had done for vampirism. The writer who was to achieve this had adopted the *nom de plume* Guy Endore and his book, *The Werewolf of Paris*, which has become famous in his own lifetime, is the nearest thing to a classic in the genre.

SIXTEEN

GUY ENDORE

The Werewolf novel can be said to have come of age with
the advent of Guy Endore. Though there had been some
laudable attempts in the longer form, there was nothing which
could faintly be regarded as a classic in the field of the novel
and such rambling narratives as those by George Reynolds
which had entertained so many in the mid-nineteenth century
would hardly appeal to the more sophisticated tastes of the
twentieth.

That a novel of the calibre of *The Werewolf of Paris* should
have come on the scene so late is somewhat unusual and worth
a moment's reflection. As we shall see in later chapters writers
of distinction had long been at work on the theme in the short
story field. The novel had been neglected.

The difference between the two forms is significant and, as
noted, has to do with the sustaining of atmosphere in the
longer. Almost alone *Dracula* is the only novel which survived
as a living work of art in the field of the vampire; in the field of
lycanthropy, *The Werewolf of Paris* is a great peak in a sea of
mediocrity.

It stands austere and solitary. In my opinion it is a well-
written work of literature, as well as an exciting and carefully
observed clinical study. Yet it has been unjustly neglected since
its first appearance in England in book form in 1934 and it is
only comparatively recently with its reappearance in paperback
that Guy Endore's gripping tale is beginning to take its rightful
place in the literature of the genre.

The author himself is a somewhat shadowy figure and facts
about him are hard to come by. A talented and erudite writer,
he seems to have created relatively few novels though he was
active in the macabre field, having published a large quantity
of well-written and finely turned short stories, many of which

were much anthologized in the '20s and '30s by leading publishers on both sides of the Atlantic.

He was also a well-known scriptwriter and collaborated on the screenplay of many distinguished films in Hollywood in the '30s and '40s. One of his best macabre pieces is the long short story *Lazarus Returns*, in which his mastery of the medium is clearly seen.

Guy Endore was born in New York in 1900. His real name was Harry Relis but he adopted the *nom de plume* as soon as he began to write. He received his early education in Vienna so it may be inferred that the Germanic influence on his prose was formed at the beginning of his life, for fantasy is at the root of the German character and is also seen in the *fin de siècle* Vienna school of music, painting, poetry and literature. A little later the German influence in the cinema was one of the greatest in fantasy and the macabre. After studying at Carnegie Technical Institute, Endore gained his degree of M.A. at Columbia University in 1924. He wrote two successful biographies of *Casanova* and *Joan of Arc* and then commenced a short series of novels, of which *The Werewolf of Paris* made his reputation in the relatively limited field of the macabre.

He was well established by the early '30s, both in the field of the novel and on the Hollywood scene, where his literate hand on the screenplays of a number of films distinguished what would otherwise have been somewhat mediocre works. Among these were, significantly, *The Mark of the Vampire*, and Tod Browning's *The Devil Doll*; in addition to the Fred Astaire film *Carefree*.

Endore, in fact, is that comparative rarity, the man whose work was so craftsmanlike, and his effects so subtly achieved that he was in danger of becoming an artist whose terms of reference almost put him outside the realms of the macabre altogether. This is clearly seen in his masterpiece, *The Werewolf of Paris*, where his effects are achieved on a delicate scale, without any of the coarseness and over-painting of horrific detail which spoil so many essays in the macabre. In fact Endore writes at the opening of his tale, "This one has neither beginning nor end, but only a perpetual unfolding, a multi-petalled blossom of strange botany".

The paragraph is a perfect description of his style; a fastidious imagination is at work here, with none of the clumsy in-

felicities or grossness of effect which mar the work of a lesser –
albeit more successful – writer like Bram Stoker.

Of course, in the ultra-sophisticated age in which we now
live, one has to be subtle to succeed on such a plane; the old
methods of the nineteenth century with their constantly
reiterated literal horrors and insistence on climax and
anti-climax would be laughed from the stage or screen. And
publishers certainly would not find it worthwhile to issue
large-scale works of that type, which no-one would want to read.

People were a little less critical in 1934, when Endore's book
appeared, but even so the passage of more than forty years has
done little to dim its effect on the modern reader. Almost alone
among novels which make their mark in the Gothic field, this
book seems rather to gain in power than to diminish.

This is partly due to the oblique manner in which it is
written and partly because of Endore's creative skill in narrative and character delineation. I shall be discussing the novel
in full in the following chapters but firstly we should look at the
surrounding circumstances and the period and background
against which it was written.

As the reader will have gathered, apart from the excellent
studies in the shorter form, there has been almost nothing of
novel length in the first thirty years of the twentieth century to
compare with *The Werewolf of Paris*.

This fact was not lost upon Hollywood film-makers and
within a year or so of publication they had produced a film on
the subject, with Endore's reputed collaboration; though
perversely they chose to release it as *The Werewolf of London*!
It bore little true relation, however, to Endore's literary
creation; the novel was a far more fastidious and original work,
which concealed its true horror until a very late stage.

Had a film been made which remained within the framework
of this author's considerable literary imagination it might have
emerged as a remarkable one indeed; a production worthy to
rank with those films by Browning, Murnau and Dreyer which
enshrined the vampire myth in celluloid.*

Something of Endore's quality as a writer and particularly as
a scenario writer can be seen in the script he wrote for *Dark
Eyes of London*, a British horror film starring Bela Lugosi, which
was made in Great Britain in 1939. Based on a novel by Edgar

*See the author's *The Vampire: In Legend, Fact and Art*.

Wallace it was one of the strongest and most horrifying films in the genre ever made in England and was in fact the first film shot in Britain to win the 'H' for horror certificate, introduced by the British Board of Film Censors in the early '30s.

Lugosi, in Endore's script, was a benevolent director of a blind institute who was also the diabolical Dr Orloff who murdered to gain the victims' insurance money. Endore was good at suggestion and the horrific implications of scenes in which pathetic blind inmates were drowned in a tank of water before being thrown into the Thames – the doctor's scene of operations is a warehouse conveniently overlooking the river – are sombre indeed.

Directed with style and flair by veteran English director Walter Summers, Endore's terrifying script has a scene in which a blind man is also made deaf by the doctor inserting electrodes in his ears. The pathetic overtones of such sequences make strong meat, even for today's audiences, and the 'H' certificate was well earned.

Lugosi's doctor meets his end when his tool, a Frankenstein-like mute played by Wilfred Walter, eventually turns on him and hurls him in the river to join his long list of victims. The final scene shows Lugosi slowly sinking into the evil Thames mud and the camera only cuts away as the sludge is oozing into his mouth. The film remains one for the strong-nerved only and well illustrates the power of Endore's imagination, as he invests Wallace's basically robust tale of murder and intrigue with all sorts of psychological and erotic undercurrents.

There is no doubt that some of Endore's more powerful ideas in such films were coarsened in translating them to the visual and more literal medium of the cinema but there were no such restrictions in his prose. There his imagination was free to roam in new directions and the modern reader who comes across works by Endore – and apart from *Werewolf* in paperback they are remarkably hard to find – will not be disappointed; that is, if craftsmanship, talent, imagination and fastidious skill are what he is seeking. These elements are always strongly present in Endore's work and, as we shall see, deeply suffused this author's greatest creation.

A modern paperback edition of Endore's tale claims on its cover, "One of the world's great classics of horror". This is a view which I myself share but it has taken many decades for people to recognize and it is still a description denied by many critics, assuming that any of them have even heard of the story.

The title may be regarded by some as catchpenny; if so this is a pity and my analysis in the next chapters will attempt to prove that this is a literate work, cunningly written and which it is no exaggeration to describe as of classic status within the genre.

With its multiplicity of characters, its evocative air of a long-ago Paris of the Commune and its telling use of obliqueness in achieving its effects, the book is a feast for those to whom the macabre with all its poetry and fantasy is an enchantment, an escape from the twentieth century with its more realistic horrors.

And yet it has a documentary realism underlying it, which gives its pages the faint smell of the charnel house and its scenes of horror must be among the most muted in all literature. Small wonder then that other, cruder novels achieved a wider reputation. But like most classics *The Werewolf of Paris* has advanced, little by little over the years and from being an obscure, cult book it has now, I feel, taken its place with such famous tales as *Frankenstein* and *Uncle Silas* as an acknowledged if minor masterwork.

A strange book, perhaps, to come from an American author who was a well-known Hollywood script-writer and an habitué of the international scene who moved in sophisticated circles. Yet if one examines it more closely, perhaps not quite so strange. Endore, as we have seen, had passed his formative years in Vienna and had lived much in Europe latterly. He was closely drawn to the world of the macabre and apart from this long novel, many of his evocative short stories reveal his fascination with the bizarre, the strange and the weird.

And, of course, he was an outstanding screenwriter of horror films, both in his native America and in Great Britain in the '30s. He was a man who appears not to have had a public persona and whose personality remains elusive. He is almost unmentioned in the memoirs of the period, both in film and literary circles yet he had been a well-known, if not famous writer on both sides of the Atlantic for decades.

His long and distinguished career merits only some two inches in the American reference work *Contemporary Authors,* though his other important books had included: *The Sword of God, Joan of Arc, King of Paris* and *Voltaire! Voltaire!* in addition to biographical works and numerous screenplays.

In 1927 he had married Henrietta Portugal and they had two children, Marcia and Gita. Guy Endore died in America in February 1970, and his passing apparently attracted as little public notice as his hard-working literary life had done.

Certainly, Guy Endore has hitherto been denied his rightful place in the history of the macabre. By the evidence of *The Werewolf of Paris* alone he emerges as a master.

SEVENTEEN

TERROR IN PARIS

One of the most fascinating books on a macabre theme ever written begins with a most incongruous prologue, set in modern Paris, and more reminiscent of Hemingway than the Gothic novella. A young American expatriate author living in the capital is trying to write non-fiction but is interrupted by Eliane, a girlfriend just over from the States, who wants to see the town.

But even this modern prologue, written in the 1930s, of course, has not dated at all and Endore mixes his casual reportage of night-life and sexual passages with erudite discussions of the Roman Festival of the Lupercales. With many writers this would misfire but with Endore it blends perfectly and one is almost imperceptibly entrapped in this jazzy prologue which is totally unlike the body of the book itself.

The opening is partly autobiographical, for Endore himself lived in Paris; he too, like the hero-narrator had studied for a Ph.D. and he is perfectly at home quoting French, German and Latin with practised ease at places in the narrative where they would naturally occur.

The narrator has been discussing with a café acquaintance certain Roman practices and now, having parted from him, is seated on a bench in the dawn light when two rag-pickers approach and lay out their treasures on the *quai* near where he is sitting. Among the broken light-bulbs and other bric-à-brac is a nineteenth-century manuscript.

He buys it for five francs and finds a handwritten account of the court martial of a man named Bertrand Chaillet in 1871. The writer's name is Aymar Galliez and the narrator is so interested in his report that he seeks out a descendant, Lieutenant Aymar Galliez. He learns little of the original Aymar save that he was wounded in the Paris street-fighting in 1848, became a political pamphleteer and later a priest, dying in 1890.

Endore begins his first chapter proper with Aymar Galliez' narrative of a particularly cruel history relating to the rivalry between two ancient French houses, Pitaval and Pitamont, whose two castles frowned at one another from the opposite sides of a valley bisected by a stream.

This is so perfectly described, with recourse to a device which the author uses sparingly, learned footnotes – that the reader might well be deceived into believing it literal truth. The deadly warfare between these two branches of the same family became so fratricidal that the populace deserted their estates, they became impoverished and had to mortgage farms and other property.

This is the situation when, one bitterly cold night, with wolves howling in the mountains, a travelling friar from Italy begs shelter within the walls of Castle Pitaval. At dead of night the monk throws off his sheepskins and murders two of his sleeping hosts, a married couple, in their chamber.

But the treacherous guest trips on a staircase and awakes the Pitavals. By morning the murders are known and the friar, unmasked as a rival Pitamont, is locked in a small cell in the bowels of the castle. The young Pitaval heir summons a stone-mason and an oubliette is constructed from an old well.

On to a stone ledge is lowered the naked figure of Jehan Pitamont: below him the well-water can be reached by a metal stoup held by a chain; apart from a cess-pit, the only other amenities are an airhole in the dome above. From a small chamber on top of the dome Pitaval servants throw meat and suet three times a week on to a grating in reach of the captive. This is the terrible fate meted out to a traitor and Jehan Pitamont resigns himself to death.*

But the instinct for life is strong and the naked captive, shivering and feverish, beguiles his time with imagining rescue by his family who would assuredly assault and capture this cursed castle. No help comes and weakened by lack of food Pitamont determines to count the hours and days. But time soon becomes meaningless, his only diversion the rare occasions

*This is almost the only situation retained *in toto* from Endore's novel in the screen adaptation *The Curse of the Werewolf*, filmed by Hammer Films in 1961, and discussed in a later chapter.

when his jailers toss him food with such sarcastic questions as to whether he requires a prayer stool or a breviary.

Endore spends several pages in detailing Pitamont's mental and physical tortures; firstly, a description of him trying to dash his head against the wall; then voluntarily starving himself and finally, all restraint cast away, his howling like a dog when his thrice-weekly food is late in arriving. His family think him dead, of course, and in the vault, which keeps an even temperature, despite the seasons outside, Pitamont endures a living death. Full fifty years pass and still he is entombed.

With this admirable opening Endore, his oblique methods already apparent, even though only an eighth of the book begun, sets the pattern for a classic work in the genre. The long ordeal of Pitamont ends in ironic fashion. The lawyer Datini forecloses the mortgages on both Pitaval and Pitamont houses and visiting Castle Pitaval with his bailiffs is received pleasantly by the surviving Pitaval and his steward.

The party are at dinner when the lawyer is startled to hear an awful howling from the depths of the castle. Pitaval merely informs him blandly that it is a pet wolf and orders the steward to take the beast some poisoned meat. The howling shortly afterwards ceases. When the former lord and his steward, dispossessed, are preparing to quit the castle, an old woman, one of the few surviving Pitamonts, appears and implores him to tell her where her "poor Jehan" is buried.

Pitaval gives her the key to the dungeon, adding, "No king ever had a more fitting tomb. Nor monk either."

Like Victor Hugo before him Endore is a master of the elliptical narrative. His chapters end in the air and we then skip several centuries to take up the history of other characters, apparently completely unrelated to those we have been reading about. But like a Swiss precision watch all these small parts fit together until in the end, the last component is placed in position, and we have the entire story.

So it is with *The Werewolf of Paris*; as the narrator says, the reader will keep company with the Pitamonts throughout the book and recognize them, despite their disguises. In the Paris of the 1850s young Lieutenant Aymar Galliez is living with his aunt and a young orphan girl Josephine, who is seduced by a drunken and lecherous priest Father Pitamont. From this unwholesome union a child is born but Galliez who at first pities the girl and is then attracted, himself becomes her lover.

A fine descriptive passage vividly delineates Aymar's whirling thoughts and indecision and reveals Endore's mastery of prose. As the young officer sits in his room, unable to write and thinking only about Josephine, he rises and goes to the casement. The passage continues: "He looked out of his window, down on the hot August boulevard. Men and women, horses and cabs, drenched in the sun, hastened by in both directions. What was the meaning of all this? His mind was empty of any thoughts. The whole world had no meaning. Nothing but hot dust, eye-searing colours, people who did not know what they were about".

The quotation is an evocative one and would not disgrace Maupassant. But it is not exceptional for this work and for this writer, whose prose is everywhere of a high literary standard; every phrase is turned with such precision as to extract the last subtle nuance of meaning.

Josephine's child is born on Christmas Eve, which Aymar's aunt refers to bitterly as a mockery of the birth of Christ, and is christened Bertrand Aymar Caillet, the first Christian name being that of Father Pitamont, the second that of the lieutenant, of course; the surname standing for the mythical designation of Josephine's 'husband', supposedly away at sea.

From the first the child is strange and unusual and to Madame Didier's horror the mother proposes to keep him and return to her native village with him. But for the time being the family remain in Paris though Madame Didier has many misgivings about the child; she points out that his eyebrows join across his nose, which she says is the sign of a low nature. She and her nephew are afraid that the boy might turn out to be like its father, the priest Pitamont, who has been transferred by his bishop and has conveniently disappeared.

Madame Didier speaks of a legend of a white deer which came each night to search for its mate, a pure young girl; another legend concerned men/wolves, who could be recognized by the hair on the palms of their hands. There is an awful silence as Madame Didier observes, "Bertrand has hair on the palms of his hands". A few days later a dismal howling like that of a dog fills the house; Aymar rushes to Bertrand's room but the child is all right. Returning to his aunt he finds she has died quietly in her chair.

Sensitive, gifted, oblique, Endore spins a story as light as a cobweb to entrap the unwary reader; it is made up of a thousand impressions; of Aymar being unable to study for the priesthood because of his crippled leg; of his selling the Paris apartment; of his again hearing a dog baying in the empty rooms as he stands thinking of his past life there.

Aymar and Bertrand, now a boy of nine, are living in the country near a small village on the Yonne. A fox has been stealing sheep and the local mayor orders Bramond, a forest guard, to shoot it. More lambs are killed and a huge dog jumps at a small child and the villagers realize they have to deal with a wolf.

Bramond, who has twice shot at the beast as it stands over its prey, without result, makes a wax mould and casts a bullet from a silver crucifix belonging to his wife. One winter night, in deep snow he fires at and wounds the wolf, which makes its escape. He follows a blood trail and is aware he himself is being stalked. He finally shoots not a wolf but a local shepherd's dog.

Bramond collapses in the snow and lies ill for weeks. The mayor congratulates him; the dog was the creature responsible for the sheep-killing. At any rate there are no more wolf attacks in the neighbourhood.

But Aymar is stupefied to find, after Josephine has reported that Bertrand is lying ill in bed, a wound in the child's leg. He squeezes out the silver bullet.

Bertrand, who is a pathetic figure, tells Aymar that he has terrible nightmares; the ex-officer is overcome with pity when the boy says he dreams of blood and thinks he is a wolf which has to kill birds and animals. And so, with Josephine's approval, he puts bars across the windows of the child's room and locks the door every night.

Endore describes in restrained terms, all the more telling, of Aymar's doubts and fears as he nightly hears snorting and the scratching of claws on the floor of Bertrand's bedroom. But each time he opens the door there is only the boy on the bed, turning feverishly in nightmare. He consults old books on lycanthropy and often takes the silver bullet out of his desk as he ruminates on Bertrand's strange Pitamont ancestry.

And, asks Endore, "Could it be that a curious concatenation of causes, a rare and strange plexus of events, to be encountered only once in centuries, might produce a monstrous exception to the ordinary course of nature?"

Sombrely, inexorably over the course of many pages and many chapters does the strange story develop, with a subtle and striking battle in Aymar's mind between his pity for Bertrand and his disgust for the thing in the bedroom; more than once he is on the point of destroying it by fire but his civilized nature recoils from this. But the tiger in Bertrand is only sleeping; while a student of medicine some years later the blood-lust overcomes him in a brothel and only Aymar's purse is able to save him from the law.

It is a happy invention of Aymar's to have a doctor diagnose anaemia in the young man and he is fed on a diet of raw meat which keeps his savage nature in check – for a time.

But things go wrong when Bertrand's mother uses the key to let him out at night, not realizing his bestial nature; a newly interred corpse is plucked from the grave and violated. The anguish suffered by the unfortunate Bertrand is nowhere more ably epitomized than in the striking Chapter Nine of Endore's masterpiece in which the young man, still unaware of his condition, ruminates on the reasons for his being kept under lock and key.

The heights of horror are reached in the laconically described scenes which follow. Bertrand's mother, awakening him with money and a packed valise for his journey to Paris to resume his studies, is mistaken for the girl in the brothel and Bertrand rapes her. As soon as he comes to himself he flees from this incestuous scene and then attacks Aymar, who seeks to prevent him leaving.

Hiding in the countryside near the village Bertrand has an overmastering desire to tear off his clothes; he sees his uncle following and attacks him. Awakening in the cold dawn he is appalled to find he has torn out the throat of his friend Jacques Bramond and realizes that he is afflicted with the curse of lycanthropy. He flees to Paris, leaving a young farmhand to be blamed for the murder of Bramond.

But Aymar has realized the truth; he leaves money for the farmhand's defence and sets out for Paris to track down the monster spawned by the Pitamont priest. The book now takes a new tangent. It is the time of the Franco-Prussian War and the Siege of Paris. Against this impressively detailed background the remainder of Endore's great drama is played out.

EIGHTEEN

THE WOLF OF THE COMMUNE

It is not possible to envisage exactly what was in Endore's mind when he wrote *The Werewolf of Paris*, for this gifted author is now dead. But it is significant that the hero/villain is called Bertrand. May it not be that Endore had read the factual reports of Sergeant Bertrand, the monstrous desecrator of cemeteries in nineteenth-century Paris, and had transmuted the vampiric real-life Bertrand into the lycanthropic beast of his book?

It is more than likely and the facts – dealt with in my own volume *The Vampire: In Legend, Fact and Art* – parallel the literary Bertrand's exploits in an astonishing manner; perhaps too closely for it to be entirely coincidence. In any event it is an interesting echo from the past and I myself like to think that the greatest lycanthrope in literature is based on one of the greatest vampiric *causes célèbres* in history.

In a neat reversal of fact into art, the vampire is metamorphosed into the lycanthrope. Well, let it be so. It is no worse for that. For Guy Endore's sure touch with the macabre is hardly needed to embellish the passages which follow, as the Grand Guignol circumstances surrounding the case of the real-life Sergeant Bertrand are hardly equalled, let alone surpassed in Gothic fiction.

General Darimon, an officer of retiring age who had married a young heiress, has lost his five-year-old daughter, a fever victim. The child is laid to rest at Père-Lachaise and here the old father comes mourning at dawn each day to keep vigil. But one morning a dog rushes past and the general collapses with shock and grief on finding the grave violated, the corpse desecrated.

Only Lieutenant Aymar Galliez, the muffled bombardment

of the German cannon investing Paris booming in his ears, realizes what has happened. As he reads the newspaper reports of cemeteries violated and further shocking crimes committed, he is on the trail of Bertrand. This tremendous canvas of the historical background is brilliantly used by Endore to bring the events described to vivid life.

He has subtly shifted the date of the real-life happenings of the Sergeant Bertrand crimes from 1849 to 1870 so that he could depict the events of the Siege of Paris which undoubtedly adds a great deal to the final chapters of this most engrossing of horrific novels.

With the bombardment and siege comes famine; Aymar seizes on newspaper reports which speak of a wolf which has invaded the suburbs. One report says a wolf has actually been captured and taken to the Jardin d'Acclimatation for identification. Aymar recognizes the name of the director of the Jardin; it is that of an old friend, Geoffroy Saint-Hilaire. Hurrying to the Zoo he is greeted cordially; instead of answering Aymar's inquiries about the wolf, the director instead invites him to dinner in an elegant household.

He is puzzled at the rich variety of food upon the table; all the guests are members of the Imperial Zoological Society. As the meal progresses Aymar realizes that the elegant phrases of the menu conceal the most extraordinary dishes, such as horse, dog's liver, minced cat and ragout of rat.

This is one of the most fascinating chapters in *The Werewolf of Paris* and Endore has based his incidents upon actual historical fact as seen during the Siege of Paris when the population of the city was reduced to near starvation. His research is thorough and esoteric and there is much moving detail as in the description of the deaths of the two elephants at the Paris Zoological Gardens, Castor and Pollux, which are slaughtered to provide butcher's meat.

This is the sort of thing which gives Endore's book such a strange flavour and it is, after all, something not often met with in the field of the macabre novel. For this reason alone, it stands pre-eminent in lycanthropic fiction.

There is a supreme irony in Endore's description of the elaborate meal prepared for the zoologists; after the tasting of each course, the description is read out. Later, while they walk back through the night, Aymar realizes his friend's apparent casualness over the matter of the wolf. He supposes the beast to have been a pet dog belonging to Galliez.

Says Saint-Hilaire, "We wanted a dog for our cook . . . And the happy thought struck me; I might take you along, and at least you would be in on his funeral."

Aymar realizes the dog has been served at the dinner he has just consumed; he is appalled at the implications and rushes off without saying good-bye. But later, reading a report of a prostitute murdered by a man in the uniform of the National Guard, he realizes that Bertrand is still very much alive.

In the turmoil and the terror caused by the Siege of Paris, the dreadful deeds of a Bertrand, dressed in the anonymous uniform of the National Guard, pass almost unnoticed. And the young man, with animal cunning, has made his arrangements to perfect the weird life he is now leading; he had enrolled in the service under a changed name. In his lodging he has fixed new locks to door and window, so that he can come and go without the *concierge* seeing him.

One morning he awakes to new terror; like most lycanthropes Bertrand knows little or nothing of the morbid compulsion which forces him to kill; he does not even know if he is physically metamorphosed when stalking his victim through the dim streets of the war-time capital.

On this occasion he finds the white arm of a male victim lying beneath his bed; in these almost casual descriptions of unspeakable horrors, Endore throws up masterly images and strikes a genuine chill into the reader. With this gruesome discovery recollection returns to Bertrand and with it, the description of another murder glimpsed obliquely and of which he is not the author.

The previous day Bertrand, in uniform, had joined in a funeral procession wending its way to Montparnasse; striking up conversation with a fellow mourner Bertrand learns that the dead man had been only fifty. He had married a young girl and Bertrand's confidant expresses suspicion at the suddenness of his friend's death and the cool attitude of the widow.

Later, feasting off charnel horrors at the grave of the dis-interred corpse Bertrand is involved in a terrible fight with the revived husband of the young girl, recovering from his drugged trance. It is this sort of gratuitous horror, related in a documentary style, which gives Endore's work its unique flavour; imparting one horror, he tops it with another so that we seem to see the Grand Guignol aspects of life in this period going on beyond the edges of the frame he has chosen for himself. This is something usually seen only in the higher forms of art and certainly this writer's work is of a superior order.

He now introduces another strand in the final third of the book; in a canteen for troops frequented by Bertrand he has noticed a young girl serving refreshments to the Guardsmen. She is a well-born young lady, barely seventeen, Mlle Sophie de Blumenberg, the daughter of a wealthy Paris banker. Laughingly ignoring the clumsy blandishments of the troops she has eyes for one man only; her constant escort, an equally aristocratic Captain of Cavalry, Barral de Montfort.

With the entrance of these new characters this unique book is nearing its close. Without involving any of the hackneyed clichés of the Frankenstein or vampire themes, Endore is constantly breaking new ground with his hard-edged historical facts and carefully researched backgrounds; and the reader sometimes forgets the lycanthropic nature of the novel as the author makes fascinating digressions without ever quite departing from his major threads.

In this he shares something of the attributes of an incomparably greater writer and an acknowledged master, Victor Hugo, whose books are like gigantic, apparently unrelated fragments, which finally come together – totally unlike life but with incomparable art and conviction.

Here is Endore vividly sketching in his heroine: "Sophie's dress of tightly laced white velvet faintly tinted with lemon, her trailing skirt of white satin and frills, as if she had stepped out of the surf and a wave had dashed after her with a foaming white crest. And out of this calyx of whiteness, her beautifully curving shoulders and bosom as if of polished bronze, her bare brown arms, her dark laughing face, her hair in ebony ringlets".

And equally deftly he sketches in her milieu: "The great apartment was quiet. The massive furniture gleamed, the brass fitttngs of scrolls and sphinxes glittered under the gas-light. Somewhere behind a door, she knew, a sleepy servant was yawning and waiting for her to depart so that he could extinguish the lights".

Improbable as it may seem the young soldier, Bertrand, his heart cleansed of his bestiality by happiness, becomes the lover of Sophie; the two, drawn together by attractions so subtle as to be almost imperceptible to others, carry on an affair under the very eyes of her family and, too late, de Montford finds his fiancée beyond his grasp.

When she visits Bertrand in his ugly room the girl finds an unexpected streak of masochism in her make-up. She begs Bertrand to hurt her in their love-making; contrary to the reader's expectation the young soldier is able to sublimate his bestiality and the lycanthropic attack upon the beautiful young woman does not take place.

There is another link with Hugo too, as the book approaches its climax; Endore dismisses the Siege of Paris, the ceding of Alsace-Lorraine, the revolution and the Commune in a few lines. We take up the story again some time later; Barral de Montfort, thwarted in love, is employed in espionage work for the new government. One is irresistibly reminded in particular of *Les Misérables* and the relationship between Jean Valjean and his pursuer Inspector Javert and the sub-plot involving Cosette and Marius. Only here the Javert rôle is represented by de Montfort and the Cosette-Marius relationship by Bertrand and Sophie.

But like his great predecessor, Hugo, this writer keeps his plot-points firmly linked to the narrative, however digressive the surface, the reader constantly being jerked back to the matter in hand. The parallel with Hugo is irresistible as when Aymar Galliez, still searching for Bertrand, returns to the narrative and, passing along a Paris street, pauses near a cat, dog and rat butcher shop, recognizing the red-faced, heavily jowled butcher with his bloodied cleaver as the former Father Pitamont.

When Aymar and Bertrand do meet, the encounter is pitched in a minor key. As a guardsman the latter is helping to excavate coffins from a crypt at the Picpus Monastery. Aymar is visiting there with a friend.

"Your speciality, isn't it?" says Aymar, indicating a coffin.

Bertrand is not embarrassed; he has an innocent eye.

"I have suffered," he tells his uncle.

Aymar reproaches him for not having written; for not having

had the decency to let him know he was still alive, "after seventeen years of good care and food".

It is on this level that the novel is so excellent; one might be reading a work by Balzac or Maupassant. The two men talk of banal trivialities, the horror which is in their thoughts left unspoken, hovering in the air around them. Bertrand tells Aymar he is cured; the love of a beautiful young woman has purged the terrible curse which beset him. Despite himself Aymar is moved.

Endore has saved one of his most shattering scenes of medical horror to this late stage of the book. Barral de Montfort, the Government spy, is still in love with Sophie. He writes her but then decides to check if the address where she is living is the real one. He finds a mean house in a mean street and tries to decide which is the window of their apartment.

He flees on seeing a candle lit behind a white curtain. It is indeed the room occupied by Sophie and Bertrand but a very different scene is being enacted there to that imagined by the lovesick young man. Bertrand is awake; he is fevered and cannot sleep. The girl looks at him pityingly. The knife is on the table, she tells him.

As the young guardsman uncovers her the reader is made aware, in Endore's fastidious prose that the beautiful girl's body is scarred with half-healed cuts. He makes a fresh incision and drinks her blood greedily, while she plays lovingly with his hair. This is a scene of tenderness and horror rare in literature and Endore here shows a profound knowledge of human psychology; the scene is compounded equally of disgust, pity and horror, the latter emotion coming from the reader's own reaction to the events.

In one moment of clear-sightedness Sophie realizes the feelings that Barral has for her; only moments before they have casually torn up the young officer's nightly love-letter to Sophie, unread. Now she sees clearly how passion may blind a person and blind him or her irrevocably to the object of that love. With incredible folly she gives herself up to Bertrand's nightly blood-lusts, while the young man himself proceeds from one excess to another.

Against the personal drama another, greater, external canvas is unfolding; the struggle of the Versailles troops to exterminate the Communards. In the face of death, the young lovers decide to die together if the worst should come. But the lycanthropic lusts have been only slumbering in Bertrand; night after night, as Sophie lies sleeping by his side, he fights against the impulse to bite into the carotid artery and slake his unnatural thirst at the fountain of life itself. One evening, his torment unbearable, he rushes out into the night to seek a new victim.

But the man he selects for his attack is young and strong, a fellow soldier; he brings Bertrand down and he is soon under arrest. So it is that Aymar is startled next morning to hear the news that a National Guardsman has tried to bite a comrade. Meanwhile, Sophie has passed a wretched day without news of her lover.

The three strands of the story come together in the finale; Aymar is reconciled with Bertrand in the asylum in which he is incarcerated; Barral is half-blinded and crippled by the mob at Sophie's instigation, who believes he has made away with his rival, Bertrand. Contrite, she agrees to marry Barral but commits suicide the night before the wedding.

The last of the Communards is eventually massacred in a grave-to-grave battle in Père Lachaise – echoes of Sergeant Bertrand here – and as a bloody dawn comes up over a terrified Paris, the civil war is at last over. Aymar is strangely thoughtful as he wanders about the city; with twenty thousand people executed by the Versailles government in one week, he realizes that a *loup-garou* like Bertrand is very mild stuff indeed compared with this holocaust. We have bred a whole race of werewolves, he thinks. And once he had thought them rare!

There is a strange irony in the ending of Endore's finest novel, and he repeats the phrase used at the beginning, about the many-petalled blossom of strange botany. And he almost plays with the reader, threatening to end the story as if the long agony of Bertrand were of no importance against the historical background he has invoked.

He says, tantalizingly, "Why should I not end here? Why should you want to know of the death of this werewolf rather than another? Consult your mortuary registers." So he brings the story to an end with a documentary flourish that is as ingenious as anything else in this unique work.

In the private asylum of Dr Dumas, Bertrand, as savage and cunning as ever, meets his predestined end in a fine, imaginative piece of bravura writing that is as inevitable as it is satisfying. Barral de Montfort, living only for revenge on Bertrand arrives too late. He stands looking at the grave, thinking that he would like to dig it up and spit in the occupant's face.

Endore has saved some of his best effects for this final portion of his detailed and carefully wrought text. There is a scene heavy with irony where Aymar discusses Bertrand's case with Dr Dumas, neither knowing the other's true feeling; the doctor cruelly repressing and harshly ill-treating his patient; Aymar, who is taking holy orders, not knowing that the superintendent believes the uncle should also be under treatment in the asylum.

In a long and beautifully written argument, the two men debate the subject of lycanthropy; the doctor sceptical and putting the scientific arguments; Aymar countering with religious doctrine and the changes of nature, such as the metamorphosis of grub into butterfly. This is one of the best-drawn scenes in the book and an example in itself of Endore's right to be regarded as an important writer.

He has saved his grimmest joke for the end. The Appendix to *The Werewolf of Paris* is a series of reports in flat, unemotional prose on the hygienic conditions in Paris cemeteries in the nineteenth century. In experiments with the Système Coupry in which corpses were reduced to their skeletal state in a short space of time and noxious gases burned, a number of bodies from the St Nazaire Cemetery were exhumed.

Endore here again uses actual reports and documents which may still be consulted today; and which give his book such vivid and unique verisimilitude. Among the ten bodies exhumed was one of a man called Bertrand, which had been in the ground for eight years. The *conservateur* of the cemetery forwarded this report to the Department of Criminal Justice.

Evidently a grave robbery or a grim joke on the part of the gravediggers. There was no human body in the coffin. Instead, nothing but the still undecomposed corpse of a dog.

NINETEEN

WOLVES AND PANTHERS

From the charnel horrors of Guy Endore's all too believable Paris of the Commune it is perhaps a relief to escape for a while to the more cosy literary terrors of writers of the early and later nineteenth century. While no work of this nature can claim to be definitive I hope in this and following chapters to discuss and point out some of the more striking tales of lycanthropy in the short-story form.

As will be remembered we made the point when discussing the longer works that the major problem of lycanthropy as a fictional exercise was the difficulty of sustaining atmosphere and with the atmosphere, belief. This is, of course, no less important in the novella or the short story, but the compression does assist a great deal and the successful works in this area are more numerous than one might think.

This is also because many first-class writers have been attracted to the theme in the short story form, including such masters as Robert Louis Stevenson, Frederick Marryat, Ambrose Bierce, Algernon Blackwood and Saki among earlier practitioners; and in more modern times, among others, F. G. Loring, Peter Fleming, Clark Ashton Smith, August Derleth, H. Warner Munn and Seabury Quinn.

When dealing with outstanding works of the earlier period, I shall point out literary highlights from various decades of the nineteenth century and give shorter notice to less important tales. This will mean some jumping about in time but will be a more satisfactory method, I feel, than proceeding in strict chronological order, as the more important stories may be dealt with together and trends and styles indicated.

For this reason I will commence my examination with an acknowledged master of the late nineteenth century, an adept at the classic ghost story and conte cruel alike, Ambrose Bierce, soldier, journalist and war-correspondent whose own fate was as mysterious as anything in his stories.

Bierce was a reticent and enigmatic figure, a sort of American version of Guy de Maupassant in his abrasive cynicism. A well-known journalist of his day, he was born in 1842 in Ohio, the son of a farmer. He worked at a number of menial jobs to keep himself alive and fought with the Union Army in the Civil War, distinguishing himself in battle and ending the conflict as an officer.

He went into journalism in San Francisco and in 1872 came to London where he worked on the staff of a magazine for four years. He published a number of books of which the most famous and justly celebrated was *In the Midst of Life*, a collection of tales of "soldiers and civilians".

Horrific, cynical and ghostly in turn they have become classics; Bierce drew richly on his grim experiences in the Civil War and a number of the tales have long been favourites of anthologists. Pre-eminent among these stories, which first appeared in 1891, are *A Horseman in the Sky*, *An Occurrence at Owl Creek Bridge*, *One of The Missing*, *A Watcher by the Dead*, *The Boarded Window* and *The Middle Toe of the Right Foot*.

The end of Bierce's life was as cryptic as the man himself. After editing his collected works, including his famous encyclopaedia of aphorisms in 1912, he left America to cover the Mexican Revolution as a war correspondent. He was attached to the army of the revolutionary Pancho Villa and disappeared on one of that leader's expeditions. Nothing was ever learned of his ultimate fate.

Known among his journalistic colleagues as 'Bitter' Bierce, he was the perfect example of the wit and cynic who was decades ahead of his time as a teller of pitiless tales; his astringent personality was perfectly suited to the form and content he chose and in works like *In the Midst of Life* he rose to high art.

And in the field of the macabre, outside this key collection, the short story *The Eyes of the Panther* is one of the most chilling pieces ever penned on the subject of lycanthropy. It must also be one of the strangest and most subtle manifestations of the human-into-beast theme ever penned; in a brief ten or so pages Bierce takes the reader by the scruff of the neck and compels him to believe.

The tale is set in a milieu this writer made very much his own:

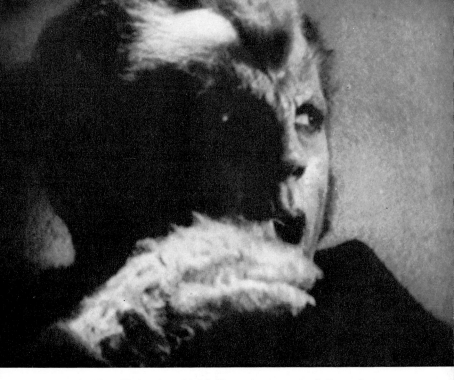

Two remarkable stills by Gerald McKee, photographed direct from the television tube during the screening of Universal's *The Werewolf of London*. *Above*, Henry Hull in his weird werewolf make-up. *Below*, Henry Hull (left, without make-up) and Warner Oland in one of the film's quieter moments

Metamorphosis—Henry Hull works on the antidote in his laboratory as he metamorphoses back into his wolfish shape in *The Werewolf of London*

The astonishing werewolf-like image designed by Jean Cocteau for his famous 1945 production of *La Belle et la Bête*. Beauty, Josette Day, the Beast, Jean Marais

the wild, untamed frontier of America at a time in the late
nineteenth century when the advent of the railway and increasing urbanization was threatening the wild places; a time
when woodsmen and farmers lived in lonely cabins on the edge
of what had recently been primaeval forest, with their women-
folk and children.

Here, at the very rim of civilization, a beautiful young girl,
Irene Marlowe, explains to her would-be-husband, the
attorney Jenner Brading, why she cannot marry him. She is
insane, she tells him; or at least that is what men would think.
"I might myself prefer to call it a case of 'possession'," she says.

She tells Brading a horrifying story of her mother, alone in a
cabin in the wilderness with her small child, while her husband
is out hunting. As twilight falls she sleeps; she awakes to see two
red eyes staring at her in the darkness of the window space. For
an incalculable time the panther stares in; it is supporting itself
by its paws on the window-sill.

As Bierce adds so tellingly, "That signified a malign interest –
not the mere gratification of an indolent curiosity". The
woman's ordeal is described in deft, economical strokes, with
not a word misused or out of place. When the tension is almost
too much for the reader to bear the woman sinks to the floor.

The hunter returns home to find his wife hopelessly insane,
the child in her arms suffocated in her embrace.

Irene Marlowe herself is born three months after that night,
her mother dying during the birth.

"Is it likely," Irene tells Brading, "that a person born under
such circumstances is like others – is what you call sane?"

One is irresistibly reminded in such incidents, told in clipped,
bare prose all the more terrifying for being so restrained, of
Maupassant, who penned a remarkably similar story, though
not with a lycanthropic theme, in *Fear*.

Brading recalls earlier newspaper stories of a panther which
had frightened village people by looking in their windows at
night; he recalls also that Irene's father was a broken man, old
before his time with some secret sorrow. There were strange
stories about Irene too; notably of her great fear of the dark;
of her solitary life with her father and friends' talk of her never
being seen after nightfall. She never, in fact, goes out at night.

This is the situation, sketched in the most casual manner, as
the interview in the forest clearing between Brading and Irene

ends. As the girl disappears into the thick undergrowth the lawyer sees two bright eyes staring at him from the darkness. He runs to warn Irene of the panther but all he sees is her grey skirt disappearing through the doorway of the house; the beast is nowhere to be seen.

Brading himself lives in a small house facing the forest; he sleeps on the ground floor with his window open in summer. One night, soon after his talk with Irene he is awakened by a noise. He seizes his revolver and waits, looking toward the bedroom window. He sees two malignant, gleaming eyes staring at him; there is unbearable tension in the room as Brading sits immobile, the eyes rising as though the beast is about to spring on him.

He fires, follows a blood trail to a clearing. Even then Bierce does not spoil his story by bald description. This master of prose brings a classic tale of lycanthropy to an end, by relating obliquely what Brading found in the clearing.

He says, "What it was is told, even to this day, upon a weather-worn headstone in the village churchyard, and for many years was attested daily at the graveside by the bent figure and sorrow-seamed face of Old Man Marlowe, to whose soul, and to the soul of his strange, unhappy child, peace. Peace and reparation."

To return to the earlier part of the nineteenth century we find one of the finest and most celebrated of werewolf tales, from the solidly dependable pen of Captain Frederick Marryat. At first sight Marryat, the well-known author of *Midshipman Easy* and *Masterman Ready*, might seem a strange source for one of the great tales of horror.

But perhaps there is something about the sea and its immensity which impels writers with this background to essay the weird from time to time. One has only to think of such masters as William Hope Hodgson; Joseph Conrad, who tried his hand at the supernatural on more than one occasion; Stevenson himself, whose contribution to the genre of lycanthropy we shall be sampling later; and W. W. Jacobs, the great humorist and nautical writer who penned one of the most horrifying of macabre tales, *The Monkey's Paw*.

So, it may be inferred, Marryat took time out from his wholesome tales of sea-adventure in the tradition of *Treasure*

Island, and traced a more sombre course. His tale *The White Wolf of the Hartz Mountains*, sometimes called *The Werewolf*, is a particularly fine one, and is extracted from a book of his called *The Phantom Ship*, published in 1839.

Extremely well written, as might be imagined, it could well have come from the pen of Sheridan Le Fanu. The story is, in fact, a self-contained chapter and none the worse for that. It is told by a man called Krantz when he and a companion are sailing in a peroqua through the islands of Malaya.

Interestingly, the narrative concerns Transylvania and a girl called Marcella. The reader will not have forgotten that Transylvania is the land of the vampire, the twin-horror figure of mythology and together with the lycanthrope, the most potent. And, as we have seen in the earlier book,* Marcella is extremely close to Mircalla, an anagram for Carmilla, the classic she-vampire of Sheridan Le Fanu's famous story of the same name, though of course Marryat's tale precedes the other in point of time.

The story, which has much about it of the conte cruel with overtones of Grimm, concerns a rich man's steward who flees from Hungary after murdering his unfaithful wife and the nobleman who was her lover. He takes refuge in a remote cottage in the Hartz Mountains of Germany where he hunts and cultivates the land near the house, providing a scanty living for himself and the three children of his ruined marriage.

There, in the depths of winter, he hears a wolf outside the window and takes up his gun to shoot it; but the animal is cunning and draws him off a long way. Instead of shooting the wolf he instead rescues two lost travellers, a dark man on horse-back, with a beautiful girl mounted behind him. They are father and daughter and the hunter gives them shelter in his home.

The daughter is, Marryat tells us, exceedingly beautiful with glossy and shining hair "bright as a mirror"; she is about twenty and when she smiles shows brilliant teeth. But there is some-thing about her eyes which makes the children uneasy and though she is kind and speaks gently to them, patting their heads, Marcella, the hunter's little daughter, will not come near her.

The stranger, the huntsman finds, is his second cousin,

The Vampire: In Legend, Fact and Art.

Wilfred of Barnsdorf. Not surprisingly, the former is attracted
by the daughter Christina and eventually asks his kinsman for
her hand in marriage. Wilfred tells the enamoured man that
he has to leave the house on "being called elsewhere"; there is
no priest and in that remote spot no facilities for the proposed
marriage.

Naturally, the father will not be satisfied until some proper
form of ceremony has been observed between them so he
marries the couple himself, binding them "by all the spirits of
the Hartz mountains, by all their power for good and for evil",
and bids the huntsman never to lift his hand against her. The
oath concludes with a proviso that causes some unease; that if
the bridegroom fails in his vow the vengeance of the spirits will
fall upon him and his children and they will be torn to pieces
by the beasts of the forest.

Little Marcella cannot restrain herself at this and bursts into
tears as her father concludes the ceremony. But the marriage,
though satisfactory from the point of view of husband and wife,
is far from happy for the children, for the new step-mother is
harsh and unkind to them, particularly to little Marcella.

The story swiftly moves to its sombre climax; the children
are terrified at their strange step-mother's nocturnal wanderings, particularly as the great white wolf hunted by their father
has returned to haunt their part of the forest.

They hear its growling under their window and on several
occasions Christina gets up in the middle of the night and goes
out into the snow and bitter cold clad only in her flimsy night-
dress. When she returns on one occasion the young boy
Caesar is terrified to see her hands and face are covered with
blood.

Marryat's story has a unique flavour all its own, and reads
today, with its undated prose and almost laconic narrative
method, as though it had been newly penned. Which probably
accounts for its perennial popularity.

Incidentally, there is a strange error in some of the copies of
this story printed in various anthologies, Christina being
referred to as the children's mother-in-law when, of course, she
is actually their step-mother. Marryat's narrative is in the
classic mould and forms the model for so much werewolf
literature that is to follow.

It is not until two of the children have been eaten by the wolf that the surviving child Krantz, the narrator of the story, has his revenge. He sees Christina in her night clothes lifting off the stones from his little sister's grave. He calls his father who finds his wife tearing ferociously at the remains of the child. He fires and kills her and is stupefied to see a huge white wolf lying where his wife had been crouching.

The father Wilfred returns and tells the huntsman that he had been married to a werewolf; in a mad rage the latter seizes his axe but the blow passes harmlessly through Wilfred's form and he realizes he has been dealing with the spirits of the Hartz Mountains.

Wilfred reminds him of his vow and says that the lives of his children are forfeit; they all will be devoured by wild beasts. Father and surviving son flee to Holland where the father soon dies of brain fever. The narrator Krantz tells his friend sorrowfully that his life is forfeit. Back in the present the pair press on in their vessel, and arrive off Sumatra. Later they put ashore to swim and obtain fresh water.

It is here, in this apparently smiling spot of forest, sunshine and natural beauty that Wilfred's curse is fulfilled; a tiger bounding from the jungle seizes the unfortunate Krantz and drags him screaming back into the forest to devour him. The sorrowing Philip reflects, "His bones will bleach in the wilderness and the spirit-hunter and his wolfish daughter are avenged". There is genuine shock in the finale and Marryat's laconic method of telling his sombre story is admirably suited to the form and adds up to one of the great lycanthropic tales.

Ironically, though his two most famous novels *Masterman Ready* and *Midshipman Easy* are, I suspect, little read today, unless by schoolchildren, *The White Wolf of the Hartz Mountains* has never been out of print for the last half century or so, surfacing in anthology after anthology. Marryat wrote little else in this field, which is a pity as on this showing alone he is a master of the form.

TWENTY

TWO MASTERS

From a literary point of view the most important story of lycanthropy in the group of nineteenth-century tales we are examining is undoubtedly *Olalla* by Robert Louis Stevenson. But because of its great length – some fifty pages of small type – it cannot be analysed in much detail here.

It is one of the finest of Stevenson's essays in the macabre of which the best known is, of course, the novel *Dr Jekyll and Mr Hyde* and a sort of companion piece to *Olalla*, *Markheim*. Stevenson's fastidious prose both illuminates and terrifies in a story which combines restraint and tension in equal proportions.

Olalla appeared in 1887, only a year after the publication of Stevenson's classic novel, and it was a period in which he was obviously finding himself entirely at home in the realm of the macabre. The story deals with the taint of lycanthropy in the blood, carried on to a new generation and, as might be imagined of anything from the pen of this gifted novelist, is thus unusual in the field.

The story is set in Spain and tells of an officer, "wounded in the good cause", who takes refuge in the mountains, on the recommendation of his doctor, at the *hacienda* of a once grand family, now come down in the world.

There is a strange condition attached to the convalescence; as the doctor remarks, the "beggars of high descent" had now found the rich too high for them and the poor too low. When poverty forced them to unfasten their door to a guest they could not do so without a most ungracious stipulation. Their guest would remain a stranger; they would give him attendance but they refused the idea of the smallest intimacy.

The Englishman is piqued at this but once in residence he becomes absorbed in the study of the strange and enigmatic family he has ventured among; the son Felipe, a superstitious youth with an undeveloped mind; the mother, a voluptuous and beautiful woman, akin to the ancient portrait of an ancestor in the visitor's room; with a great mass of copper-coloured hair and continually good-tempered and smiling, though he notes in her the degeneration of the blood of this ancient house.

And the third member of the family, Olalla the daughter; a girl in whom there is none of the degenerate strain of the mother; a girl at once intelligent and beautiful but in whom there is a secret sadness of the soul.

The drama is played out in wild and savage mountain scenery surrounding the *residencia*; a great house of a Moorish character where the guest's bare apartment is approached by a stone staircase. It is within these walls that he is to spend some of the most extraordinary moments of his life.

A black wind blows for ten days and the nerves of all in the *residencia* become taut and jangled; Olalla herself is not introduced until quite late in the story, though Stevenson often hints at her presence; the young officer finds many volumes in Latin belonging to her and reads her poetry.

Olalla and the young officer, when they do meet, find themselves drifting into a love-affair until one night he is awakened by appalling and savage cries in the house. He finds he is locked in his room and spends a wretched night listening to the brutish howls and incoherent moaning, filled with sickness and horror.

He questions both Olalla and Felipe about the matter but is met with evasive and unconvincing explanations; likewise the priest who occasionally visits the house is unhelpful. The climax of the story comes when the officer receives a note from the girl in which she begs him to leave "for the sake of Him who died".

The effect of this is disastrous; the young man is already an invalid, convalescent from a wound; he commences to shake and, as if in a dream, attempts to open the window and instead, thrusts his hand through the glass. Blood spurts from his wrist and he rushes downstairs for help.

In the great climactic scene of the novella and one in which the lycanthropic nature of the house's enigma is revealed, the mother is seen to be the secret source of the horror which envelops the place. The corrupting taint of bad blood, as evinced in the cruel portrait of the ancestress hanging in the narrator's room, comes to the surface and the ravening hunger of the sleeping beast is seen through the full force of Stevenson's pen and hits the reader with a shock almost as great as that suffered by the unfortunate young officer.

Stevenson continues, " 'I have cut myself', I said, 'and rather badly. See!' And I held out my two hands from which the blood was oozing and dripping.

"Her great eyes opened wide, the pupils shrank into points; a veil seemed to fall from her face, and leave it sharply expressive and yet inscrutable. And as I still stood marvelling a little at her disturbance, she came swiftly up to me, and stooped and caught me by the hand; and the next moment my hand was at her mouth, and she had bitten me to the bone.

"The pang of the bite, and sudden spirting of blood and the monstrous horror of the act, flashed through me all in one, and I beat her back; and she sprang at me again and again, with bestial cries, cries that I recognized, such cries as had awakened me on the night of the high wind.

"Her strength was like that of madness; mine was rapidly ebbing with the loss of blood; my mind besides was whirling with the abhorrent strangeness of the onslaught, and I was already forced against the wall, when Olalla ran betwixt us, and Felipe, following at a bound, pinned down his mother on the floor."

The horrific shock of this great scene, both *dénouement* and enigma in one, is nowhere else matched in the story, the remainder of which can be briefly encapsulated. Though still in love with the girl the young officer hesitates to link his destiny with one whose blood is so corrupted. He shrinks from the family connection and Olalla herself, in a tender scene in which she binds his wound, speaks of the evil endemic in the portrait and her own tainted sources.

Like so many of Poe's heroines she comes of a doomed race; she tells her lover, "And shall I – that dwell apart in the house of the dead, my body, loathing its ways – shall I repeat the spell? Shall I bind another spirit, reluctant as my own, into this bewitched and tempest-broken tenement that I now suffer in? Shall I hand down this cursed vessel of humanity, charge it with fresh life as with fresh poison, and dash it, like a fire, in the faces of posterity?"

Sadly, she tells the officer her race shall cease from off the earth and that he must leave. In a muted ending, the lover goes instead to another village from whose peak he can see the *residencia* far below. It is here he has a confrontation with a countryman whose friend has perished within the walls of the *hacienda*. The man says that in the old days the church would have burned such a nest of basilisks.

But his friend would not go unpunished; one day soon the smoke of that house would rise to heaven. It is on this plateau too that the officer has a final poignant meeting with Olalla; she says the country people are murmuring about their liaison. His continued presence would bring danger to himself as well as those at the *residencia*. Sorrowfully, the officer takes his leave; turning back once he sees Olalla leaning against the massive crucifix whose tortured Christ stonily contemplates the plain below.

Stevenson, with the exception of *Jekyll and Hyde*, wrote nothing better in the genre than *Olalla*: in the complexities of the story, with its lycanthropic theme and brooding horror of corrupted blood passed on from generation to generation, may be glimpsed something of his own tortured life.

For Stevenson's own blood was tainted, his own life tortured and distorted not only by his own illnesses but by those of his wife, who was mentally ill for some years and which increased Stevenson's worries during the final period of his own short existence.

He told his stepson Lloyd Osbourne that he had a "tortured soul" and longed for death; his youth was dissipated and may have helped to undermine his health, never robust. As a young man he was a hashish-smoker and a womanizer, frequenting the brothels of Edinburgh, where he had been born in 1850.

He first studied law but gave this up; he was only thirty when he began to have the massive lung haemorrhages that overshadowed his life and which were thought to be of tubercular origin.

On the island of Valaima in Samoa where he went in a vain attempt to cure his maladies, his last years were clouded by his own and his wife Fanny's poor health. He was tragically young, only forty-four, when he died of an apoplectic stroke in 1894, and much great work would undoubtedly have emanated from his pen had he been spared into old age.

It was his tragedy – and the world's – that further macabre masterpieces in the same genre as *Olalla* have been forever lost.

Although slightly out of period, it would be appropriate at this point to deal with the work of Algernon Blackwood, one of the great masters of macabre literature. Though Blackwood did not publish any work until slightly after the turn of the present century, he was born as far back as 1869 and though his enormously long life extended into the world of broadcasting after the Second World War, he was in the Victorian mould and his leisurely, polished prose reflected this earlier age.

Blackwood's tale *The Camp of the Dog*, together with another companion story, *Running Wolf*, is one of a number of his pieces which are concerned with the theme of man into beast. This was, in fact, one of Blackwood's obsessions and a fortunate one for millions of readers over the past seventy years, as they inspired some of his finest work.

Wolves, leopards and cats were among the were-type animals which featured in many of his most chilling stories and both *The Camp of the Dog* and *Running Wolf* must be awarded a high place among them. The evocatively titled *Camp of the Dog* is set on an island, as in a number of this writer's tales, this time in Sweden, where the narrator, a friend of Blackwood's famous character Dr John Silence is taking a camping holiday.

The story is one of Blackwood's best and reflects his preoccupation with the outdoors and the wild places of the earth, where he had, in fact, passed much of his adventurous life. He probably gained a taste for the woodlands and great spaces of his stories from his early years as a student at the Moravian School in Germany's Black Forest.

After completing his education at Wellington College and Edinburgh University, he spent the years of his youth in adventuring in remote places, trying his hand at gold-mining, prospecting, farming in Canada; running a hotel and he even spent a period in North America as a down-and-out. Some of these experiences were related in his book *Adventures Before Forty*.

Later he became a journalist, working on the staff of the *New York Sun* and on the *New York Times*. He was already thirty-seven when he published his first collection of macabre tales in 1906. *The Empty House* was a success and from then on he devoted himself entirely to literature, writing literally hundreds of first-rate ghost stories as well as novels and volumes of travel and reminiscence.

In the course of his extremely long life – he was approaching ninety when he died – he continued to travel and between the wars, and also after the Second World War, he enchanted millions of people by relating his own stories, in simple, unaffected style through the medium of BBC Radio.

Unlike most tales of its type *The Camp of the Dog* takes place in blinding hot weather in July, "the air clear as crystal, the sea a cobalt blue". Blackwood's originality is also indicated in this early tale by his narrator commenting, on their arrival in this idyllic spot, the island in Sweden: "We realized for the first time that the horror of trains and houses was far behind us, the fever of men and cities, the weariness of streets and confined spaces."

For once Dr John Silence is not with his friend – they are to meet in Berlin – but the doctor says prophetically when the train leaves Victoria that they will meet as arranged, unless he should send for Silence sooner. Something does happen, and Silence is sent for. The tale is really a novella of some sixty pages of closely packed type and Blackwood, as befits a master of the craft, proceeds in leisurely fashion, sketching in the characters of the people camping together in the wilderness. Town-bred people, a vicar and his family, in fact, who take on quite different aspects when the veneer of civilization is left far behind.

A member of the party, a Canadian called Sangree is attracted to the ecclesiastic's daughter, Joan, but despite his outward niceness she senses something repellent about him; something that the narrator himself is unconscious of. They discuss the problem one evening in camp when the girl confides in him; but later that night he catches Sangree staring at Joan and it seems to him as if a shadow runs across and transforms his face.

The incident is all the more curious because the cleric, who has just offered up his usual evening prayers, adds a surprising rider on this occasion; to the effect that no evil thing should come to disturb them in the night-time.

In pleasing prose Blackwood delineates the lazy, contented routine of the camp in the days that follow but this idyll is disturbed, first by small, indefinable things as experienced by Hubbard, the narrator; and then by Joan herself who tells the others that one night she heard the howling of a dog. It had come scratching round her tent and there, sure enough, are the marks on the ground made by its paws.

The brute has also been pawing round Sangree's tent as well; in this apparently innocuous fashion does terror obtrude into this commonplace, sunlit setting. The situation becomes more explicit when the camp is awakened by screams in the night; Joan's tent is found to be torn by the marauding beast and a full-scale search is made.

Later, the beast bounds over the sleeping form of Sangree himself. When Silence, summoned by Hubbard, arrives he listens to the recital of events and says, in his matter of fact way, that they have to deal with a werewolf. Just as Holmes and Watson cope with events of the everyday world, so does Silence pit himself against the bizarre and the occult, things that threaten that everyday world from somewhere outside.

So far the story might seem a typical product of many such on lycanthropic themes from the pens of less gifted authors. Sangree is the source of the emanation of evil, of course. Both Silence and the reader are aware of this.

But Blackwood's compelling gift, like that of a far more talented writer, Somerset Maugham, is readability; and there is a freshness and unforced naturalism about his writing which compels belief in his themes.

We have already spoken of the sparkling atmosphere of the lakes and the glittering quality of the scenery. Silence soon pinpoints this in Blackwood's deft phrases. He speaks of a wonderful region, but with something lacking. Hubbard says it has a superficial, glittering prettiness.

"John Silence nodded his head with approval.

" 'Exactly,' he said. 'The picturesqueness of stage scenery that is not real, not alive. It's like a landscape by a clever painter, yet without true imagination. Soulless – that's the word you wanted.' "

Ingeniously, by logical steps, Silence deduces that Sangree is a victim of atavistic forces; he has been cast back into his ancestral past – he is of Red Indian descent – in his passion and devotion to the girl, Joan. His physical desire to reach the heart of the loved object was "nothing more than the aspiration for union", as Silence says.

In a long and atmospheric finale, Dr Silence solves the

problem but unlike most such tales there is a happy ending which, if running against the grain of lycanthropic literature, does at least satisfy the reader. Sangree and Joan, irresistibly drawn together, are deeply in love. The figure of the dog, materializing in the camp one night, is seen to bear the visage of Sangree. The girl answers his wild cries from across the lake.

Sangree's own body, lying on its bunk, is curiously deflated as its beast-double roams the night. Another occupant of the camp, Maloney, shoots Sangree in his metamorphosis, but he is only wounded. He recovers and he and Joan look forward to a new life together in one of the most unusual stories of its kind in all such literature.

The cure, says Silence, is not to quell such savage force but to direct it to better outlets. A more traditional solution to the problem was arrived at by another and very different writer to Blackwood.

TWENTY-ONE

THE WHITE WOLF

He was Sir Gilbert Campbell, a little-known nineteenth-century writer, who specialized in short stories on macabre themes, but one in the mainstream of Victorian tradition. Biographical details are sparse but certainly he is the author of one of the best lycanthropic tales in the Marryat mould.

His *The White Wolf of Kostopchin* first appeared in a collection of macabre stories, *Wild and Weird*, which was published in London in 1889. It seems to have attracted little attention at the time but is a solidly constructed work of late Victorian craftsmanship and well worth wider notice. Students of the macabre should be grateful to Mr Brian Frost who rescued it from obscurity and published it in an excellent paperback collection of fictional werewolf tales, *The Book of the Werewolf*, in 1973.

The story takes place in Lithuania and is in the tradition which made the vampire theme a perennial favourite among nineteenth-century writers. It can be briefly summarized here but is worth more than a passing comment.

The chief character, a dissolute nobleman banished to his estate in Poland at the *diktat* of the Emperor, lives in idleness amid the ruins of his once considerable empire, surrounded only by a few serfs and accompanied by his two small children Alexis and Katrina. Paul Sergevitch is the archetype of all Chekov characters, in fact, and the writing, while not distinguished, rises to far higher levels than the majority of such tales of the period.

In fact there is a fine chill of fear to the story his steward Michal tells him; of his encounter with a pack of half-famished wolves at the edge of a swamp the previous night; led by a white she-wolf which followed him all the way to his home. He says, in terms which strike the right chord of terror, "As I am a living man, that white devil followed me the whole distance, keeping fifty paces in the rear, and every now and then licking her lips with a sound that made my flesh creep".

It will be noted that this fictional narrative bears a remarkable resemblance to the adventure of the two magistrates of the Gironde detailed in Chapter Five. It would be interesting to know if Sir Gilbert had ever read the account and whether he drew on it for his striking story. Certainly it enhances a remarkably fine tale and one of the best in the genre.

In one of the most original scenes in all the literature of the werewolf a great *battue* is formed and the serfs, the Prince at their head, beat the woodlands. Suddenly there is uproar and one of the beaters, a young lad, is found bleeding from severe wounds; he tells them the wolf ran into a nearby thicket. The Prince and his men are about to set fire to the woodland when a sweet voice is heard and a beautiful young woman emerges.

Sir Gilbert's description of her gives an idea of the excellence of his style: "As the bushes divided, a fair woman, wrapped in a mantle of soft white fur, with a fantastically shaped travelling cap of green velvet upon her head, stood before them. She was exquisitely fair, and her long Titian red hair hung in dishevelled masses over her shoulders".

She says the wolf passed close by her but despite further searches the beaters are unable to flush the animal out; the girl, whose name is Ravina, is a political refugee and is immediately given refuge by Sergevitch, who is much taken with her beauty.

Although it is, of course, obvious from the development of the story what the plot will be, Sir Gilbert lavishes much fascinating detail on the tale which makes it one of the best of its kind; the servant Michal's terror at the woman and her gleaming teeth; the small son's unease; Katrina's trust and the discovery that the beautiful stranger has gold-mounted wolves' claws as a necklet.

It is interesting, in passing, to note that whereas the vampire of fiction is usually a handsome male preying on beautiful female victims, the werewolf is very often a beautiful woman who preys on males or small children. The sexual connotations in such stories are one of their most potent strands, though they should not be over-estimated; as is the current fashion in almost everything in art or fiction which can be twisted to reveal sexual undertones or aberrations.

Sir Gilbert's telling detail as Ravina settles in to the Prince's household is woven together to make an absorbing study which really cries out for translation to the cinema; if it were done properly it could well be the best filmic treatment of a lycanthropic theme so far.

The strange attraction of Paul's little daughter to the beautiful woman is emphasized by the Prince himself, who observes, with unconscious irony, "You have quite obtained possession of her heart".

"Not yet," the woman replies, with a strange, cold smile and the visual image of the tragic victims of the white wolf, whose hearts had been physically torn from their breasts, immediately flickers into the mind.

Sir Gilbert's originality is attested by the sombre conclusion of his tale which rivals Bram Stoker's *Dracula* in its Grand Guignol effects. Enamoured of this strange woman the Prince begs her to marry him; she agrees to remain in the house, in her own suite of apartments, for a probationary period, visiting Paul for two hours every evening.

But the servant Michal breaks the idyll by declaring that he has seen the white wolf slipping into the girl's apartment; lusty axe-blows from the serfs break down the door but Ravina appears in a frenzy of anger and orders them out. There is no wolf there, she declares, and orders Paul to forbid the old man the house.

Despite this order the faithful old man keeps watch on the mansion and surprises the wolf-woman attempting to make an incision in the breast of the unconscious Katrina with a sharp knife. In a van Helsing-like confrontation Michal bursts in and saves the child's life. Keeping the wolf-woman at bay with his crucifix he tells the sorceress he is removing the child from danger. He abandons the Prince to his fate and tells Ravina that if she breathes a word of what has happened he will return with the villagers and burn the house to the ground.

In a finale as original as anything in this field of literature the Lord of Kostopchin meets his predestined end; the beautiful Ravina says she will give him the answer to his proposal of marriage if he will meet her at a remote yew-tree on the estate that night. But the father is followed by the child Alexis, who has always hated Ravina.

Agreeing to Paul's proposal of marriage at the trysting place,

A take in progress for Hammer Films' *The Curse of the Werewolf*. Star Oliver Reed as the anguished Leon in what is probably the cinema's best essay in lycanthropy to date. Cameraman Len Harris is on the right

The remarkable make-up created for Oliver Reed in Hammer Films'
The Curse of the Werewolf. The film was restrained, however, in that
Reed appeared only in brief flashes in long shot in this elaborate
guise

Ravina ironically asks for his heart. When he agrees she springs on him and tearing that organ from his breast commences to devour it.

The boy Alexis then shoots Ravina dead with his father's pistol; later, the peasants find the white wolf dead with a half-devoured human heart between its paws. Old Michal comes out of hiding and brother and sister are reunited, bringing one of the most effective and absorbing tales of its kind to an end.

Nothing else in this nineteenth-century group of stories we are considering quite comes up to *The White Wolf of Kostopchin*. Many of the other tales which appeared in journals, magazines and anthologies of the time had flashes of inspiration but the general level was not high and invention, together with narrative skill, was sadly lacking in most of them.

A master, Rudyard Kipling, had briefly glanced at the theme in his *The Mark of the Beast* (1891), published in *Life's Handicap*, but the tale, which concerned the transmigration of souls, was not really germane to the mainstream of lycanthropic literature and is mentioned merely in passing. It was an effectively gruesome story, however, and concerned an Englishman in India who was cursed by a leper priest, as a result of which a beast's soul took possession of his body.

More typical of the generally low level were such stories as those by the Hon. Mrs Greene, *Bound by a Spell* (1885); H. Beaugrand's *The Werewolves* (1898); and Mrs Crowe's piece, one of the earliest in the field, *The Story of a Weir-Wolf* (1846), in which the theme was muddled with witchcraft.

Disappointing too were other essays in the form, such as Eden Philpotts' *Loup-Garou!* published in 1899. Philpotts was more at home with his bucolic comedies such as *The Farmer's Wife* and though the miracle had been achieved by W. W. Jacobs, a humorous writer who created a masterpiece of terror in *The Monkey's Paw*, Philpotts lacked the magic touch and his attempt at lycanthropic horror, incongruously set in the West Indies, was a failure.

As already mentioned, a fine tale in the true canon, in which the theme was treated obliquely, was Algernon Blackwood's *Running Wolf*, a companion piece to *The Camp of the Dog*; and Blackwood also published a number of other excellent stories germane to the theme.

Before the nineteenth century was quite out there came a final flare of the candle, before the genre faded, only really to be revived in the full sense of the term, in the period following the Second World War. In the earlier part of the nineteenth century, it is true, there had been some first-rate individual tales in which the wolf-theme has been evoked, though perhaps it would be exaggerating to call most of them true werewolf stories, as has sometimes been claimed.

Among the best may be mentioned the Rev. Sabine Baring-Gould's collection of 1865, *The Book of Werewolves*; and the French writing team of Erkmann-Chatrian produced *The Man-Wolf* (*Hugues-Le-Loup*) a few years later in 1869.

The Rev. Baring-Gould was the perfect example of the English cleric-eccentric, and in the mainstream of those clerics of our own day who both cherish and write detective-fiction. Extremely well known in the Victorian age, though almost forgotten today, Baring-Gould was a collector as well as a writer of macabre tales.

Much more interesting, however, was *The Man-Wolf*, which had an impressive Gothic castle setting and considerable skill was displayed by the writing team in evoking the atmosphere of the curse of lycanthropy, which had been transmitted from one generation to another. Wisely, Erkmann-Chatrian wrote no more werewolf tales. Once is enough in the domain of the macabre; would that other writers in the field had shown similar restraint, for the market was to become flooded with cheap imitations with the dawn of the new century.

In the peripheral group of authors who glanced at the theme should perhaps be mentioned Guy de Maupassant with his *The White Wolf* and, as noted, even the Gothic novelist, William Beckford, had made some use of the theme in his *Vathek*, written as early as 1777. Guy de Maupassant (1850–1893), one of the world's greatest masters of the short story, who was to die tragically young of syphilis, also wrote one of the finest tales with a vampiric background, *The Horla*.*

The late nineteenth-century flowering of short-story writers inspired by lycanthropy as a literary device, also produced Count Eric Stenbock's *The Other Side*.

Stenbock was a Russian nobleman, resident in England, who led a disordered life like Maupassant, and died young, ruining

*His life is briefly sketched in "*The Vampire*": *In Legend, Fact and Art*.

his health with drink and drugs. The handful of short stories of horror and the macabre he left behind, all showed a mastery of the form, no doubt coloured by his own existence on the edge of madness.

The Other Side (1894) was reputed to have been based on a lycanthropic legend current in France in the Middle Ages, and featured a stream, on the far bank of which dwelt wolves and werewolves, which pursue the hero of the tale as in a nightmare.

Almost contemporaneous with this was an interesting novella written by that rare being, a female macabre writer. The Gothic novel of some eighty years earlier, of course, had been strong on female writers like Mary Shelley and Mrs Radclyffe, and was to be so again in the twentieth century.

But at the period of which we are speaking, the last decade of the nineteenth century, macabre writers like Clemence Houseman were a fairly scarce breed. Her novelette *The Werewolf*, which appeared in 1895, has a number of points of interest. The story is told in a sort of stylized, medieval-type prose, rather reminscent of that latter-day fantasist of gifted imagination, the prolific Robert E. Howard, who died in his thirties. It is a mannered, convoluted style which would pall over the length of a novel but is perfectly suited to its purpose here.

It begins in a manner strangely reminiscent of *The White Wolf of Kostopchin* and as it appeared only six years after the tale by Sir Gilbert one cannot help wondering if the earlier piece had not provided the inspiration. It is none the worse for that, of course, and in its manner and style is highly original.

Set in the Middle Ages the opening of the tale sketches in an evening at a great farm hall with its occupants busy spinning, weaving and talking by the fire; in what had perhaps become a cliché even by the time Clemence Houseman came to write the story, a child's cry is three times heard at the door; on each occasion, when the door is opened, there is nothing there and no tracks in the snow.

Later, a beautiful young woman is found at the door and given shelter for the night. But one of the brothers of the house, Christian, a mighty hunter, hastening homeward comes upon the tracks of a wolf and traces it as far as the farm porch.

Unlike most characters in this type of story he enters the hall and on seeing the girl immediately suspects that she is a werewolf; the interest and surprise in the story lie in the manner in which the author solves the technical problems she has set herself.

Only the great dog Tyr, banished to the hearth; and Christian, twin-brother of Sweyn, the handsome athlete whom he hero-worships, know the truth about the girl who is sharing their roof. The tension in the story arises from the fact that the loved brother is enamoured of the beautiful stranger and, sceptical of the younger brother's allegations, swears him to silence.

But after the disappearance of the child Rol – presumably eaten by a wolf and never seen again – Christian determines on revenge. In finely described passages, he runs to a distant church to fetch holy water from the font; but his brother guesses his intent to do ill to the girl, White Fell, and they fight. The flask of holy water shatters against the door as the girl rushes out of the farm on hearing a hunting horn.

The finale, which features the three-hour pursuit across the frozen wastes of the wolf-woman by Christian, ending in the death of them both and the metamorphosis of White Fell back into her wolf shape, has an epic quality and recalls the Norse legends or, perhaps even more vividly, the pursuit of the monster into the wastes of the Antarctic in Mary Shelley's *Frankenstein* in its starkness and simplicity.

Here the writing matches the theme exactly and we are given, in this strange and unique story by a little-known woman writer, a minor classic in the genre.

With the advent of the twentieth century the floodgates were to be opened and many strange versions of the man-monster, ranging in style from the classic pattern to the edge of science-fiction, were to emerge.

TWENTY-TWO

SAKI AND OTHERS

Humour, one would have thought, would not have found much of a toe-hold in the sombre world of the lycanthrope. Yet such a modern master as the late James Thurber saluted the potency of the myth in a classic cartoon in which a hostess, one of Thurber's quintessential unattractive females is introducing a gigantic smiling figure to a small, bald and rather confused man.

Says the hostess, "I want you to know Mr Thrawn, Mr Simms. Mr Thrawn claims to be a werewolf!"

But there is an uneasy echo in the laugh evoked by this superb piece of nonsense and the werewolf figure of Thurber's cartoon has a disturbing quality beneath the surface of the joke.

This is the power the myth releases in the short-story writer who is a master of his craft and which has been canalized into tales of terrifying potency in the best of them. It is perhaps appropriate to begin in the twentieth-century short-story field with work which was contemporaneous with those authors of longer stories I have already examined.

Blackwood's contribution has already been dealt with; he was one of the first on the scene as the twentieth century dawned and was working at the peak of his imaginative power in the short-story form. But others were emerging who were to make even more subtle and elliptical offerings to the genre.

Indeed, this is one of the difficulties for the chronicler of such tales; there was such a wealth of material as the century advanced, much of it of very high level, that selection was a major problem if the book was not to degenerate into a mere catalogue.

A link between the older school and the newer to emerge between the two World Wars, was a typically effective tale from the pen of the gifted and cynical Herbert Hector Munro, who became famous under his pen-name of "Saki".

Munro, born in 1870 and already over age when the First World War broke out, volunteered for the trenches where he acquitted himself gallantly. Like his doomed contemporary the macabre and ghost-story writer William Hope Hodgson, who also volunteered for the front, he was killed in action (in 1916), at the age of forty-six.

In *Gabriel-Ernest* he created one of the most vivid and unnerving lycanthrope-type tales which, as with most of his short stories, has never been out of print since publication early this century. Like its companion piece *Sredni Vashtar*, the story of the giant polecat-ferret which tore out the throat of the youthful hero's hated relative, *Gabriel-Ernest* has alarming undertones, which make this author's creations still malevolently alive after more than seventy years.

Economy and surprise are Saki's strongest suits and his gifts are nowhere more evident in this direction than in *Gabriel-Ernest*, which is a mere seven pages long. Yet within this compression there is often more pure terror evoked than in many a fifty-page novella.

But Saki gently guys the werewolf myth in this sardonic trifle. The irony for which this writer is noted is fully flavoured in the enigmatic conversation the landowner Van Cheele carries on with the strange, naked boy he finds sprawling by the pool in his woods.

Says the proprietor, "I can't have you staying here in these woods."

"I fancy you'd rather have me here than in your house," says the boy.

The acid humour of the situation is a Saki speciality which gives his best tales their bite and flavour. Out of a few bald incidents he constructs a werewolf tale which is at once a comedy, a horror story and a criticism of the genre. He is not interested in atmosphere or the mechanics of the legend. His strange boy is next seen in Van Cheele's drawing-room but though the canary and the pet dog know better and cry their alarm in their respective ways, the boy's aunt mothers the child.

She adopts and clothes the foundling, christening him Gabriel-Ernest and giving him an orphan boy to take care of. Giving him an orphan boy for his tea in effect, for there are screams on the hill and clothing found on the banks of the mill-stream. Neither Gabriel-Ernest nor the child are ever seen again.

But the aunt assumes that the child has fallen in and that Gabriel-Ernest has gallantly given his own life in attempting to save him from drowning. She even gets up a fund for a memorial brass to the boy's gallantry in the parish church.

The tale closes with a typical Saki paragraph; Van Cheele gave way to his aunt in most things but he flatly refused to subscribe to the Gabriel-Ernest memorial.

Saki was undoubtedly drawn to the man/beast theme because he uses it on other occasions, notably in *Laura*, in which the dead Amanda first materializes as an otter and then as a "naked brown Nubian boy".

A far different writer though just as effective was the late Peter Fleming whose sole but most effective contribution to the genre was an equally celebrated story, *The Kill*.

Fleming, novelist and explorer, was the brother of the more famous but less distinguished Ian Fleming, whose meretricious James Bond books had astonishing success.

Peter Fleming was an altogether more finished artist and his fastidious prose makes of *The Kill* a minor but memorable essay in the macabre. The story, essentially an atmosphere piece, concentrates on the enigmatic conversation between two strangers stranded in the lonely waiting room at a West of England railway station on a cold winter's night.

The writing is thick and dense and Fleming's carefully used adjectives powerfully reinforce the poetic atmosphere of his story. The stove gives out a "hot, thick smell"; there is a "pale leprous flush" of a light shining through the window; and the key figure in the story has a "black halo of nonchalance" about him.

The younger man resents being stranded in this God-forsaken place and is thus not averse when his companion offers him a ready ear. His interest quickens when the stranger says he came there to hunt. The young man introduces himself as a nephew of Lord Fleer, who keeps a well-known pack of hounds nearby.

His uncle had told him a strange story; many years before he had had a child by his Welsh housekeeper. Dying, she had cursed him by saying that the child would take revenge on anybody else he made heir to Fleer over his natural son.

Lord Fleer noticed the child had the third finger on each hand longer than the second; the superstitious country people said it was the sign of a werewolf. Lord Fleer disregarded his mistress' advice; the boy was taken in by a keeper on the estate and ran away at the age of ten. He made a Belgian woman refugee, Germaine, his heir.

Recently sheep on the estate had been killed by having their throats torn out; Lord Fleer is worried. He is certain that it is his son killing the sheep. They had found a man's footprints in the meadow.

"His business is not with sheep," he tells his nephew, who is glad he is not the heir. But the Belgian, Germaine Vom, has been found the previous day with her throat torn out like the sheep. The young man tells his companion that by the death of the Belgian he is heir to Fleer.

The stranger in the waiting room rises with a strange smile; he removes his bowler hat. The nephew notices that his third finger is longer than the second.

There is something strangely satisfying in such a story where all the pieces come together sweetly for the finale; the narrative too is told in elegant prose and underplayed throughout; deadpan almost, so that the shock of the finale is all the greater. One of the best of werewolf stories, Fleming's modern cautionary tale has been heavily anthologized.

These are among the highlights of modern werewolf fiction in the short-story field and though they are not chosen at random they are by no means alone in their quality; the standard of craftsmanship is high in general as one advances into the twentieth century and the subject is one which has absorbed many able and diverse minds in the field of literature.

It is difficult to select among such a wealth of material and perhaps it might be better if trends were indicated and individual examples selected here and there to give the flavour of a particular piece.

Impetus was given to the macabre story in general and the werewolf legend in particular by such American pulp magazines as *Weird Tales* which flourished in the '20s and '30s of this century. Perhaps its high tide was from 1925 to 1935 and certainly some of the most celebrated tales of terror, including those by Lovecraft, August Derleth, Robert Bloch and others equally celebrated, first saw print between its covers.

Of course, a great many short stories of the old *Weird Tales* genre in the '20s are too numerous and too slight to be dealt with here. But variants of an evergreen theme worth mentioning are Mary Elizabeth Counselman's *The Cat Woman* (1933), a literary equivalent of Val Lewton's cinematic studies *The Cat People* and *The Curse of the Cat People*, in which the human-into-beast theme was evoked compellingly; Howard Wandrei's wolf-girl story *The Hand of the O'Mecca* (1935) and Robert Bloch's *The Black Kiss* (1937), written in collaboration with Henry Kuttner.

In the true *Weird Tales* tradition were Seabury Quinn's *The Phantom Farmhouse*, filmed by Universal Pictures for their Night Gallery TV series in the early '70s; and *The Wolf of St Bonnot*, which appeared in 1930. The two Quinn pieces, the latter featuring Quinn's famous detective Jules de Grandin, were ably partnered by August Derleth's *The Werewolf of Tottenham*, one of his celebrated Solar Pons adventures. Pons was a pastiche of Sherlock Holmes which Derleth, a prolific American author with nearly two hundred books to his credit, first invented in the '20s as a homage to Conan Doyle, with whom he has been in correspondence.

Derleth, who published and encouraged me in my own career as a macabre writer, once told me that Pons would have been better known but for the fact that Sir Arthur's son, Adrian, prevented August from having the books published in England. Though they have long been available in England in the original American editions they are only now to be published in the United Kingdom, some fifty years after Pons and his Watson, Dr Lyndon Parker, first began their Pontine adventures.

The Werewolf of Tottenham, which was later collected between hard covers in the eight or so volumes of the *Pontine Canon*, is an evocative tale; it concerns not the area of London as might have been thought, but a remote village in Yorkshire where a number of people have been murdered, their throats torn out. The atmosphere, as befits one of Pons' best adventures, has all the trappings of the werewolf legend but, as might be imagined, Pons finds a human agency behind the series of diabolical murders.

A Renaissance man who gave ever-generous help to the struggling writer, August Derleth was poet, essayist, publisher, regional novelist, detective story writer, editor, film and TV script writer, book reviewer, champion of Lovecraft whom he literally brought to literary respectability; a prolific anthologist of ghost story collections; one of the world's foremost collectors of comic strips; creator of another interesting detective, Judge Peck; biographer; and author of nature studies. As a journalist he contributed literally thousands of pieces to journals, newspapers and magazines all over the world.

He died in 1971 of heart complications, at the premature age of sixty-two, literally worn out after a lifetime of service to literature. Though he considered his Solar Pons stories as little more than pastiches and could turn them out with astonishing facility, they may, like Conan Doyle before him, do much to make his memory green in after years and the *Canon* deserves a secure place alongside the works of the Master.

Another name familiar to *Weird Tales* and Derleth's imprint Arkham House, was Greye La Spina, a lady whose pen had more than a touch of baleful fire. Her novel *Invaders of the Dark*, which originally appeared as a serial in 1925 and was later published by Arkham is in the true lycanthropic mould and her *The Devil's Pool* (1932), another werewolf piece, is perhaps overdue for revival.

Other interesting werewolf stories from the old *Weird Tales* school of writers are H. Warner Munn's *The Werewolf of Ponkert* (1925), which is full of horrific detail; the werewolf story *par excellence*, with all the stops pulled out. Lycanthropy was a favourite theme with Munn, who was the author of one of the greatest contes cruels outside Poe, *The Chain*; he also penned *The Return of the Master* (1927) and *The Werewolf's Daughter* (1928), both of which still make excellent reading.

Quinn, whom I have already mentioned, was also addicted to the theme. He was drawn to lycanthropy again and again and his most successful essays in this field were *Fortune's Fools* (1938); *The Blood Flower* (1927); *The Thing in the Fog* (1933); and *The Gentle Werewolf* (1940). Another *Weird Tales* luminary was Robert E. Howard who died by his own hand tragically young; among his prolific output of fantastic books detailing the adventures of such heroes as Conan the Cimmerian, were evocative werewolf stories such as *In the Forest of Villeferre* (1925); and *Wolfshead*, which appeared the following year.

There is little left for the modern writer in the field except surprise. My own contribution to the genre *Cry Wolf*, was written in 1968 for an American anthology and relies entirely on the surprise of its *dénouement*, in the manner of Peter Fleming.

And yet something has been lost with the sheer prolificity of modern writers concentrating on this ancient theme. Something of craftsmanship and atmosphere has disappeared in all but the best of them. Two writers of an older school are worth some consideration at this stage.

The first is a little-known writer of the '30s, F. G. Loring, who appears to be known solely by the much re-printed story, *The Tomb of Sarah*. He is, however, to judge by this one example, a master craftsman in the field of macabre literature and the piece compels a genuine shudder in the reader which is the hallmark of a comparative few, headed by Poe, Lovecraft, E. F. Benson and M. R. James.

Curiously enough, the story in question, has been anthologized under both the headings of vampirism and lycanthropy. Let the reader judge for himself. The tale purports to be the diary of a church restorer "of about sixty years ago", which relates to the restoring and enlarging of the chancel of a church in the West Country. The tale is a scholarly and well-turned piece of writing which would have delighted Dr M. R. James, who was a specialist in this field.

During the course of the work the labourers have to move a tomb belonging to the ancient family of the Kenyons; the inscription on it is an inspired piece of invention on Loring's part and makes an effective companion piece to Stoker's equally forbidding inscription in *Dracula's Guest* in which the Countess Dolingen of Gratz found "the dead travel fast".

The inscription on the Tomb of Sarah runs, "SARAH, 1630. For the sake of the dead and the welfare of the living, let this sepulchre remain untouched and its occupant undisturbed until the Coming of Christ. In the name of the Father, the Son and the Holy Ghost".

Despite this solemn and forbidding exhortation the restorers have little choice; the ground beneath the tomb has so sunk that the church is in danger.

The legend, the narrator finds, says that the Countess Sarah was murdered for her evil deeds; she had lived in a nearby castle on the road to Bristol and was reputed to have been a were-woman, her only companion being a familiar in the shape of an Asiatic wolf.

Loring, who was a Naval Commander, has a subtle way of communicating unease and terror and the story is one of the very best of its kind, being mainly concerned with atmosphere; the whole situation conveyed in prosaic, matter-of-fact diary entries.

He does in fact use both the legends of vampirism and lycanthropy, as he refers to the Countess Sarah as a were-woman and uses the motif of a gigantic dog or wolf which first appears from the tomb and terrorizes the neighbourhood.

But later the narrator and the rector of the parish put paid to the animated corpse by the time-honoured methods of destroying a vampire; that is by the use of the stake.

In fact, *The Tomb of Sarah* belongs to both mythologies; it is a splendidly narrated tale, from the discovery of the Countess, crouched in her tomb with a rope round her neck; to the appearance of the great dog which lopes from out the mist surrounding the churchyard.

The Tomb of Sarah was a story which thrilled in childhood and I find it still as potent today. Another in the same mould as Loring was Oliver Onions, who wrote a number of the great classic tales of terror, including *Rooum*; *Phantas* and, perhaps his best, *The Beckoning Fair One*.

He ventured into the field of lycanthropy with an extremely rare tale *The Master of the House*, which appeared as early as 1929. In fastidious prose Onions told a brooding tale of horror which is among the best in the field. As far as I know it was his only venture in the genre. As I have said elsewhere most writers in the macabre field find a need to evoke the man-beast theme once; most of them have no need to do so again. Few are successful a second time. One feels that Onions might have been, had he so desired. With the two writers mentioned should also be grouped one of a later generation, Anthony Boucher, a distinguished practitioner in the field who penned some notable tales. His *The Compleat Werewolf*, which appeared in 1942, is in the true canon.

The werewolf story can be brought briefly up to date. At the time of writing there seems to be little sign of slackening on the part of those writers of short stories who wish to evoke the theme. As I indicated earlier, there is little left now save surprise. There is a bewildering richness and variety, sprinkled throughout the several hundred anthologies which have been published in the United Kingdom and America since the end of the Second World War.

It would be impossible to list them all, even if it were desirable to do so. Manly Wade Wellman, the American practitioner, was early in the field in the '30s with such stories as *The Horror Undying* and he continued the tradition on through the '50s with such tales as *The Last Grave of Lill Warran*.

James Blish, another familiar and distinguished name in American macabre and science-fiction fields published his excellent novella *There Shall Be No Darkness* in 1950; and the old *Weird Tales* tradition is carried on in more recent times by writers like the evergreen Clark Ashton Smith with *Monsters in the Night*.

A newer generation brings a more casual style and the shock revelation to such modern tales as *Mrs Kaye* by Beverly Haaf and *Pia!* by John Donaldson.

The range is extraordinary and many unexpected writers have been attracted to the theme; from that superb craftsman of the thriller Geoffrey Household, who wrote *Taboo* in the '30s to today's famous sci-fi writer Clifford Simak with *The Werewolf Principle*. Nothing could be more incongruous than the juxtaposition of the Western writer Max Brand and the English novelist Hugh Walpole, yet both penned werewolf tales in their time.

There seems nowhere else to take the theme today; certainly, there is already evidence that science-fiction writers are resurrecting that hairy old friend among the unfamiliar settings of alien stars and planets. Or perhaps an even newer generation of writers will find it necessary to return to well-crafted stories set in opulent nineteenth-century *milieu*. We shall have to wait and see.

In the meantime the filmic monsters spawned by the legend of the werewolf are waiting to beguile us.

In Art: The Cinema

"Even a man who is pure in heart
  And says his prayers by night,
  Can become a wolf when the wolfsbane blooms
  And the autumn moon is bright."

From Curt Siodmak's script of *The Wolf Man*
(Universal Pictures, 1941)

TWENTY-THREE

ILL MET BY MOONLIGHT

The cinema took up the theme of lycanthropy fairly late. Though an American film called *The Werewolf* had been made as early as 1913 it was only a short feature, hardly more than a one-reeler and is now irretrievably lost. The vampire had been celebrated in major films from 1922 onwards and afterwards monsters, mummies, ghosts, ghouls and other assorted fiends had rushed with increasing speed from the world's film studios, notably those of Germany and America.

But it was not until the mid-'30s that the American sound film created an essay on the lycanthrope; it would be nice to report that the production was an undoubted masterpiece but that would be far from the truth. It was a disappointing effort and that mainly due to the principal actor, somewhat pedestrian direction and a reluctance to attack the theme with sufficient *brio*.

All the more unfortunate because the piece was handsomely mounted, given first-rate players and extremely well photographed. And it had the advantage of Guy Endore himself, who reputedly had a hand in the script. Perversely, his literary masterpiece, *The Werewolf of Paris* had now become *The Werewolf of London* and, naturally enough, bore no resemblance at all to his original story.

But we should not be too surprised at that and undoubtedly had America's major horror studio of the '30s, Universal, not been behind the production, the result would have been even less distinguished. The film has some good moments and even two or three striking ones; but with more care and less concentration on the mannered comedy relief could have been an outstanding essay in the macabre.

Strangely enough, it was not until the '60s and the advent of Hammer Films, that the lycanthrope was to receive more subtle treatment. The '30s essays always featured an actor heavily made up in fur and with sharp teeth, whereas a more imaginative approach, using a wolf for the attacks on humans and a human being without make-up for the "normal" sequences, would have been far more impressive.

Even better would have been a gallery of suspects with no hint of the werewolf's identity; the *dénouement* at the end of the film would have come with twice the shock. So far as I know, even at the time of writing, this has never been done.

The two major drawbacks of the 1935 Universal production of *The Werewolf of London* were the pedestrian direction of Stuart Walker, with little style or pace; and the central performance of Henry Hull in the Jekyll-Hyde rôle of the scientist/lycanthrope.

Hull was ill at ease in such a macabre film. An excellent actor, he was at his best playing fiery newspaper editors in major Westerns or historical pieces, and reportedly he had little patience with the long make-up sessions at the hands of Universal's wizard Jack Pierce, who had made such a frightening transformation of Karloff's features for the *Frankenstein* series.

Instead, even in full lycanthropic cry, he looked more like a pug-dog suffering from five-o'clock shadow, than the sinister beast of legend, and the ludicrous effect was even more heightened in the cape and strange flapped cap the costume department dug up.

This is a pity, for the film starts promisingly, even brilliantly, with Dr Glendon's expedition to Tibet to find a strange plant, the *mariphasa lupino lumino*, which blooms only in moonlight. Botanically, the idea is not so fantastic today as it then seemed in the mid-'30s.

Though obviously a studio-bound set, Universal's Tibet had a strange beauty, the fur-clad figures setting out against freezing winds which whip the snow from the distant peaks. Glendon finds his plant but while gathering it he is attacked by a half-seen figure swathed in furs. The two fight and Glendon is bitten in the struggle.

This ends the prologue and Glendon is then seen in London society as an affluent man of affairs with an elegant town house – complete with laboratory, of course – many wealthy friends and a beautiful wife. Valerie Hobson, fresh from her triumphs as Henry Frankenstein's lady in *Bride of Frankenstein* a few years earlier, brings a poignant, wistful beauty to her rôle as a girl who has married unwisely and who flirts throughout with her old flame, the rather stodgy Lester Matthews, who provides the expected 'Scotland Yard' boyfriend in this type of film.

The production takes off a little with its well-designed conservatory scenes – the conservatory replaces and makes a much-needed change from the over-used mad scientist's laboratory – where elaborate lamps simulate moonlight to germinate the strange seeds Glendon has brought back from Tibet.

The subdued playing of J. M. Kerrigan as Glendon's assistant, straw-hatted and suitably botanical, and his exchanges with Glendon in the white-painted glasshouse setting, are some of the most enjoyable in the film, and the excellent, high-key camera work, with its long, gliding tracking shots give the film a distinction which it only occasionally attains elsewhere.

The entrance of Warner Oland as an inscrutable savant, Dr Yogami of the unlikely-sounding 'University of Carpathia', is an excellent touch and this first-rate artiste gives the film a badly needed lift in its middle sections, for Hull unfortunately, has not sufficient presence to carry the central rôle and is obviously out of his element.

Other things too act against the production; the presence in the cast of fine supporting actresses like Spring Byington and Ethel Griffies, instead of strengthening it, actually demolish its horrific structure because their comedy relief, which incidentally goes on far too long, effectively dissipates whatever tension the director has been able to build up.

There are other hilarious and unintentional gaffes too, which Universal, with its ignorance of British police procedures, should have left to those better qualified than themselves. A police constable who continually talks about "cracked arches" on the beat, when he means "fallen arches"; the cosy police set-up, like something out of a Will Hay film, with the two Scotland Yard chiefs being uncle and nephew (not helped by Lawrence Grant's stodgy portrayal as the former); and, worst of all, English police cars rushing to the rescue with American sirens wailing and motor-cycle outriders!

What then, one might ask, is left, with such glaring failures;

surprisingly, quite a few virtues. I shall attempt to outline them in the remainder of this chapter.

As the reader may have guessed by now, Dr Glendon has been bitten by a werewolf during his search for the wonderful plant in Tibet. With the aid of Kerrigan he is engaged in finding the antidote; as the hair on his hands becomes swarthier (in none too skilful dissolves) he and Kerrigan struggle to persuade the stubborn bulbs to flower with the aid of artificial moonlight.

No wonder Miss Hobson becomes so irritable. "What are you doing in there, Henry?" she exclaims petulantly at one point, unable to penetrate the fastnesses of the conservatory. What indeed! But one or two genuine chills are at hand. There is a sort of open day at the house at which some of Glendon's botanical marvels are on display.

At one point Kerrigan comes out to feed a giant Venus fly-trap with a live frog. There is a telling close-up of this while Spring Byington exclaims, "How revolting!" in thrilled tones. And then Dr Yogami turns up unannounced. Oland, with his heavy build, thick moustache and light-coloured suit has never been better than in this half-sinister, half-pathetic performance. He too is a lycanthrope and he is seeking cuttings from Glendon's magical plant, which is the only known antidote. "We met in Tibet," he explains.

The audience has already guessed, of course, that it was Oland who bit Hull in Tibet but it will take the good doctor another five reels to realize that. He discusses his experiments politely with Yogami and when the savant reappears a few days later and begs for some cuttings "to save two lives", Glendon bars the way to his laboratory and peremptorily refuses. He will give his findings to the world in due course.

He fails to realize that Yogami is talking about his own plight and that of Glendon himself; for Oland brings to his rôle something of the pathos – the self-realization of the true lycanthrope that is so conspicuously lacking in the characterization of Glendon – and it is Hull's inadequacy and the effortless strength of Oland's performance beside it that gives the production its imbalance.

Oland is operating within his true milieu; the framework of the macabre film and the mystery thriller which he had made so much his own in long years of Charlie Chan characterizations and the polish of his playing makes Hull, badly out of his depth, seem even more colourless.

But then follows one of the film's few highlights which lifts it for a few moments into genuine horror and one is left speculating on what the production could have been with a little more care and thought. Hull returns to the laboratory and he and Kerrigan busy themselves with the mariphasa and the "moonlight" lamps. Bulbs flower in time-lapse photography and the doctor then notices that his hands are beginning to show the classical darkening with hair which is the prelude to one of his appalling transformations.

He hastily returns to the study of his house. On a cushion near his chair his pet cat sits, contented and lazily licking its paws.

However, the animal senses that there is something amiss with its master. Glendon reaches out to stroke his pet. In seconds the cat is roused to fury. It gives an extraordinary performance, arching its back, spitting and flexing its claws in rage. It is an impressive moment, imaginatively treated by director Stuart Walker's camera, broken into big close-ups and cross-cut with Glendon's alarmed reactions.

The cat is undoubtedly reacting to stimuli outside camera range but these are astonishing moments which elevate the film briefly to heights of terror. But it is significant that Hull does little to achieve this result. His reactions are conventional. The burden of the scene is on the cat and its 'acting' abilities and the close-up camera and the skill of the editor do the rest.

There are two camera styles in the film in fact; an appropriately glossy and high-key treatment with plenty of white paint and rugs for the domestic interiors; and low-key, gauzy camerawork for the night scenes and misty exteriors.

Dr Yogami, it will be remembered, had asked for two blossoms of the mariphasa; "Two blossoms for two souls," as he puts it. And, he had added significantly, "Tomorrow is too late".

Too late for Hull undoubtedly but not too late for Oland, who breaks into the conservatory that night and snips off the life-saving blooms. But they are, however, only a temporary remedy for the lycanthrope who returns to his beastly state at inopportune moments.

The next of these comes at one of those frequent white tie and tails parties which characters in this sort of film were throwing throughout the '30s. Hull is transformed in a series of long tracking shots through his house, the make-up being changed between shots, so that the slow metamorphosis, so beloved in more sophisticated productions, never takes place. Instead, looking slightly Mephistophelean, he lopes off and shortly afterwards the howl of a wolf is heard through the night air.

Oland is discovered at this point with the socialite of Spring Byington – Miss Hobson's aunt in the film – on one of those improbable balconies overlooking a Thames suggested only by shadows and spotlamps and which certainly never existed outside a Hollywood dream. Much might have been made of this division between the rich and the under-privileged, with the Thames between, for the dialogue refers to that "poor quarter across the water" – Whitechapel? Wapping? – and into which Glendon himself, unknown to his wife, must soon plunge in his flight from discovery.

"What is that?" asks Miss Byington as the wolf howl sounds again.

"A lost soul," says Oland with sad truth.

This impressive actor here and in similar scenes supplies all the "presence" and expertise that should have been at the film's core and it is a thousand pities that Universal did not simply replace Hull when he objected to the long make-up sessions.

A few moments later and in another world altogether apparently, murder is done as a prostitute in Hollywood's idea of a foggy Wapping, the atmospheric "Goose Lane", is ripped to pieces by Glendon during some goat-like caperings.

The scene, as indicated, does not square with the earlier material as the night was clear during the balcony scenes a few seconds before. But night fogs come up quickly in Universal country and one had perhaps better not be too carping. Even here Hull does little but rush slavering at the camera and the studio sound department takes case of the rest.

In his Holmes-like cape and flapped cap Hull then takes up his abode in a Dickensian-style waterside pub where we are to be treated to the tedious and endless ramblings of two old crones. One had hoped that Hull in his lycanthropic mood would have swiftly disposed of these two bibulous ladies but unfortunately he never gets round to this. Instead, he lies in his room, uttering hideous cries, while the alarmed women wander up and down the stairs declaiming their interminable monologues.

The script then goes completely wild back at the Hull mansion as Miss Hobson and her Scotland Yard boyfriend insist on riding by moonlight. London here is treated as though it might be eighteenth-century heathland and throughout there is no trace of traffic, buses or noise and indeed, how can there be, when the whole farrago takes place in California?

But it is fatal to what remains of the film's style; one half – the high-key part taking place in modern, well-lit mansions and the other in Mayhew country where the costumes, particularly in the low dives, are slightly Dickensian though the whole action takes place in the year 1935.

The production takes a nose-dive soon after Glendon warns his wife about riding by night; quite reasonably she asserts her freedom and Glendon, for her own safety, takes refuge in seedy lodgings, reinforcing the Jekyll and Hyde parallel. Paradoxically, the best sequences occur when Hull is not on screen or, as in the case of the cat episode, when the motivation for terror is coming from some other source.

One such occurs at the London Zoo of the film when the wolves are understandably uneasy at the brute-beast prowling – but not seen – in the undergrowth and the keeper who goes to investigate is torn to pieces. This is treated quite excitingly, though a platinum blonde Beverly Hills floozie who is vamping the wolf-keeper is wildly off-key.

But the prowling camera and the wolves' unease as Walker's lens pans along the cages does convey genuine tension and ante-dates a similar sequence in *The Quatermass Xperiment* by more than twenty years. The escaped wolf red-herring which follows naturally puts the obtuse Scotland Yard officials completely off the scent and in the uproar Glendon retreats to his country estate where he has one of his employees lock him into the conveniently barred room of an outlying chalet.

But there is a full moon and to confound things Miss Hobson takes her former fiancé for a moonlight drive to visit their country place; he is anxious to see the old house again, where he and the heroine spent happier days before she married Hull.

Their idyllic wandering in the woods is interrupted by the lycanthropic Glendon, who breaks out of his room and attacks the pair.

The Yard man beats off his assailant and rescues the girl but is convinced he has recognized Glendon beneath his hirsute disguise.

But he is unable to convince his even more obtuse uncle, who, it will be remembered, is the head of Scotland Yard. The script throws up a good plot-point here with the ripping to death of a chamber-maid at a hotel many miles from Hull's estate and at the same time as the attack on Miss Hobson and her companion.

The police set off in full cry in search of the killer-wolf though once again Hollywood falters, the film's makers apparently not knowing that a different set of police would take over this latest murder. The culprit is Dr Yogami, of course, who has metamorphosed back into his beastly shape and has taken it out on the chamber-maid.

Hull returns to his laboratory where he searches desperately for the antidote. In one of the best scenes in this short – seventy-five minutes – and uneven film, he becomes aware that he is not alone. He creeps through the conservatory and finds Oland snipping the precious buds of his life-giving mariphasa. The two men fight and Oland is killed, Hull being transformed back into his wolf shape.

Hull then goes completely berserk and attempts to kill his wife too. The police burst in just in time and shoot down the wretched werewolf on the stairs as he is about to spring on the appalled Miss Hobson. Glendon is surprisingly dignified. Dying on the floor he thanks his executioners for the bullet. As life ebbs from him the brutish face slowly fades away to leave the calm features of Dr Glendon.

This is quite impressively done and the film could have ended there most effectively. Unfortunately, implausibility again creeps in and in stodgy final lines Lawrence Grant declaims, "In my report I shall say I shot him by accident while protecting his wife!"

This implies an unusual degree of corruption on the part of Scotland Yard, quite apart from the charge of manslaughter which would have been preferred against Grant had this been so!

If it appears that I am taking a sledgehammer to demolish an unworthy target, it is merely because of my disappointment at these inept touches, for this could have been a classic study in Grand Guignol with more care, better plotting and another leading player. As it is it still works intermittently and the fine camera work and the acting of some excellent players, notably Warner Oland, still bring the occasional chill to the screen.

There was to be a gap of another six years before a more worthwhile essay in the genre came to life in the cinema. The principal actor bore a famous name and was to become associated with the werewolf for the remainder of his life.

TWENTY-FOUR

WOLFSBANE AND PENTAGRAM

His name was Lon Chaney, of course. Not the more famous and infinitely more gifted Lon Chaney Sr, but his son, the massive bull-framed Lon Chaney Jr who had at first acted under the name of Creighton Chaney to avoid cashing in on a celebrated name. Chaney was never a highly gifted actor but he brought to his wolfman a pathetic, tortured quality so that it is no exaggeration to say that his was the most sympathetic monster in the whole pantheon of cinema's horror creatures.

The highlight of his career was undoubtedly his playing of the brutish, child-like Lenny in both the stage and film versions of John Steinbeck's famous novel, *Of Mice and Men* in 1939.

He never afterwards quite regained these heights, though the new film made him in great demand for many parts. Like Bela Lugosi before him he was not selective enough and appeared in too many poor, cheaply made movies, so that in less than a decade he lost much of his reputation; though he regained status somewhat many years later with parts in films like *High Noon*.

But his name had considerable lustre in 1941 when, only some eighteen months after the film version of the Steinbeck piece, he was signed by Universal for *The Wolf Man*, the first in a long series of lycanthropic movies which were to become increasingly ineffective over the years.

But in *The Wolf Man* he was in distinguished company and unlike Henry Hull he was an actor willing to submit to hours of special effects make-up at the hands of Jack Pierce so that the film could be considered a qualified success.

Qualified, because it was on small details that the production foundered though it was much better directed, better acted by its large cast, and much more excitingly handled than *The Werewolf of London*.

The camera work was more atmospheric, the sets more opulent and spacious and the tracking shots more impressive and sophisticated. Apart from the British-made *Curse of the Werewolf* more than two decades afterwards, it was the most careful and thoughtful essay the cinema had ever attempted in the genre and as such merits more than cursory study.

Perhaps it might be better to deal with its flaws first and with the many excellences later, as the latter far outweigh the former. Curt Siodmak's screenplay is literate and well-organized but like many Hollywood people of his time he had little or no idea of British locations, customs or social *mores*. His Wales as interpreted by Universal bears no resemblance to the reality; there is no attempt to give the cast the proper accents and neither the scenery – mostly studio sets, it is true – nor the décor, buildings or even the signposts are recognizably Welsh.

There is, in any case, little point in the setting as there is nothing particularly Welsh in the legend of the werewolf. The height of ludicrousness is reached with a band of Eastern European gypsies, with heavy accents, who occupy much of the screen time.

We are not told why this exotic band should be encamped in Wales and their flimsy costumes, the women in low-cut blouses and with bare arms, would be more appropriate to the Caribbean than a damp and misty Celtic setting!

These are minor flaws perhaps but there are other, more important errors. Chaney's accent is explained by saying that he has spent twenty years in Canada; that will just about pass but Siodmak or the Universal story department have again got their police facts hopelessly twisted.

The Chief Constable is a man called Captain Montford. He would undoubtedly have been a retired army captain who had accepted the post. He is treated by his "posse" throughout as though he is a police captain, a rank unknown in the British Isles: And it is doubtful whether someone of such exalted rank as Chief Constable of a shire would personally lead a search for a murderer. The investigations would probably have been headed by a local officer of Superintendent rank or possibly a Scotland Yard man.

A more unfortunate gaffe is the character of the gamekeeper on the palatial estate. He is portrayed by the impeccably old-school-tie figure of Patric Knowles who, with his immaculately cut tweeds, stands out like a sore thumb.

A key scene has him smoking his pipe sitting on a table in the baronial hall as a social equal of the local notables and pontificating on the crimes to Sir John and his cronies. Better to have made Knowles a retired army officer too, probably a major, and have made him the estate manager. Strange that big studios like Universal could not merely have asked their predominantly English casts about the social usage of their settings.

These reservations apart, there is much to commend and though the director, George Waggner, was never more than a routine Hollywood craftsman, his handling of the events is at least competent and the film occasionally rises to creditable heights of terror.

The production opens promisingly with Chaney as Lawrence Talbot returning to his Welsh ancestral home after many years abroad. Talbot Castle is one of those pieces of Hollywood Gothic at which Universal was particularly adept and this opulent setting of massive baronial hall and Sir John's observatory, where he carries on his hobby of astronomy, is impressive and sets the tone for a mainly superior essay in filmic terror.

The piece gains in depth through the performance of Claude Rains, one of the cinema's finest actors, as Talbot's father; these low-keyed sequences casually introduce the theme and Larry's return to his old home, where he is also welcomed by Sir John's friend, Captain Montford, played by another distinguished actor Ralph Bellamy, raise considerable expectations.

A massive crate is delivered to the castle: it contains Sir John's latest telescope and the son's New World experience is soon put to good use installing the equipment in the laboratory. Testing the optics on the surrounding countryside he accidentally focuses on the upper window of an antique shop in the village, and is entranced by the vision of a pretty girl, Gwen Conliffe, daughter of the owner.

He later visits the shop and on meeting Evelyn Ankers finds his initial attraction reinforced. He buys from her stock a large walking-stick with a strange silver wolf's head for a handle and ornamented with a five-pointed star. The girl tells him something of the local legends and quotes the effectively composed verse of scriptwriter Siodmak which heralds the coming chill.

Says Miss Ankers, deeply versed in gypsy lore, "Even a man who is pure in heart, And says his prayers by night, May become a wolf when the wolfsbane blooms, And the autumn moon is bright''.

This jingle is saved from echoes of Will Hay rustics by the way it is put over in its context and by the discretion of the playing and direction, so that when it is repeated later by Sir John and other members of the cast it seems to gain an added doom-laden quantity. Unknowing, Talbot has heard his own fate pronounced.

He hastens to make an appointment with the delectable Miss Ankers and is not at all put out to learn that she is engaged to the gamekeeper played by Patric Knowles. He arranges to meet her that evening to visit the gypsy encampment nearby and pausing only to exchange a few words with her father – another muted performance by J. M. Kerrigan, taking a step up from *Werewolf of London* – he hastens back to the castle.

This slow opening, covering two days or so, is perfectly apposite in the film's build-up and Waggner also introduces the sympathetic presence of another Hollywood dependable, Warren William, a former Arsène Lupin, as the local doctor, who doubles as police surgeon. The audience is now ready for the first set-piece, which begins with Chaney and Ankers' visit to the fair that night.

There are distinguished precedents for this fair sequence, from *The Cabinet of Doctor Caligari* onwards, and Waggner is not slow to seize his opportunities. The mist swirls past gaunt branches as Talbot meets the girl but he is disconcerted to find she has brought a friend Jenny (Fay Helm).

There is a gay and light-hearted scene as the gypsies dance by torchlight and then we are on to more sombre material with warning looks from crone Maria Ouspenskaya as the trio cross by her caravan. They agree to have their palms read by none other than our old friend Bela Lugosi, who makes a brief guest appearance, along with many other strong players. He recoils as he sees the sign of the pentagram materialize in Jenny's palm, realizing he has seen the forewarning of her death.

For Bela is a lycanthrope and, according to the mythology invented by Siodmak for the film, has recognized his next victim. The girl leaves the caravan, the others having gone on and Bela is next glimpsed, his head in his hands as the howl of a wolf echoes through the misty night.

Ouspenskaya, who is Bela's mother and knows his affliction,

is understandably alarmed. But before she can do anything murder and horror are erupting in the Universal fog. Jenny, walking past one of the gaunt, dead trees which are Universal's speciality, is attacked and savaged by a great dog which leaps at her. Strolling a little farther off in the woods Larry and Gwen hear the girl's screams.

Larry dashes to her rescue and sees not a dog but a wolf savaging the girl on the ground. As it springs at him he strikes it with his silver-headed stick and rains blow after blow on its head. This is a powerfully realized scene and Waggner's camera, discreetly framed by the fork of a tree, concentrates on Chaney beating downwards in the mist.

But the wolf has bitten his chest and as Larry staggers away he is himself, without realizing it, afflicted with the curse of the werewolf. The police are quickly on the scene but when higher authority is summoned a bizarre state of affairs is disclosed. The girl Gwen is dead, her throat torn out. By the tree, where he left the corpse of the wolf, Larry now sees the body of Bela, the gypsy fortune-teller whose skull has been crushed by the silver-handled stick, now covered with blood and hair.

An appalled Larry tells his story to Montford, who listens with increasing scepticism; when Talbot says the wolf savaged him, Dr Lloyd examines him but there is now no trace of a wound. The doctor tells the police his patient must have complete rest, as he is obviously suffering from shock.

But Talbot suspects that Maleva, Bela's mother, knows a great deal more about the affair than anyone suspects. He slips from his room and later finds his way to the castle vault where Bela's coffin has been placed awaiting burial. He hears someone coming and conceals himself in a dark niche where he observes Maleva saying a gypsy prayer over her son's body.

This is an excellent sequence, with well-composed images and there is another telling moment a short while later when the gamekeeper's dog indicates its dislike for Talbot by growling and uneasy behaviour. Waggner's direction also encompasses deft and subtle touches which are almost more effective than the big setpieces.

Lon Chaney himself brings a pathetic edge to his rôle as a man torn between his desire to do good and the brutish instincts released by the bite of the lycanthrope; this is given emphasis at the fair when he finds himself unable to shoot the image of a tin wolf at the rifle-range. Maleva herself, in the hands of Ouspenskaya, a fine and gifted actress, formerly of the Moscow Arts Theatre, who appeared in some of Hollywood's best films, is drawn to him and warns him against the evil which threatens.

She gives him a charm to wear over his heart; this pentagram symbol he in turn gives to Gwen, knowing it will keep her from harm at his hands. Thus, unlike most macabre situations, the peculiar nature of the lycanthropic disease has the victim/ monster trying to protect his own potential victim. The film has now arrived at a stage where Grand Guignol is about to be given its head.

At the next full moon, Talbot, despite himself, is again transformed into the brutish beast he so despises. The fur grows on the palms of his hands – the audience is given only detail shots here, which add to the effect – and his face visibly thickens and coarsens. With a bestial howl he then leaves the castle and roams the night, his fur glistening in the light of the moon.

He murders and savages the sexton digging Bela's grave in the misty churchyard and then lopes off as the alarm is given. In the morning as Talbot awakes in anguish in his palatial bedroom in the castle, his clothes torn and stained, his face strained and stubbled with beard, the police are already in the grounds. They have followed the wolf tracks to Castle Talbot itself. Larry is appalled to find the mark of the pentagram on his chest.

At church that Sunday Talbot is uneasy and preoccupied. He walks up the steps with his family and lingers in the porch. The church set is extraordinarily lavish, even for a Universal macabre production, and looks as though it might have been left over from the Laughton production of *The Hunchback of Notre Dame*, turned at R.K.O. Radio two years earlier.

Larry is repelled by the symbols of Christianity and is unable to advance any further into the interior; he retreats to the square outside, visibly shaken and now knows himself to be damned. The scene is an effective one and arouses echoes of a similar incident in Murnau's *Faust*, where the Mephistopheles of Emil Jannings is unable to enter the cathedral for the Mass.

Talbot has been warned by the old gypsy woman that her son was a lycanthrope and that he too, having been bitten, has become one in his turn. Larry is still inclined to scoff and asks his father about the superstition. Sir John quotes Greek folklore to him and says that a man might imagine he had become a beast.

But he derides the superstition that supposes physical change to take place. Only Dr Lloyd, in the sympathetic persona of Warren William takes Larry's obsession seriously. He advises him to leave the neighbourhood. Fortunately for the audience, he ignores the advice.

The next night of the full moon he is again transformed and walks the misty woods looking for victims. But Captain Montford and the gamekeeper have set traps for the wolf and the werewolf finds his leg caught in a jagged trap. When he comes to he is again transformed into Talbot; he is saved by Maleva who drives her cart out and helps him to escape from the law. He walks limping through the police searchers, saying he was out on the hunt too and sprained his ankle.

Back at the antique shop he reveals his love for Gwen and tries to warn her of his affliction; she wants to go away with him but he refuses. They discuss the charm which hangs around her neck and Larry sees with sick horror that the sign of the pentagram has now appeared in the palm of Gwen's hand; she will be his next victim.

He confesses to his father but Sir John puts his agitation and wild story down to his disturbed mental condition following the death of Bela; he tries to rationalize his son's fears. Eventually, as preparations are made for the wolf hunt in the local woods, he agrees to Larry's suggestion that he should be bound to a chair and locked in his room while the search for the wild beast continues.

In a well-directed and edited finale, Larry breaks out and hunts Gwen through the misty Universal woods. He is about to savage her when the police appear. In a repetition of the sequence earlier in the film where Larry killed Bela, Sir John rains blow after blow on the monster's head with Larry's own silver-handled stick.

As the thing on the ground dies the police come up and with Montford and Dr Lloyd kneeling in the light of torches, the horrified Sir John sees the corpse before him slowly metamorphose back into the tranquil features of his own son.

Maleva adds a sad postscript to the legend as she draws near. She murmurs, "As the rain enters the soil, so the river enters the sea. As tears run to a predestined end." And she adds that Larry will now find peace for all eternity.

So ended what was to prove the best film on a lycanthropic theme until the advent of the Hammer essay more than two decades later. Though there were faults and blemishes of style, these were largely vitiated by the polish of the playing; the pace and expertise of the direction; and by the atmospheric camera work. The main settings, of the Castle, antique shop, village and the church were lavish and of high quality, and the story, with its legendary framework, was ingeniously composed.

It was certainly the best thing Chaney was to do in the field and though there was a spate of werewolf films from Universal in the ensuing years, none came up to the standard of the first.

By any standard, too, this was one of the most distinguished casts any horror film was to have; and though one cannot equate the principals with Karloff, Basil Rathbone, Charles Laughton, Leslie Banks, Ernest Thesiger, and the other, primarily macabre talents, who graced the great horror movies of the '30s, it is no mean roster Hollywood's major horror studio assembled to re-tell this ancient legend of one of the most fearsome beasts ever spawned from the mists of time.

Indeed, Lon Chaney was to walk the night again before two years were out, when he was to be reunited with many of the cast of the first film, together with some distinguished additions. We shall follow the further adventures of the Wolf Man in the next chapter.

TWENTY-FIVE

THE WOLFMAN COMETH

Lon Chaney Jr, was born Creighton Chaney in California in 1904. His father, the great Lon Chaney was then only in his early twenties and not yet the international star, famous for his macabre and horrifying screen rôles, with which he was to make the whole world shudder in the '20s. The young Chaney suffered from this situation for many years and living in his father's shadow made him want to branch out for himself.

It was with this in view that he stuck to his family name of Creighton Chaney when he became an actor and it took a long time before the studios were able to persuade him to try to take over the mantle of his father. The elder Chaney in fact, had been strongly opposed to his son's career in films. The boy was only fourteen when he confessed to his ambition to become an actor.

But Lon Chaney Sr was horrified at the idea and the son was removed from his studies at Hollywood High School and sent to a business college far from the studios and showbiz atmosphere of Beverly Hills. Incredibly, the man who was to become almost as well-known as his father in horror rôles in the sound cinema, was an executive in a water-heater corporation before the call of the cameras became too strong.

He gave up business life on taking a successful test for R.K.O. Radio Pictures in 1932. Though he made brief appearances in some good films, such as the 1933 *Lucky Devils*, an interesting story of First World War pilots who become stunt men in the movies, with William Boyd – later to become "Hopalong Cassidy" – he was condemned for more than six years to a long succession of routine Westerns, dramas, thrillers and adventure yarns, in many of which he played villains or even bit parts.

It was David O. Selznick who originally asked him to take his father's name but much to his credit young Chaney refused.

But later, with the horror boom beginning in the late '30s he did give in, though even then recognition was slow in coming.

His big opportunity came in 1939 when the play of Steinbeck's *Of Mice and Men* transferred from Broadway to Los Angeles and Broderick Crawford, who played Lennie, left the cast to make a film. Chaney auditioned for the part, got it and went on to a spectacular success in both stage and screen versions. His film *Lennie* is a moving portrayal even today, more than three decades afterwards.

Sadly, it was to be his first and best film as a star, though there were other highlights made within the next few years, including a spectacular performance as a prehistoric tribal leader in Hal Roach's *One Million B.C.* in 1940. As we have seen, his stock was still high when he made the definitive *Wolf Man* in 1941. Though he had come down a step or two Chaney was still an impressive actor, and even in the sequels which we are about to discuss, there were occasional flashes of brilliance.

Unfortunately, as so often happened with Universal at this period, uninspired thinking and a desire to cash in on once famous names, resulted in a severe lowering of standards for Chaney's second portrayal as Larry Talbot. Even the title of this 1943 film makes the heart sink. *Frankenstein Meets the Wolf Man* fully lived down to its expectations and the choice of an almost unknown and totally undistinguished director, Roy William Neill did not help.

Ironically, the film was a minute longer than the originating vehicle *The Wolf Man*, and had an equally distinguished cast, largely wasted in unrewarding rôles. Again though, the production values were good and there was some evocative photography of Universal's celebrated misty landscapes.

Particularly impressive was the laboratory set, apparently refurbished from the exploded wreck which we last saw in *Bride of Frankenstein* some eight years earlier; but the story was atrocious. Nevertheless, like so many of these films, it began promisingly with grave-robbers disturbing the Talbot vault in Wales, where, it will be remembered, the unfortunate Larry had been struck down by his father with the silver-headed cane two years before.

This scene is well and imaginatively handled, with its groping, furtive movements from the vault-robbers, and the evocative, low-key lighting. But as they disturb the contents of the coffin Larry Talbot too is disturbed and within a very short space of time he is off on new charnel adventures.

Maria Ouspenskaya reappears as Maleva and taking what might well be regarded as her foster child under her protection, transports him from a studio Wales to the happier atmosphere of the Transylvanian-style Vasaria, in the hope that Baron Frankenstein may be able to effect his release. Note that Talbot is hoping for release, not cure.

It says a lot for Chaney's presence that he is able sometimes to transmute the unpromising material he is given and make a pathetic, even anguished figure of the lycanthrope. There are many splendid artistes in this sequel, including Patric Knowles, now upgraded to Baron Frankenstein; and Ilona Massey as a Baroness.

But Neill's limp direction misfires more than once, particularly in a potentially horrific scene in which Talbot and Maleva find the body of Frankenstein's monster – this time played by Bela Lugosi in a quite convincing makeup – entombed in the ice beneath the vaults of Castle Frankenstein.

"Oh, this must be the monster," he mumbles mildly as though he had just found a lost door-key, and all tension is dissipated in a wave of laughter from the audience. Which is a pity for there are many good things in the film, even given its silly premises.

Apart from the strong players already mentioned the studio packed the cast with outstanding character actors like Lionel Atwill and Dwight Frye, the original Jonathan Harker in *Dracula*; and the dwarf from the entire *Frankenstein* series, though this time he is promoted to villager. Dennis Hoey played the romantic lead.

But the cast were not entirely unhappy when the fatal lever in Frankenstein's laboratory was pulled to blow the castle to pieces; with the monster wrecking what is left of the place and Larry Talbot again turning back into hairy beastliness, the goodies flee as the villagers blow up a convenient dam to inundate the nest of monsters. Poor stuff when compared with the original or even with *Werewolf of London* but audiences were glad to get it in the austerity of the mid-war years.

Omitting for the moment other minor, wolf-man films in which the original Lawrence Talbot did not appear, it was to be more than a year before Chaney again donned the thick fur and sharp tusks of the undying Talbot.

This was in Universal's 1944 *House of Frankenstein*, an even more unlikely mish-mash, which I have already had cause to mention in my Vampire book. The film, somewhat limply directed by Erle C. Kenton was merely an excuse to bring Frankenstein's monster, the Wolf Man and Count Dracula all together in one adventure! Acting on the old show-business adage that nothing succeeds like excess.

The opposite was the result; it was quite the silliest of productions, though there was one of the finest line-ups of talent ever seen in a film of this type. Not only the master, Boris Karloff himself, who declined to don the monster make-up yet again, playing instead the scientist to the monster of Glenn Strange; but Chaney as Lawrence Talbot; John Carradine as Count Dracula; J. Carrol Naish, Anne Gwynne, Peter Coe, Lionel Atwill, George Zucco, Sig Rumann, Elena Verdugo and Philip Van Zandt.

It was almost like a roll-call of Hollywood macabre specialists, lacking only Bela Lugosi, Rathbone, Dwight Frye and Ernest Thesiger to make the complete roster. Naish played the hunchback rôle essayed by Frye in earlier years; Atwill the Central European police inspector; and Zucco a sort of latter-day Caligari, a fairground showroom in whose chamber of horrors the monsters manifest themselves. Karloff escaped from gaol to find Larry Talbot and Frankenstein's monster frozen beneath the ruins.

One cannot but suspect Curt Siodmak of having his tongue in his cheek when he dreamed up this sequence for in the earlier film, it will be remembered, Chaney had himself found the monster (played in that instance by Lugosi) in deep-freeze. Resuscitated, Larry soon finds a lycanthropic mood stealing over him and in furry glory is shot by the silver bullet of his sweetheart, Elena Verdugo.

Chaney was rapidly descending in status to accept such a part after the prominence of the first two films in the series. And his running time was brief, as the director had a great many other monsters to accommodate in his limited seventy-one minutes.

Apart from a television appearance Chaney Jr made his penultimate appearance as the pathetic Talbot in the next of the Universal series, typically entitled *House of Dracula*. But remarkably enough it was to be an improvement on what had gone before and tired audiences, at war's end in 1945, were enthusiastic at fantasy which briefly removed them from bleak reality.

Kenton as director did a little better in this latter film which at least starred Lon Chaney and gave the central performance to the cavortings of the wolf man. And again, there were the comforting figures of distinguished supporting actors who formed a cosy little club in the Universal horror movies of the '30s; John Carradine, having his second shot at Dracula; Lionel Atwill too; Ludwig Stossel; Martha O'Driscoll in the romantic lead, with Onslow Stevens and Glenn Strange for good measure as Frankenstein's monster. A good deal to cram into a mere sixty-seven minutes this time but the result was at least an improvement on *House of Frankenstein*.

Onslow Stephens made his only incursion into the horror genre with his effective mad scientist who resuscitates both wolf man and monster with the inevitable disastrous results. But once again there was the promising opening which is never quite fulfilled by anything which follows.

Police official Lionel Atwill summons Dr Franz Edelmann to the ancient gaol in Vasaria where he has a strange captive. It is none other than the unfortunate Talbot, raving and bestial, the moonlight glinting on the bars of his cell, metamorphosed yet again in all his lycanthropic hairiness. Much against commonsense Edelmann decides to remove his strange patient to his laboratory in the castle above the village for examination.

These earlier scenes, particularly those shot in the impressive laboratory sets raise considerable anticipation but, as so often happens in this series, the script – this time by Edward Lowe – degenerates into a welter of climaxes, though the film is at least more integrated than the others.

Edelmann finds a cure for Larry with the application of a special mould but he is not so fortunate with the Dracula of John Carradine. The once-noble Count knocks at the castle door one night begging to be cured and in a scene reminiscent of a National Health patient asking to be taken on to a G.P.'s panel, is accepted for treatment. But the complicated procedure misfires.

The film ends up with Edelmann turned into a vampire,

Dracula dissolving into nothingness and the crazed doctor reviving the monster. In a twist on previous efforts, Larry shoots the doctor and the monster wrecks the laboratory, which once again goes up in flames.

Even then Larry Talbot was not finished. He was to be resuscitated one more time for a dismal encounter with Abbott and Costello. In fact, Charles Barton's 1948 *Abbott and Costello Meet Frankenstein* was a sort of Marx Brothers compendium of Universal's entire range of monsters. Lon Chaney was billed lead with the two comics as Larry Talbot once more and he must have felt at home with Bela Lugosi as Dracula; Glenn Strange in the Frankenstein monster make-up; and with Vincent Price as the voice of the Invisible Man!

Also involved in this mish-mash, which is not worth analysing, were Lenore Aubert, Jane Randolph and Frank Ferguson. Funny it certainly was, in places, and Abbott and Costello could be very funny at times, but it was not Grand Guignol and made a sad exit for a lycanthropic monster who had started out so promisingly and brightly in the moonlight only seven years earlier.

Yet Lon Chaney was to be remembered by the portrayal of the tragic lycanthrope all his life and he at least certainly regarded the rôle as his own. He died in 1973 at the age of sixty-eight, still regarding the Talbot rôles and his New York Critics' Award for the Broadway production *Of Mice and Men*, together with the subsequent screen performance as the highlights of his career.

He once referred to the rôle as "my baby" and if artistry be measured in patience, painful adherence to one's professional standards and integrity of performance, Chaney must at least be reckoned as a first-rate craftsman. He endured agonies in the six-hour sessions at the hands of Jack Pierce for his complicated make-up as the lycanthrope.

His worst time was during the long and complex cartoon-like procedure of the actual changes of features in front of the camera. These began in the early hours of the morning and with lab-tests and twenty-one changes of make-up, occupied over twenty hours! Larry Talbot had the field to himself and created the definitive lycanthrope which set the standard for all subsequent performers. It is time now to discuss some lesser efforts in the genre.

Sensing that Universal was about to cash in on a lucrative market with its lycanthropic movies, Harry Cohn's Columbia studios had been fairly early in the field with their *Return of the Vampire* directed in 1943 by the veteran Lew Landers and released almost simultaneously with the second Lon Chaney Wolfman film.

Columbia had, in fact, assembled an exceptionally strong cast, utilizing no less a name than Bela Lugosi himself in the lead rôle of the vampire, Armand Tesla. The film was strong too, on distinguished leading ladies, who included Frieda Inescort, Nina Foch and Jeanne Bates.

The script-writers were unwise, however, to update the theme to the Second World War. A graveyard is bombed by the Germans during the blitz and the explosions disturb the grave of Count Tesla of Rumania, a vampire who returns to plague the unfortunate citizens of London.

An ingenious plot point has workmen sent to clear up the cemetery mistaking the stake through the Count's body for a piece of shrapnel and removing it, thus exposing the capital to even graver dangers than the Nazis.

He fastens on Nina Foch, making her a vampire and in turn transforms actor Matt Willis into another hairy lycanthrope, Andreas Obry. This *mélange*, which carried an 'H' certificate, was not inexpertly done and there were some excitements in the sixty-nine minute production which was, however, despite the ever-real horrors of the blitz, still cut by the British censor, who objected to Lugosi's body melting at the end to reveal his skeleton!

As in the case of Larry Talbot, Willis eventually rebels at the excesses he is being compelled to take part in and drags the Count's sleeping body into the sunlight. The photographic effects in the film, apart from the finale, which was excised from the print in England anyway, were not outstanding, the wolf-man's transformations taking place off screen.

But production values and photography were good and the cast was further strengthened by actors like Gilbert Emery, Roland Varno, Miles Mander and former Mack Sennett comic Billy Bevan who was to have a long career in serious drama playing bewildered policemen, ticket collectors and taxi-drivers.

Nina Foch was promoted by Columbia in the next of their series, *Cry of the Werewolf*, in which she seems to be the screen's first female lycanthrope. An excellent actress, she scored as the heroine Celeste La Tour, a gypsy queen from Hungary, who had the curse passed on to her by her mother.

This 1944 production, intelligently directed by Henry Levin ran only to sixty-three minutes, the average length of the '30s horror films, but was further distinguished by not having the star turn physically into a hairy monster before our eyes. Instead, she turned into a real wolf off screen. Though this might have been disappointing for *aficionados* of the genre, it was more true to legend. This was probably the reason it received only an 'A' certificate at the time.

Miss Foch finally perished in traditional style but not before there were a few genuine shudders. Excellent supporting players included Osa Massen and the formidable Blanche Yurka among the females; and Barton MacLane, Stephen Crane, Ivan Triesault, John Abbott and Fritz Leiber among the males. A rarity today, the film would be worth revival on television.

Columbia were to leave the werewolf alone for more than a decade but in 1956 the script-writers dusted off their wolfsbane and silver bullets for another excursion in *The Werewolf*, an undistinguished production directed by a routine craftsman, Fred F. Sears, against an unlikely American backwoods setting.

The main trouble with this seventy-eight minute 'B' feature was the almost completely unknown cast, only Joyce Holden being a familiar name. Even the nominal "star", the film's producer Steven Rich seemed to have come from nowhere and to have disappeared shortly afterwards and his rather turgid performance as the werewolf of the title certainly did not help. If Columbia hoped to initiate a new cycle they must have been disappointed and the film had only limited release. Only the transformations had any impact and a re-viewing of the film on British television in 1975 confirmed its soporific character.

A new low was reached the following year when American International fathered a monstrosity in *I Was a Teenage Werewolf*, presumably to cash in on the juvenile market. This seventy-six minute yarn featured Michael Landon as a high-school student who became a werewolf and attacked and

savaged pretty girls. The whole thing was hardly taken seriously, even by director Gene Fowler, and despite some better-
than-average artistes, including Whit Bissell, is best forgotten.

MGM went one better, if that be the word, with *Werewolf in
a Girls' Dormitory* in 1963. Another unknown director Richard
Benson directed an equally obscure cast, whose plot is perfectly
described by its title. A sad attempt to mingle horror and sex.
MGM were never really horror specialists in any event – apart
from a few Lon Chaney silent films – and the cycle mercifully
died here, though a distinguished film on lycanthropy had been
produced in England a little earlier.

Since the early '60s forays into the world of the pentagram
and the silver bullet have been few and far between. As
indicated, the theme of the feral child received distinguished
treatment at the hands of the French film maker, Truffaut,
though that lies outside the range of this chapter.

One of the best latter-day werewolf films was, as noted, *The
Beast Must Die*, based on a story by science-fiction writer James
Blish. As early as 1942 Twentieth Century Fox had produced
what was described as a superior essay in the werewolf genre,
The Undying Monster. The film was directed by John Brahm but
as I have been unable to trace a copy in order to arrange a
viewing, I am unable to comment.

The theme has been but sparingly evoked in recent years.
Columbia's dreary 1956 programmer, *The Werewolf*, briefly
re-surfaced on British TV early in 1975 and disappeared without leaving a ripple. It looked even more dismal then than it
had appeared in the cinema.

But in 1973 appeared a send-up of the werewolf theme in the
unlikely guise of a farce based on political corruption in The
White House and the Watergate Affair. *The Werewolf of
Washington*, directed by Milton Moses Ginsberg, takes all the
dearly-loved clichés of lycanthropic cinema and stages them
gleefully in the corridors of power.

This lavish colour production is probably the only con-
sciously orientated comedy in the genre and was welcomed with
the enthusiasm it deserved, though inevitably as memories of
Watergate fade so must its hilarious impact. Starring Dean
Stockwell and including in its cast the well-known dwarf actor
Michael Dunn, the tale, acted out against Presidential aircraft
and the White House itself, sees Stockwell as a Nixon aide who

becomes a werewolf at full moon and wreaks havoc in the capital and the Capitol.

Its thinly disguised real-life characters gave it an added edge and it is likely to be the definitive and most witty essay in this particular sphere, a lycanthropic equivalent of Roman Polanski's equally gleeful send-up of vampirism in *The Dance of the Vampires*.

Perhaps the best traditional werewolf story of modern times comes, most appropriately, from Hammer Films. *The Curse of the Werewolf* is examined in detail in the next chapter.

TWENTY-SIX

HORROR IN SPAIN

As we have seen, the nearest thing to a classic in the cinema of the '30s on the werewolf theme was the Lon Chaney piece *The Wolf Man*. But a production which came very late on the scene has already, in just over a decade, become something of a legend for its integrity, restraint and brilliantly depicted atmosphere.

This was *The Curse of the Werewolf*, produced by the British company Hammer Films, whose studios at Bray-on-Thames have probably over the past twenty years turned out more horror films than any other studio. The new werewolf work, released in 1961, was directed by Terence Fisher, a veteran in the field, who had been responsible for some of the most striking Frankenstein and Dracula productions.

Fisher, in fact, had directed Hammer's first *Dracula* film in 1958 and he was also to pioneer the theme of lycanthropy at this studio as, curiously, *The Curse of the Werewolf* seems to have been Hammer Films' first and, so far, only essay in the genre. Fisher brought to it all the flair and craftsmanship which had made his name a familiar one to enthusiasts of the macabre and a more than usually distinguished cast gave frightening authority to the sombre theme.

The film was, naturally enough, based on Guy Endore's *Werewolf of Paris*, though the script-writer, John Elder, seemed to have abandoned most of its plot motivations and subtle horror, retaining only a few scenes and motifs from Endore's original. Indeed, the setting itself had been completely changed and the piece was now set in eighteenth-century Spain, which gave the Bray craftsmen excellent opportunities to embellish the settings with plaster work and other rococo ornamentation.

The film, in fact, gained a great deal from this transposition and Hammer virtually created a new and unfamiliar work in a genre which, though not as over-exposed as Frankenstein and Dracula, was in danger of becoming somewhat hackneyed. The Technicolor camerawork and the set designs themselves were particularly impressive and the result was a sumptuously mounted excursion into the macabre which will long stand as a high peak in the field.

Apart from the anguished performance of Oliver Reed, the actor nephew of film director Carol Reed, who came to prominence in the central rôle in this film and whose performance will be analysed later, the piece also has two other outstanding horror creations; the scabrous beggar of Richard Wordsworth who sires the monster; and the magnificent Anthony Dawson as the sadistic, lecherous and decadent nobleman, the Marques Siniestro, who dominates the long prologue of the film with a performance which draws heavily on the Marquis de Sade in its mannerisms.

An already strong cast is further enhanced by excellent performances from Clifford Evans, Ewen Solon, and Catherine Feller. For the specialist one of the character parts, that of a forest guard, is taken by Warren Mitchell – a big-screen dependable for many years before he sprang to national fame in Britain as the loud-mouthed Alf Garnett in television's *Till Death Us Do Part* series.

The Curse of the Werewolf opens sumptuously with a banquet at the castle of the sinister Marques. While he and his decadent friends dine in almost sybaritic luxury, the beggar of Richard Wordsworth approaches and is told, in a cruel joke, that those in need are welcome at the castle. The bewildered beggar is overwhelmed with the splendour of the palace and takes his jesting reception seriously.

The elegant camerawork lingers on the lush delights of both the women guests and the delicacies on the banqueting table as the tattered beggar is led before the master of the house. Anthony Dawson, a British actor who has had a distinguished career in both Hollywood and the British cinema, has never been better than in these scenes as the arrogant nobleman, slim and pale-faced, taunts the starving scarecrow before him.

Dawson has given many fine portrayals, from the would-be killer who is himself stabbed to death in Hitchcock's *Dial M for Murder* to the sinister but innocent presence in *Midnight Lace*, but he has seldom had such opportunities afforded him as in

The Curse of the Werewolf, and his sadism comes vividly to life
in the figure of the evil, burning-eyed debauchee.

In a long sequence the beggar is alternately humiliated and
rewarded and is forced to sing and dance grotesquely in return
for scraps from the table. It is in fact the Marques's wedding
night and the sumptuous bride (the nubile Josephine Llewellyn)
gives added point to the scenes which follow. As the wedding
guests' talk and actions become even more wild and heated, so
does the beggar's half-exhausted prancings, inflamed by the
wine he is ill-advisedly plied with.

Finally, when Dawson and his bride are about to retire for
the night the beggar oversteps himself by an ironic and clumsy
verbal jest; in a rage, the mercurial Marques orders the beggar
to be cast into the castle's dungeons. There he is straightaway
conveyed and there, for years, he is allowed to rot, apparently
forgotten by everyone in the great house above. These are
among the best scenes in the film which is, in effect, an extended
conte cruel with much more insight into psychological suffering
than is usual with this type of production.

Richard Wordsworth gives a performance which ranks
alongside that of Dawson and the film's nominal star, Oliver
Reed himself. Covered with mud, sores and with long, matted
beard and hair his bestial howls and animal noises as the years
pass and his incarceration continues, make the spectator believe
absolutely in the story. These details, combined with his pointed
teeth and the rolling of his bloodshot eyes, are used to chilling
effect in the pivotal scene of the film's long introduction.

The Marques Siniestro himself is now, with the passing of the
years, an old and disgusting roué, still absorbed with the lusts of
the flesh. His wife has long since forsaken him and he now
makes what sport he is able among the more complaisant of his
servant girls. With his white, pitted face and senile gait
Anthony Dawson rises to even greater heights of excellence in
these scenes. He has now cast his eyes upon a mute servant girl
in his palace, played by Yvonne Romain.

But she repulses his advances and he has her cast into the
dungeon, where she is placed in the same cell with the beggar.
In a truly horrifying sequence the beggar rapes her; from their
union the werewolf, Leon, is to be born. When the half-drunken
jailer proves inattentive the girl escapes and stabs the Marques
to death. The fleeing girl is found exhausted by the Professor

Alfredo of Clifford Evans, the only truly sympathetic character in the film. A scholar and a liberal, he takes the girl into his household.

She is tended by the professor's housekeeper and eventually dies giving birth to a child. All this and the main narrative of the film is hardly begun. The child, Leon, whom we first see at the age of six, is sympathetically played by the young actor Justin Walter and it is mainly due to his skilful acting and that of Oliver Reed as the adult Leon that the audience feels more sympathy than usual with the tormented being who becomes the werewolf.

In fact the film is a sort of compendium of all the lycan-thropic ingredients, from the tormented disgust of the monster/victim to the growing of hair on the palms of the hands and the frightening transformation into the man-beast at the full moon. The psychological implications of the situation are subtly underlined by the playing, direction and camerawork so that we are far removed from the cruder manifestations of the genre as evinced in the earlier performances of such actors as Lon Chaney Jr.

The child has terrible dreams and the professor, who is given all the authority of the veteran actor Clifford Evans' gifted playing, suspects something of the truth. Warren Mitchell, as the forest guard, confides in the villagers that a wolf has been troubling the sheep and he boasts that he will shoot it before long. One night he hears the snarl of a wolf and, aiming care-fully, is convinced that he has killed the beast. But he finds only blood upon the spot. He hurries back to the village.

Meanwhile, the professor and his housekeeper find Leon wounded. The terrified child begs to be placed under restraint and the professor has bars placed across his wondow. A priest consulted murmurs conventional banalities and the stage is now set for the absorbing last half of a film which is at once more literate, humane and subtle than most other productions of its kind.

With the entrance of Oliver Reed the production gathers momentum towards its sombre finale. Reed has, of course, since *The Curse of the Werewolf*, emerged as one of the most powerful and potent artistes of the modern cinema. Even when the werewolf piece was made he had already served a long and arduous apprenticeship in dozens of films, in a number of which he had played the lead. *The Curse of the Werewolf* was to bring him to wide general notice and he was ideally suited to the part with his husky build, animal good looks and ferocious style of playing.

Leon obtains permission from the professor to leave the only home he has ever known and go to work for the owner of a vineyard in a town some distance away. Much against his better judgement the professor agrees and the young man is apprenticed to a *hacienda*, where he works long hours with another apprentice, washing bottles and labelling the wine.

The cast is further strengthened at this point by the appearance of the New Zealand actor Ewen Solon – best known perhaps for his TV appearances as Lucas in the Maigret series – as the lame and unsympathetic owner of the vineyard. Leon falls foul of his employer and to complicate matters falls in love with his daughter, Christina, played by Catherine Feller. This actress also gives an unusually sympathetic performance which makes Leon's situation all the more poignant. The young lovers plan to elope but before they can do so it is the time of full moon.

Leon suffers another attack while having an evening out at a sordid dance hall and murders one of the prostitutes, who invites him to her room. Again, Fisher is rather more subtle than usual, relying on shadow effects, brutish growls and the anguish on the woman's face, in contrast to the more usual horrors. In a night of hideous terror Leon murders his apprentice friend and, hunted by the townspeople, takes refuge with his adopted father.

The professor shields him but decides to keep him chained. Unable to resist the impulses associated with his terrible disease Leon again flees; Christina is meanwhile searching for Leon and his true nature is revealed to her by the professor. She is certain that together they can find a cure for him but Leon and his true nature is revealed to her by the professor. being together when Leon, transformed into a creature of terrifying strength, escapes from his cell.

Howling demoniacally at the full moon he terrifies the village, but a posse of the moronic villagers so beloved of film-makers pursue him and he is trapped in the belfry of the church. There is a curious and moving moment when he calls down to his father in the crowd to kill him with the silver bullet which was originally cast by the forest guard.

In a finale in which terror is balanced with pity Clifford Evans enters the bell-tower, a shot cracks out and the werewolf is dead. A great deal of the credit for the success of this elegant and absorbing film must go to Oliver Reed, then a young actor of only twenty-four, who gave a powerful and anguished performance, notable for its subtle approach rather than crude horrors.

He was seldom glimpsed as the man-beast, these effects being reserved for key moments. The usual time-lapse photography denoted the growth of hair on his hands and body and the full make-up made striking use of matted, silvery-black hair which looked even more impressive in Technicolor.

The Spanish locations, though obviously the work of the Hammer set-designers, were lavish and convincing, particularly those of the Marques's palace, and the more unfamiliar backgrounds made a refreshingly unhackneyed setting for the frightening narrative.

This, combined with the excellent script, acting and the elliptical way the camera told the story, added up to one of the best of the werewolf pictures; its success is underlined by the fact that it has become a perennial favourite on television screens during the last few years.

The talents of Fisher and his team of actors led by Reed, Evans, Dawson and Wordsworth had combined, improbably as it might seem, to produce the nearest thing to a classic on lycanthropy which the screen has so far seen.

TWENTY-SEVEN

DAYBREAK

The moonlight is waning now. The night wind moans through the tree-tops, tossing the pine-branches and on the lower slopes of the mountain ruffling the leaves of the wolfsbane which grows there. The faint, far-off howl of a wolf sounds across the valley, re-echoing from crag to crag, until it fades in the distance.

The beast, its night's hunting over, seeks its lair before the hours of daylight overtake it. One of man's oldest enemies, cunning, strong, ever vigilant, the wolf, as I have endeavoured to show in this study, demands respect not only for its courage but for its loyalty and family feeling for those in its own pack.

And it is the wolf, with its deeds of ferocity, its prowling during the night hours, which brought fear to the heart of the primitive peasant. So that for hundreds of years man, huddled at his fireside, only timber and earth walls and a simple iron latch between him and the prowlers of the night, feared and hated the yellow-eyed prowler.

The wolf in its turn gave substance to the older, more primal fears of the werewolf, the *loup-garou* of legend who was turned by an ancient curse into a monster himself, doomed to roam the night, tearing and slaying and bringing the fearsome taint to those he attacked.

Unlike the undead dead, the vampire who had first to infect his prey, the unfortunate lycanthrope could fall victim to the curse through no fault of his own, a factor which added a new dimension of terror to the condition. Wandering at the light of the full moon, the wretched werewolf/victim could find rest only through the silver bullet or the stake.

I have traced the lycanthrope's tragic destiny through the Gothic tales of the nineteenth century and the classic short stories of the nineteenth and twentieth centuries; to the full flowering of the theme in such novels as Guy Endore's *Werewolf of Paris*.

In the cinema too, though there has been nothing to equal the theme in literature, I have examined such productions as *The Werewolf of London*; the *Wolfman* films of the late Lon Chaney Jr and modern exercises like Hammer's *Curse of the Werewolf*, the nearest thing to a cinema classic on the theme, with an anguished performance by Oliver Reed.

The legend of the werewolf was further embellished by the plight of medical victims of a rare disease, congenital porphyria, whose existence in medieval times gave rise to persecutions, mass hysteria and orgies of torture and blood-letting. With their photosensitivity to light and the sores and excoriations of the skin, the wretched victims of this type of porphyria, with their red-stained teeth and propensity to wander about at night, when the light no longer exacerbated their condition, fell ready-made victims to superstition, merciless judges and ruthless public opinion.

In our own time the link between this disease and the wave of judicial inquisitions in the Dark Ages, has been pin-pointed by the young physician, Dr Lee Illis in a pioneering paper which for the first time puts forward a convincing reason for the motivation behind some of these terrible events and has shed more light on a dark corner of medieval superstition and bigotry.

The strange figure of the wolf-child has been glimpsed too, moving far off among the trees, and adding his own sombre and vivid strand to the strange and terrible legend. The feral child, abandoned by his parents and brought up among wolves and other wild beasts, living as an animal, unable to talk or walk upright and possessing the ability to live in the wild, has been hovering on the fringes of the civilized world for centuries.

In such classic cases as Victor of Aveyron and Kaspar Hauser, the fact has been even stranger than fiction and the terrible events underlying Kaspar's story and his tragic and mysterious murder will probably now never be solved. Shining like a bright light among these pathetic and bizarre histories which continue even to our own day, is the work of Dr Jean Itard, the pioneer psychologist who treated and eased the lot of Victor of Aveyron and made a major contribution to medical literature with his long reports and study of this classic case-history of the eighteenth century.

Apart from learned works and discussion in medical papers and research, Itard's work was little-known to the general public until François Truffaut's intelligent and humane film *L'Enfant Sauvage* appeared in the late sixties, with the director himself giving an outstanding performance in the rôle of Itard.

The wolf, the wolf-child and the victim of the werewolf disease have each formed a strand of the legend of the werewolf itself, one of the strangest and most terrible myths of mankind, which stands almost alone with the vampire as being one of the primal sources of terror and a figure which has inspired universal horror and loathing among human beings for thousands of years.

And almost alone too among the hobgoblins of the mind – vampire, werewolf, witch, demon, sorcerer, fiend, and monster – the victim of lycanthropy is a figure which evokes pity as well as terror. This is because he was as much victim as predator.

The moonlight is fading fast. Day is breaking beyond the distant mountains. A crackling echoes through the silence, down in the darkness of a thicket. A figure emerges furtively from the fringe of the forest.

Stubbled hair covers the face, red-rimmed eyes stare mindlessly from their sockets, and the creature's clothes are damp, stained with mud and torn. He rips at a sapling with gnarled and claw-like hands and then hurls himself to the ground, racked with a paroxysm of sobs. The fit passes. It is becoming lighter.

The figure on the ground stirs and moans as a soft wind rustles the grasses. A face turns upward toward the light. It is that of a young man whose fresh complexion yet bears the ravages of the night. The cheeks are white and blanched and the eyes gleam with the fires of the pit.

The youth staggers to his feet and brushes his hands across his face. His fingers are cut and sore and there is a long slash across one wrist which still oozes blood. Furtively, the young man repairs the damage to his person and clothing as best he can. His shirt is gaping wide and open to the wind of dawn. As he goes to re-lace it the growing light gleams on a strange mark near his throat.

It is blackened as though burnt into the flesh. The youth hastily draws his clothing across the five-pointed star – the pentagram which denotes the mark of the beast. He shrugs into a sheepskin jacket and then, his step firmer, his breathing easier, strides out across the hill.

The wind freshens, waving the tips of the wolfsbane on the lower slopes. A new day is beginning, the strengthening sunlight banishing the fears and terrors of the night. The figure of the shepherd is minute now, a mere dot against the vast green of the upward slope of the hill. The village lies that way.

Two hawks fly upwards, using the freshening breeze to carry them on strong wings, as they seek their prey on the ground below. The sunlight spreads across the hill, the shadows fleeing before it. The creaking of a farm-cart sounds along the track and the distant bleat of sheep.

Only in the churchyard beyond the village, hemmed in by dank evergreen trees, do the shadows linger. Then they too disappear before the revivifying rays of the sun. Day breaks and the terrors of the night recede. The werewolf – with the vampire and the other demons of the dark – is resting and the world is at peace.

SELECTED BIBLIOGRAPHY

MEDICAL STUDIES

Dr Lee Illis, *On Porphyria and the Aetiology of Werwolves* (Royal Society of Medicine, 1963).

Pierre-Joseph Bonnaterre, *Notice Historique sur le Sauvage de l'Aveyron* (France, 1800).

Robert Eisler, *Man into Wolf* (New York, 1947).

Frank Hamel, *Human Animals* (U.S.A., 1915).

Lucien Malson, *Wolf Children* (Longmans Green, 1952; London, 1973).

Goldberg and Rimington, *Diseases of Porphyrin Metabolism* (U.S.A., 1962).

G. C. Ferriss, *Sanichar, the Wolf-Boy of India* (New York, 1902).

Arnold Gesell, *Wolf Child and Human Child* (London, 1941).

Carl Von Linne (Linnaeus), *Systema Naturae* (Stockholm, 1758).

Dr Jean Itard, *De l'Education d'un Homme Sauvage ou des Premiers Developpements Physiques et Moraux du Jeune Sauvage de l'Aveyron* (Paris, 1801).

J. A. L. Singh, R. M. Zingg, *Wolf Children and Feral Man* (New York, 1942).

H. G. Lindberg, *Kaspar Hauser* (London, 1833).

NON-FICTION

Valentin Ball, *Jungle Life in India* (London, 1880).

WORKS OF SCHOLARSHIP

Pennethorne Hughes, *Witchcraft* (Pelican Books, 1952).

Sir Walter Scott, *Demonology and Witchcraft* (John Murray, 1830).

Restif de la Bretonne, *Mémoires* (France, c. 1785).

Dr Montague Summers, *The Werewolf* (Kegan Paul, Trench and Trubner, c. 1930).

Witchcraft and Black Magic (Rider, London, 1946).

The Vampire in Europe (Kegan Paul, Trench and Trubner, 1929).

The Vampire: His Kith and Kin (Kegan Paul, Trench and Trubner, 1928).

T. Muller. *Historia Danica* (Copenhagen, 1839).

Radu Florescu, Raymond T. McNally, *Dracula: A Biography* (Robert Hale, 1974).

Jules Michelet, *Satanism and Witchcraft* (Arco Publications Ltd, London, 1958).

Heinrich Kramer, James Sprenger, *Malleus Maleficarum* (Germany, 1486). (English translation, Dr Montague Summers, Arrow Books, London, 1971).

Jean Bodin, *De la Démonomanie des Sorciers* (Paris, 1580).

H. P. Lovecraft, "Supernatural Horror in Literature" (essay in *Dagon and other Macabre Tales*, Gollancz, 1967).

Rollo Ahmed, *The Black Art* (John Long, 1936).

James Pope Hennessy, *Robert Louis Stevenson* (Cape, 1974).

William Seabrook, *The Magic Island* (Harrap, 1929).

WORKS OF FICTION

Anon, *William and the Werewolf* (France, fourteenth century; translated into English, 1350).

N. Weber, *The Tribunal of Blood* (London, 1806).

Charles Maturin, *The Albigenses* (London, 1824).

George W. M. Reynolds, *Wagner the Wehr-Wolf* (London, 1857).

Mrs Crowe, *A Story of a Weir-Wolf* (London, 1846).

Alexandre Dumas, *The Wolf Leader* (Paris, 1857).

Jack London, *Love of Life* (Paul Elek, 1946).

Brian J. Frost (Ed.), *Book of the Werewolf* (Sphere Books, 1973).

William Beckford, *Vathek* (France, 1787; New English Library, 1966).

Denis Gifford, *A Pictorial History of Horror Movies* (Paul Hamlyn, 1973).

Drake Douglas, *Horrors* (John Baker, 1967).

Alex Hamilton (Ed.), *The Cold Embrace* (Corgi Books, 1966).

F. G. Loring, *The Tomb of Sarah* (*Prince of Darkness*, John Westhouse, 1946).

Douglas Hill (Ed.), *Way of the Werewolf* (Panther, 1966).

Sam Moskowitz (Ed.), *Horrors Unknown* (Kaye and Ward, 1972).

Joel E. Siegel, *Val Lewton: The Reality of Terror* (Secker and Warburg B.F.I., 1972).

Ivan Butler, *The Horror Film* (Zwemmer, 1967).

Marie de France, *The Werewolf* (London, 1966).

Guy Endore, *The Werewolf of Paris* (John Long, 1934).

Frederick Marryat, *The White Wolf of the Hartz Mountains* (*The Phantom Ship*, London, 1839).

Basil Copper, *Cry Wolf* (*Vampires, Werewolves and other Monsters*, Curtis Books, New York, 1974; *When Footsteps Echo*, Robert Hale, 1975).

Peter Fleming, *The Kill* (*Book of the Werewolf*, Ed. Brian J. Frost, Sphere Books, 1973).

Seabury Quinn, *The Phantom Farmhouse* (*Weird Tales*, 1923).
  The Wolf of St Bonnot (*Weird Tales*, 1930).
  The Blood Flower (*Weird Tales*, 1927).
  Fortune's Fools (*Weird Tales*, 1938).
  The Thing in the Fog (*Weird Tales*, 1933).
  The Gentle Werewolf (*Weird Tales*, 1940).

Saki (H. H. Munro), *Gabriel-Ernest* (*Reginald in Russia*, London, 1910).

Claude Seignolle, *The Galoupe* (*Récits Diaboliques*, France, n.d.).

Jane Rice, *The Refugee* (*Unknown Worlds*, U.S., 1943).

Gerald Bliss, *The Door of the Unreal* (London, 1905).

August Derleth, *The Adventure of the Tottenham Werewolf* (*The Memoirs of Solar Pons*, Mycroft and Moran, U.S., 1951).

Bruce Elliott, *Wolves Don't Cry* (Mercury Press Inc., 1953).

Algernon Blackwood, *Running Wolf* (*The Willows and other Queer Tales*, Collins, c. 1936).
  The Camp of the Dog (*Selected Tales of Algernon Blackwood*, Penguin, 1942).

Ambrose Bierce, *The Eyes of the Panther* (*In the Midst of Life*, U.S., 1891; Penguin, 1939).

Sir Gilbert Campbell, *The White Wolf of Kostopchin* (*Wild and Weird*, London, 1889).

Elliott O'Donnell, *Mere Maxim* (*Werewolves*, London, 1912).

Abraham Merritt, *The Drone*, (*Weird Tales*, 1934).

Manly Bannister, *Eena* (*Weird Tales*, 1947).

Beverly Haaf, *Mrs Kaye* (U.S., 1968).

Dale C. Donaldson, *Pia!* (U.S., 1969).

Rev. Sabine Baring-Gould, *The Book of Werewolves* (London, 1865).

Count Eric Stenbock, *The Other Side* (London, 1894).

Rudyard Kipling, *The Mark of the Beast* (London, 1891).

Clemence Houseman, *The Werewolf* (London, 1895).

Erkmann-Chatrian, *The Man-Wolf* (France, n.d.).

Greye La Spina, *Invaders from the Dark* (U.S., n.d.)

H. Warner Munn, *The Werewolf of Ponkert* (*Weird Tales*, 1925).
  The Return of the Master (*Weird Tales*, 1927).
  The Werewolf's Daughter (*Weird Tales*, 1928).

B. Chandler, *Frontier of the Dark* (U.S., 1952).

Clark Ashton Smith, *Monsters in the Night* (U.S., 1954).

Jerome Bixby, *The Young One* (U.S., 1954).

Gordon Dickson, *The Girl Who Played Wolf* (U.S., 1958).

H. Bedford Jones, *The Wolf Man* (U.S., 1963).

Anthony Boucher, *The Compleat Werewolf* (U.S., 1942).

James Blish, *There Shall Be No Darkness* (U.S., 1950).

David Garnett, *Lady into Fox* (London, 1922).

Arthur Salmon, *The Were-Wolf* (U.S., 1927).

Robert E. Howard, *In the Forest of Villeferre* (*Weird Tales*, 1925). *Wolfshead* (*Weird Tales*, 1926).

Manly Wade Wellman, *The Werewolf Snarls* (*Weird Tales*, 1937). *The Horror Undying* (*Weird Tales*, 1936). *The Last Grave of Lill Warran* (U.S., 1951). *The Hairy Ones Shall Dance* (U.S., 1938).

Gladys Trenery (G. G. Pendarves), *Werewolf of the Sahara* (U.S., 1936).

Lireve Monet, *Norn* (U.S., 1936).

Theda Kenyon, *The House of the Golden Eyes* (U.S., 1930).

Howard Wandrei, *The Hand of the O'Mecca* (U.S., 1935).

Mary Elizabeth Counselman, *The Cat Woman* (U.S., 1933).

Robert Bloch (with Henry Kuttner), *The Black Kiss* (U.S., 1937).

Jack Williamson, *Wolves of Darkness* (U.S., 1932).

Max Brand, *The Werewolf* (U.S., 1926).

Madame Aino Kallas, *The Wolf Bride* (U.S., 1930).

Hugh Walpole, *Tarnhelm* (London, 1933).

Geoffrey Household, *Taboo* (London, *c*. 1935).

Clifford Simak, *The Werewolf Principle* (U.S., 1965).

Alex Hamilton, *Canis Lupus Sapiens* (London, 1966).

Sutherland Menzies, *Hugues, the Wer-Wolf* (*Victorian Ghost Stories*, London, 1934).

James Thurber, *Men, Women and Dogs* (Hamish Hamilton, 1943).

OTHER SOURCES
The Times.
Times Literary Supplement.
The Daily Telegraph.

SELECTED FILMOGRAPHY

The Werewolf (U.S.A., 1913. 1 reel).

The Werewolf of London (Universal Pictures, 1935. Directed by Stuart Walker).

Leading Players: Henry Hull, Warner Oland, Valerie Hobson, Lester Matthews, J. M. Kerrigan, Spring Byington, Ethel Griffies, Lawrence Grant.

The Wolf Man (Universal Pictures, 1941. Directed by George Waggner. Make-up, Jack P. Pierce).

Leading Players: Lawrence Talbot, Lon Chaney Jr: Sir John Talbot, Claude Rains: Captain Montford, Ralph Bellamy: Gamekeeper, Patric Knowles: Doctor, Warren William: Gwen Conliffe, Evelyn Ankers: Mr Conliffe, J. M. Kerrigan: Maleva, Maria Ouspenskaya: Bela, Bela Lugosi: Jenny, Fay Helm.

The Undying Monster (Twentieth Century Fox, 1942. Directed by John Brahm).

Leading Player: John Howard.

Frankenstein Meets the Wolf Man (Universal Pictures, 1943. Directed by Roy William Neill).

Leading Players: Lon Chaney Jr (as Lawrence Talbot); Bela Lugosi, Lionel Atwill, Dwight Frye, Maria Ouspenskaya, Patric Knowles, Ilona Massey, Dennis Hoey.

House of Frankenstein (Universal Pictures, 1944. Directed by Erle C. Kenton).

Leading Players: Lon Chaney Jr (as Lawrence Talbot), John Carradine (Count Dracula), Boris Karloff (Baron Frankenstein), Glenn Strange (The Monster), J. Carroll Naish, Anne Gwynne, Peter Coe, Lionel Atwill, George Zucco, Sig Rumann, Elena Verdugo, Phillip Van Zandt.

House of Dracula (Universal Pictures, 1945. Directed by Erle C. Kenton).

Leading Players: Lon Chaney Jr (as Lawrence Talbot), John Carradine (Count Dracula), Lionel Atwill, Ludwig Stossel, Martha O'Driscoll, Onslow Stevens, Glenn Strange (The Monster).

Abbott and Costello Meet Frankenstein (Universal Pictures, 1948. Directed by Charles Barton).

Leading Players: Bud Abbott, Lou Costello, Lon Chaney Jr (as Lawrence Talbot), Bela Lugosi (Count Dracula), Glenn Strange (The Monster), Vincent Price (The Invisible Man), Lenore Aubert, Jane Randolph, Frank Ferguson.

COLUMBIA SERIES

The Return of the Vampire (Columbia Pictures, 1943. Directed by Lew Landers).

Leading Players: Matt Willis (Andreas Obry, The Wolfman), Bela Lugosi (Count Armand Tesla), Frieda Inescourt, Nina Foch, Jeanne Bates, Gilbert Emery, Roland Varno, Miles Mander, Billy Bevan.

Cry of the Werewolf (Columbia Pictures, 1944. Directed by Henry Levin).

Leading Players: Nina Foch (Celeste La Tour, The Wolf Woman), Osa Massen, Blanche Yurka, Barton Maclane, Stephen Crane, Ivan Triesault, John Abbott, Fritz Leiber.

The Werewolf (Columbia Pictures, 1956. Directed by Fred F. Sears).

Leading Players: Steven Rich, Joyce Holden.

I Was a Teenage Werewolf (Universal-International, 1957. Directed by Gene Fowler).

Leading Players: Michael Landon, Whit Bissell.

The Curse of the Werewolf (Hammer Films, 1961. Directed by Terence Fisher).

Leading Players: Leon, Oliver Reed; Marques Siniestro, Anthony Dawson; Beggar, Richard Wordsworth; Professor, Clifford Evans; Forest Guard, Warren Mitchell; and with: Ewen Solon, Catherine Feller, Yvonne Romain.

Werewolf in a Girls' Dormitory (M.G.M., 1963. Directed by Richard Benson).

The Werewolf of Washington (U.S.A., 1973. Directed by Milton Moses Ginsberg).

Leading Players: Dean Stockwell, Michael Dunn.

The Beast Must Die (Amicus, 1974. Producer, Milton Subotsky, from the novel by James Blish).

INDEX